Bible Studies
The Twelve Prophets
Hosea to Malachi

Second Edition

James Malm

ISBN: 978-1-989208-10-6

Copyright © 2018 James Malm
All Rights Reserved
Unless otherwise noted all scripture quotes are from
the King James Version of the Bible

Dedication

This work is dedicated to the Great God whose house is eternity; the Father and Sovereign of all that exists and the sum of all Truth, Wisdom, Love, Justice and Mercy.

May God's house be filled with children whose chief joy is to be like Him!

Visit Our Website

theshininglight.info

Table of Contents

Introduction 7

Hosea **11**

    Hosea Introduction 12
    Hosea 1 14
    Hosea 2 18
    Hosea 3 23
    Hosea 4 25
    Hosea 5 32
    Hosea 6 36
    Hosea 7 39
    Hosea 8 44
    Hosea 9 49
    Hosea 10 53
    Hosea 11 57
    Hosea 12 60
    Hosea 13 63
    Hosea 14 66

Joel **69**

    Joel 1 70
    Joel 2 75
    Joel 3 82

AMOS **87**

    Amos 1 89
    Amos 2 94
    Amos 3 98
    Amos 4 102
    Amos 5 106
    Amos 6 111
    Amos 7 115
    Amos 8 120
    Amos 9 125

Obadiah **131**

Obadiah	132

Jonah **139**

Jonah 1	140
Jonah 2	143
Jonah 3	146
Jonah 4	148

Micah **151**

Micah 1	152
Micah 2	156
Micah 3	159
Micah 4	162
Micah 5	165
Micah 6	168
Micah 7	171

Nahum **175**

Introduction:	176
Nahum 1	180
Nahum 2	184
Nahum 3	187

Habakkuk **191**

Introduction	192
Habakkuk 1	194
Habakkuk 2	197
Habakkuk 3	201

Zephaniah **203**

Zephaniah	204
Zephaniah 2	209
Zephaniah 3	212

Haggai **217**

Introduction	218
Haggai 1	221
Haggai 2	227

Zechariah **233**

    Zechariah 1 234
    Zechariah 2 240
    Zechariah 3 242
    Zechariah 4 245
    Zechariah 5 251
    Zechariah 6 254
    Zechariah 7 259
    Zechariah 8 262
    Zechariah 9 267
    Zechariah 10 271
    Zechariah 11 274
    Zechariah 12 279
    Zechariah 13 283
    Zechariah 14 285

Malachi **291**

    Introduction 292
    Malachi 1 294
    Malachi 2 302
    Malachi 3 310
    Malachi 4 316

Introduction

Generally, the biblical prophetic books are divided between the longer books called the Major Prophets [Isaiah - Jeremiah - Lamentations - Ezekiel - Daniel], and the 12 shorter books called the Minor Prophets.

This is a study into the twelve shorter prophetic books sometimes called the Minor Prophets: Hosea - Joel - Amos - Obadiah - Jonah - Micah - Nahum - Habakkuk- Zephaniah - Haggai - Zechariah and Malachi.

The twelve Minor Prophets conclude the Old Testament prophets and each of them concerns the reasons for the latter day tribulation, the tribulation itself, the future of various nations, the early millennium or about the coming of Messiah.

Definitions and explanations

In dating I will often use the letter "c"; this means circa or approximately.

Physical Israel was called out from bondage in Egypt and is an allegorical example of God spiritually calling people out of bondage to sin. Therefore everything written about physical Israel and physical Judah, also applies spiritually to those that God is calling out of bondage to sin.

As Physical Israel / Judah were corrected when they turned away from God; so professing Christians as a kind of spiritual Israel will be corrected if they are not faithfully diligent to keep and live by every Word of God.

2 Timothy 3:16 All scripture *is* given by inspiration of God, and **is profitable for doctrine, for reproof, for correction, for instruction in righteousness:**

1 Corinthians 10:5 But with many of them God was not well pleased: for they were overthrown in the wilderness. **10:6** Now these things were [recorded as examples for our instruction] our examples, to the intent we should not lust after evil things, as they also lusted

God is not a respecter of persons and God will require the same things of Christians that he requires of physical Israel and Judah; which is a passionate Christ-like zeal to live by every Word of God

The English word "church" can mean a building or a corporate entity which is deceptive since the biblical word "Ekklesia" [which is rendered "church" in English], means neither of these things. The word "Ekklesia" in its religious application means all those called out to God who faithfully live by Every Word of God (Mat 4:4])

I will be using the word Ekklesia as well as brethren, spiritual Israel, brotherhood, assemblies and other general terms to refer to professing Christians and to point out lessons applicable to all professing Christians.

Israel /Judah were one nation until God separated ten tribes of Israel off from Judah/Benjamin for the sins of Solomon.

1 Kings 11:29 And it came to pass at that time when Jeroboam went out of Jerusalem, that the prophet Ahijah the Shilonite found him in the way; and he had clad himself with a new garment; and they two were alone in the field: **11:30** And Ahijah caught the new garment that was on him, and rent it in twelve pieces:

11:31 And he said to Jeroboam, Take thee ten pieces: for thus saith the LORD, the God of Israel, Behold, I will rend the kingdom out of the hand of Solomon, and will give ten tribes to thee:

11:32 (But he shall have one tribe for my servant David's sake, and for Jerusalem's sake, the city which I have chosen out of all the tribes of Israel:)

Since that time, the scriptures address Judah with Benjamin as the kingdom of Judah and the ten tribes as the kingdom of Israel or Samaria, as two separate peoples who will be reunited at the coming of Christ.

The tribe of Levi being the tribe of God was scattered throughout both kingdoms but mainly remained with Judah because of Judah's possession of Jerusalem.

~ 10 ~

Hosea

Hosea Introduction

The book of Hosea is about the vast unending love of God for his wife [physical Israel, which marriage ended at the death of the Husband who had given up his Godhood to be made flesh as Jesus Christ; and about the vast love of Messiah for his New Covenant bride of those called into a kind of spiritual Israel (Jer 31:31 and Eze 37:26) and about his unspeakable agony at their continual idolatry and adulteries against him.

Hosea is told to take a wife from among the whores to illustrate the situation of the continual adulteries of Israel against her deeply loving God-Husband.

A true Christian is part of a holy nation a kind of spiritual Israel.

1 Peter 2:9 But ye are a chosen generation, a royal priesthood, an **holy nation**, a peculiar [Set Apart to God] people; that ye should shew forth the praises of him who hath called you out of darkness [of bondage to sin] into his marvellous light [the Light of the Word of God];

Hosea's historical context is the time just before the captivity of Israel in c 721 B.C., and has God pleading with Israel to stop her idolatries and spiritual adulteries and return to be faithful to him. These prophecies are dual also referring to today's physical and spiritual Israel just before our latter day correction.

Hosea also prophesies that in these latter days Israel will yet repent and turn to love and be faithful to God.

Besides physical Israel this is also a prophecy of the New Covenant. God also loves Spiritual Israel and God is in a similar deep agony of spirit over today's Spiritual Ekklesia's spiritual adulteries with idols of men, following and obeying them instead of faithfully living by EVERY WORD of God.

This was recorded and preserved for us and for our instruction today, so that when BOTH physical and spiritual Israel are corrected in the soon coming great tribulation; we will turn to our God in deep sincere repentance to cleave to him alone forever more.

History: Jeroboam II (Hebrew: ירבעם השני or יָרָבְעָם; Greek: Ιεροβοάμ; Latin: *Jeroboam*) was the son and successor of Jehoash, (alternatively spelled Joash), and the fourteenth king of the ancient Kingdom of Israel, over which he ruled for forty-one years. His reign was contemporary with those of Amaziah (*2 Kings* 14:23) and Uzziah (15:1), kings of Judah. He was victorious over the Syrians (13:4; 14:26, 27), conquered Damascus (14:28), and extended Israel to its former limits, from "the entering of Hamath to the sea of the plain" (14:25; *Amos* 6:14).

William F. Albright has dated his reign to 786 BC – 746 BC, while E. R. Thiele says he was coregent with Jehoash 793 BC to 782 BC and sole ruler 782 BC to 753 BC.

Jeroboam's reign was also the period of the prophets Hosea, Joel, Jonah and Amos, all of whom condemned the idolatry, materialism and selfishness of the Israelite elite of their day.

Remember that all physical sins, especially idolatry and adultery; have their spiritual counterparts of disloyalty to the Word of God to whom the Spiritual Ekklesia is called.

This warning prophecy was not meant exclusively for the ancients, but for latter day physical and spiritual Israel as well, else it would not have been recorded for US today.

Just like physical Israel was full of idolatry and sin at that time; today's physical Israel is full of sin; and today's professing Christianity [Spiritual Israel] is full of the same sin in its spiritual context: following idols of men and exalting the words of men above the Word of God.

Hosea 1

Hosea 1:1 The word of the LORD that came unto Hosea, the son of Beeri, in the days of Uzziah, Jotham, Ahaz, and Hezekiah, kings of Judah, and in the days of Jeroboam the son of Joash, king of Israel.

1:2 The beginning of the word of the LORD by Hosea. And the LORD said to Hosea, **Go, take unto thee a wife of whoredoms and children of whoredoms**: for the land [the nation of Israel] hath committed great whoredom, departing from the LORD.

God set up Hosea as an analogy of himself and his relationship with physical Israel and his relationship with today's professing Christians; commanding Hosea to marry a whore, analogous to the continual spiritual adultery and idolatry of today's Ekklesia, just before our rejection and correction by God.

This is also a lesson for latter day physical Israel and today's Spiritual Ekklesia, who are full of gross physical and spiritual idolatry and adultery just before our correction in the latter day tribulation.

Hosea is a message to Mosaic Israel and it is a message to spiritual Israel today.

Almighty God will not tolerate our following idols of men and exalting them above any zeal to live by God's Word any longer: God is about to withdraw his blessings and protection and allow us to be thoroughly corrected to humble us and turn us to HIM.

HOSEA is a message to today's Professing Christianity, the Spiritual Israel of TODAY!

1:3 So he went and took Gomer the daughter of Diblaim; which conceived, and bare him a son.

God declares that he will end the kingdom of Israel and send them into captivity for their wickedness, and God will again correct the latter day proud nations of physical Israel and the called out of spiritual Israel as well.

1:4 And the LORD said unto him, Call his name Jezreel; for yet a little while, and I **will avenge the blood of Jezreel upon the house of Jehu**, and **will cause to cease the kingdom of the house of Israel**.

Jehu slew the priests of Baal, yet he was lukewarm and allowed the golden calves to be worshipped and much idolatry in Israel. This is just like today's Ekklesia making a pretense of condemning sin while following idols of men today.

A Word About Idols

The rulers of the people knew that idols are dumb inanimate nothing, so why did they lead the people to worship them? So that they could then teach the people their own doctrine and lead the people to follow themselves by claiming that their gods had so declared.

An idol cannot declare a doctrine! The priest declares his own doctrine and then attributes it to the idol, in that way distracting the people into actually following themselves. An idol is just smoke and mirrors to distract and manipulate people into following its priesthood, thereby controlling and enslaving the people to follow the priests.

Idols are only symbols of false teachings.

Today, we also have our idols: They are called corporate Churches, traditions of men and exalted leaders! We are told that such and such is "God's Church" and that we must be loyal to it and to its leaders. Then the leaders teach whatever they want and the brethren swallow it up, thinking it is God's Word.

We must prove ALL things by the Word of God and follow men ONLY as they follow God! If Israel had done that they would never have been led astray.

If we do NOT prove ALL things and hold fast to God's Word, we shall be rejected by our espoused Husband into great correction, just as physical Israel was also rejected into captivity!

1:5 And it shall come to pass at that day, that I will break the bow of Israel, in the valley of Jezreel.

Because of Israel's idolatry God would later break Israel in Jezreel [by the invading Assyrians], and lead them into captivity, rejecting them from off the land. In the same way God will reject physical Israel and spiritual Israel [today's Ekklesia] today and cast them into great tribulation to bring them to sincere repentance.

1:6 And she conceived again, and bare a daughter. And God said unto him, Call her name Loruhamah: for **I will no more have mercy upon the house of Israel; but I will utterly take them away.**

God declares that his mercy and patience with Mosaic Israel, and with the idolatrous latter day Spiritual Ekklesia is at an end. God will correct the guilty and he will save those faithful to him.

1:7 But I will have mercy upon the house of Judah [Israel went into captivity years before Judah did, Judah being saved by God at that time because of the righteous deeds of the good king Hezekiah]**, and will save them by the LORD their God, and will not save them by bow, nor by sword, nor by battle, by horses, nor by horsemen.**

1:8 Now when she had weaned Loruhamah, she conceived, and bare a son.

Loammi is to be a type of Israel when they are rejected by God for their continual sins against him; yet God promises that when Israel does sincerely repent he will accept them back. The same thing is true of today's spiritual Israel who will be corrected for a short time and when they sincerely turn to the Eternal with a whole heart they will be accepted by him.

The lesson is that God will correct those he loves in order to save them.

1:9 Then said God, Call his name Loammi: for **ye are not my people, and I will not be your God.**

This is a rejection of physical Israel, and the rejection of today's Spiritual Ekklesia in Revelation 3:15.

1:10 Yet the number of the children of Israel shall be as the sand of the sea, which cannot be measured nor numbered; and **it shall come to pass,**

that in the place where it was said unto them, Ye are not my people, there it shall be said unto them, Ye are the sons of the living God.

This will happen when Messiah the Christ comes and Israel and Judah will again be united together under the resurrected king David while Messiah the Christ rules the whole earth.

1:11 Then shall **the children of Judah and the children of Israel be gathered together, and appoint themselves one head,** and they shall come up out of the land: for great shall be the day of Jezreel.

This is a promise that after being rejected for a time, Israel will sincerely repent and be brought into the New Covenant of Jeremiah 31:31 and shall be united with Judea once again.

This is also a prophecy that in the tribulation, today's Spiritual Laodicea WILL sincerely repent and turn away from her idolatry of following idols of men, and will worship the Living God! And a prophecy that all the faithful will then be united under ONE KING; The Lord of Hosts is HIS NAME!

What follows is a plea for physical and spiritual Israel to repent from their whoredoms after other gods and idols.

It is a plea for physical and spiritual Israel to set aside their whoring [selling themselves to follow others] after their false traditions, leaders and organizations; to turn back to their espoused Husband in passionate love and zeal for his will and law; lest we be rejected by our espoused Husband Jesus Christ and thrown into the furnace of affliction.

Hosea 2

Hosea 2:1 Say ye unto your brethren, Ammi; and to your sisters, Ruhamah.

The adulteries of physical and Spiritual Israel have come between us and our Husband so that we are an unclean thing to him.

2:2 Plead with your mother, plead: for she is not [no longer] my wife, neither am I her husband: let her therefore put away her whoredoms out of her sight, and her adulteries from between her breasts;

If we do not repent quickly, God will remove all our blessings and he will reveal all of our sins.

2:3 Lest I strip her naked, and set her as in the day that she was born, and make her as a wilderness, and set her like a dry land, and slay her with thirst.

2:4 And I will not have mercy upon her children [spiritually the converts to our spiritual adulteries]; for they be the children of whoredoms.

2:5 For their mother hath played the harlot: she that conceived them hath done shamefully: for she said, I will go after my lovers, that give me my bread and my water, my wool and my flax, mine oil and my drink.

God will neither have mercy on us nor on our converts; for we love our increase and our mammon and our turning away from our Husband! We have perverted the Gospel of warning and repentance into a inoffensive to sinners business model quest for supporters, selling ourselves for their mammon; we have turned from zeal to live by every Word of God to a zeal for idols men and false traditions.

Because we are not zealous to live by EVERY WORD of God, Almighty God will not bless us in our doings.

2:6 Therefore, behold, I will hedge up thy way with thorns, and make a wall, that she shall not find her paths.

Because today's Ekklesia seeks the love, support and approval of the worldly and does not love God enough to be zealous to keep his Word; our doings will NOT prosper. Today we are divided, confused and separated from our God because of our compromising and idolatry of men, false traditions and our spiritual adultery against the Husband of our Baptismal commitment!

2:7 And she shall follow after her lovers, but she shall not overtake them; and she shall seek them, but shall not find them: then shall she say, I will go and return to my first husband; for then was it better with me than now.

Therefore we are under a curse and our ways will not bring us gain but only sorrows, we will be divided and our increase shall be cursed for our faithlessness and whoring after our idols of men and false teachings; until we are corrected in the furnace of affliction and turn back to our God.

We have forgotten the source of our blessings and have been lifted up with pride, thinking that we are full of godliness and have need of nothing spiritually.

2:8 For she did not know that I gave her corn [grain], and wine, and oil, and multiplied her silver and gold, which they prepared for Baal

Today we are devoted to our idols of men, corporate churches and false traditions.

2:9 Therefore will I return, and take away my corn [grain] in the time [of harvest] thereof, and my wine in the season thereof, and will recover my wool and my flax given to cover her nakedness.

We have forgotten that our blessing come from our God who blesses those who are faithful zealous and obedient to him! Therefore our God will withdraw his blessings from us until we turn back to him. That includes the blessings on the Ekklesia in terms of spiritual understanding as well as in physical things. Because we reject a good understanding of godly things to follow our idols of men, the understanding of spiritual things has been kept back from the called out

Our Husband will permit the shame of our nakedness [our sinfulness] to be revealed; until we sincerely repent and seek the righteousness of his law; then we will be covered with the atoning sacrifice and the pure white linen garments of God's righteousness.

2:10 And now will I discover her lewdness in the sight of her lovers, and none shall deliver her out of mine hand.

Today most reject God's New Moons and routinely pollute God's Sabbaths; therefore God will take all joy far away from us in the furnace of extreme correction.

2:11 I will also cause all her mirth to cease, her feast days, her new moons, and her Sabbath's, and all her solemn feasts.

2:12 And I will destroy her vines and her fig trees, whereof she hath said, These are my rewards that my lovers have given me: and I will make them a forest, and the beasts of the field shall eat them.

Just as physical Israel lost all the blessings of God in that day: All our rejoicings and pleasant things will cease and be taken away during today's tribulation because of our idolatry and our idols of men and false traditions.

2:13 And I will visit upon her the days of Baalim [God will correct our leaders and elders for compromising with God's Word to lead men into sin for reward like Baalim did.], wherein she burned incense to them, and she decked herself with her earrings and her jewels, and she went after her lovers, and forgat me, saith the LORD.

God will take away our pleasant things which we have gained through our idolatry: our organizational unity has already dissolved into hundreds of schisms because we have rejected the source and the only way to unity; which is complete unity of every person with God. God will make our apostate social club churches desolate because of our sins in the hope that we might remember HIM!

Then we will remember him and he will reveal himself to us; calling out to us to sincerely repent; and forgiving and delivering those who turn to him with wholehearted zeal.

2:14 Therefore, behold, I will allure her, and bring her into the wilderness, and speak comfortably unto her.

2:15 And I will give her her vineyards from thence, and the valley of Achor for a door of hope: and she shall sing there, as in the days of her youth, and as in the day when she came up out of the land of Egypt.

2:16 And it shall be at that day, saith the LORD, that thou shalt call me Ishi [beloved Husband; a personal name meaning, "my deliverer, or my salvation."]; and shalt call me no more Baali [lord master].

2:17 For I will take away the names of Baalim [remove all thoughts of following idols of men from our minds, for out of the mind the mouth speaks] out of her mouth, and they shall no more be remembered by their name.

And in that day all Israel shall be saved:

> **Joel 2:30** And I will shew wonders in the heavens and in the earth, blood, and fire, and pillars of smoke. **2:31** The sun shall be turned into darkness, and the moon into blood, before the great and terrible day of the LORD come.
>
> **2:32 And it shall come to pass, that whosoever shall call on the name of the LORD shall be delivered: for in mount Zion and in Jerusalem shall be deliverance**, as the LORD hath said, and in the remnant whom the LORD shall call.

Now God speaks of the New Covenant and God's Spirit changing the whole earth when Messiah comes and teaches about physical Israel which was married to God, which marriage ended with the death of the Husband; and who will yet be betrothed to God in a New Covenant (Is 11, Is 65, Eze 34:25, Eze 37:26, Jer 31:31).

Hosea 2:18 And in that day will I make a covenant for them with the beasts of the field and with the fowls of heaven, and with the creeping things of the ground: and I will break the bow and the sword and the battle out of the earth, and will make them to lie down safely.

2:19 And I will betroth thee unto me for ever; yea, I will betroth thee unto me in righteousness, and in judgment, and in lovingkindness, and in mercies.

2:20 I will even betroth thee unto me in faithfulness: and thou shalt know the LORD.

At that time all repentant flesh will be grafted into the New Covenant that God will make with physical Israel, and will become part of a new Spiritual Israel the bride of Messiah the Christ!

In that day God will hear the people from heaven and they on the earth shall hear and obey his voice.

2:21 And it shall come to pass in that day, I will hear, saith the LORD, I will hear [God will hear the people from heaven] the heavens, and they [the people on the earth will hear and obey God] shall hear the earth;

2:22 And the earth shall hear [All flesh shall hear and obey God and be filled with his blessings] the corn [grain], and the wine, and the oil; and they [all nations shall see and follow the example of Israel in repentance unto godliness] shall hear Jezreel [Israel].

2:23 And I will sow her [Israel will be planted a Godly people] **unto me** in the earth; and **I will have mercy upon her that had not obtained mercy; and I will say to them which were not** [had been rejected from being] **my people, Thou art my people; and they shall say, Thou art my God.**

At that time those which have gone astray will be repentant and reconciled to God; and ALL the earth will be reconciled to God the Father and the Son through sincere wholehearted repentance from all sin and idolatry and the application of the Passover sacrifice of Jesus Christ!

Hosea 3

God commanded Hosea to love a woman who would be an adulteress against him, as an allegory of God's marriage to adulterous physical and spiritual Israel; so that Hosea will understand what it is like to be married to an unfaithful spouse.

Hosea 3:1 Then said the LORD unto me, Go yet, love a woman beloved of her friend, yet an adulteress, [as an allegory of God's love for unfaithful physical and spiritual Israel] **according to the love of the LORD toward the children of Israel, who look to other gods, and love flagons of wine.**

3:2 So I bought her to me for fifteen pieces of silver, and for an homer of barley, and an half homer of barley:

Hosea purchased a wife with a dowry of silver, which is also an allegory that Christ purchased us as his bride [although at the much higher price of his life]

3:3 And I said unto her, Thou shalt abide for me many days; thou shalt not play the harlot, and thou shalt not be for another man: so will I also be for thee [they entered a marriage covenant].

Hosea is commanded to take a wife and to love her even though she would be an adulteress; to set an example of the love of Christ for his adulteress wife, Israel; and the love of Christ for his straying people who are spiritual adulterers.

3:4 For the children of Israel shall abide many days [years] without a king [referring to God as the king], and without a prince [referring to the high priest], and without a sacrifice [without an atonement for sin], and [over time God well destroy their idols and false gods] without an image, and without an ephod, and without teraphim:

Most of Israel was and is estranged from God, until Messiah comes to reign over them.

3:5 Afterward shall the children of Israel return, and seek the LORD their God, and David their king; and shall fear the LORD and his goodness in the latter days.

God is consistent; if physical Israel beloved of Christ, is rejected for their idolatry; so Spiritual Israel Beloved of Christ, will be rejected by Christ for OUR idolatry (Rev 3).

Hosea 4

Hosea 4:1 Hear the word of the LORD, ye children of Israel: for the LORD hath a controversy with the inhabitants of the land, because **there is no truth, nor mercy, nor knowledge of God** in the land.

4:2 By swearing, and lying, and killing, and stealing, and committing adultery, they break out, and blood toucheth blood.

It is the same in today's Spiritual Ekklesia, we reject truth and knowledge of godly things for false traditions; we are full of spiritual adultery with our idols of men and leaders rob God's tithes for personal extravagances by the organizations. We are full of ourselves convinced of our own righteousness justifying all that we do; and the stink of our self-righteousness reaches up to high heaven.

The teaching of tolerance for sin, our idolizing of men and our rampant Sabbath breaking have robbed us of our potential eternal lives, leading us into destruction and death.

> **Ezekiel 34:2** Son of man, prophesy against the shepherds of [physical AND spiritual] Israel, prophesy, and say unto them, Thus saith the Lord GOD unto the shepherds; Woe be to the shepherds of Israel that do feed themselves! should not the shepherds feed the flocks?

Spiritually speaking today's Spiritually Ekklesia is murdering their own people, leading men along the path to destruction, when they should be teaching the path to life.

Hosea 4:3 Therefore shall the land mourn, and every one that dwelleth therein shall languish, with the beasts of the field, and with the **fowls of heaven**; yea, the **fishes of the sea also shall be taken away**.

We see this today with influenza, the oceans being emptied of fish, and the food stocks being diminished? Today's issues are only a small foretaste of what lies ahead in the tribulation.

Where is the godly man who strives for God against the wickedness in today's Assemblies?

4:4 Yet let no man strive, nor reprove another: for thy people are as they that strive with the [true man of God] priest.

Just as Almighty God sent ancient Israel into captivity he will send modern physical and spiritual Israel into captivity for committing the very same sins; pride, adultery against God with idols and polluting God's Holy Sabbath Day.

4:5 Therefore shalt thou fall in the day, and the [false] prophet also shall fall with thee in the night, and I will destroy thy mother.

Today's physical Israel and Judah reject the knowledge of God for their own ways and traditions, while the spiritual Israel of the Called Out also rejects the increase in knowledge that God has promised in Daniel 12 and is revealing in these last days. Therefore Almighty God will reject both physical and spiritual Israel, because we have first rejected him by rejecting God's Word.

I warn the leaders and elders of today's Spiritual Ekklesia who reject the knowledge that God is revealing and who teach the brethren to follow themselves as idols of men; that they will surely be rejected by God and cast into great correction.

4:6 My people are destroyed for lack of knowledge: **because thou hast rejected knowledge, I will also reject thee, that thou shalt be no priest to me: seeing thou hast forgotten the law of thy God, I will also forget thy children.**

God will forget the organizations that we have fathered,

Because we call the Sabbath holy while teaching men to pollute the Sabbath; and we teach the brethren to idolize men and false traditions;

committing spiritual adultery against the Husband of our Baptismal commitment, such men will be rejected and removed as shepherds of God's Flock.

Most of today's leaders and elders are extremely wicked, loving to teach the brethren to follow themselves into sin

4:7 As they were increased, so they sinned against me: therefore will I change their glory into shame.

4:8 They eat up [they relish to teach the brethren to sin by making idols of men] the sin of my people, and **they set their heart on their iniquity. 4:9** And there shall be, like people, like priest: and I will punish them for their ways, and reward them their doings.

These leaders count numbers and mammon as gain and prostitute themselves for such physical gain: Brushing aside the practical application of God's Word for carnal gain. Changing the Gospel of warning and repentance into an inoffensive business model presentation of the wonders of the Kingdom; while not teaching the way into that Kingdom.

We have increased our wickedness all the more and have left off of any zeal for living by Every Word of God.

4:10 For they shall eat, and not have enough: they shall commit whoredom, and shall not increase: because they have **left off** [refused] **to take heed to the LORD.**

The spiritual adultery of listening to others instead of being zealous to live by EVERY WORD of God; has intoxicated us with pride like alcohol intoxicates.

4:11 Whoredom and wine and new wine take away the heart.

We have been deceived into thinking that physical gain is godliness and we have separated ourselves from him to seek that physical gain. Therefore the gain shall never be enough to fill our needs, until we understand that we have been seduced by the deceitfulness of mammon.

> **1 Timothy 6:3** If any man teach otherwise, and consent not to wholesome words, even the words of our Lord Jesus Christ, and to the doctrine which is according to godliness; **6:4** He is proud, knowing nothing, but doting about questions and strifes of words, whereof cometh envy, strife, railings, evil surmisings, **6:5** Perverse disputings [against God's commandments, teaching to compromise with the Word of God] of men of corrupt minds, and destitute of the

truth [of God], supposing that gain is godliness: from such withdraw thyself. **6:6** But godliness with contentment is great gain.

Hosea 4:12 My people ask counsel at their stocks, and their staff declareth unto them: for the spirit of whoredoms hath caused them to err, and they have gone a whoring from under their God.

What is a whore? Let us look beyond the sexual and we shall see that a whore is a mercenary who has NO loyalties and will sell herself to whoever will pay her price.

A whore is a woman who's loyalty is for sale: While whoredom is the act of selling that loyalty.

We espoused ourselves to a Husband at our baptism; we committed ourselves to be ONE with him: To be of the same mind and spirit, to live by the same principles and laws, to internalize the very mind of our Lord and to become completely united in mind and spirit with HIM!

If we then follow any other we have betrayed the loyalty we vowed to our Husband! We are idolaters, and in the emotional and spiritual sense we have become adulterers and have committed whoredom!

If we idolize anyone or anything above the Word of our God and above his will; we are apostates and rebellious adulterous wives; UNFIT for entering the marriage of the Lamb as his bride!

4:13 They sacrifice upon the tops of the mountains, and burn incense upon the hills, under oaks and poplars and elms, because the shadow thereof is good: therefore your daughters shall commit whoredom, and your spouses shall commit adultery.

By not worshiping God at his Temple the ancient people worshiped as they saw fit instead of doing as God commanded them. Today the called out also worship as they see fit instead of as God commands us.

ALL united Israel was commanded to sacrifice where? AT the House of God, the Temple: and NOT on every high hill.

Jeroboam was afraid that if the people put God first and went to God's Temple in Jerusalem, that he would lose control of the people.

So it is with today's Spiritual Ekklesia; they see the brethren following and serving and living by every Word of God as a personal threat to their pride and vaunted opinion of themselves and their false traditions.

> **1 Kings 12;26** And Jeroboam said in his heart, **Now shall the kingdom return to the house of David: 12:27 If this people go up to do sacrifice in the house of the LORD at Jerusalem, then shall the heart of this people turn again unto their lord, even unto Rehoboam king of Judah**, and they shall kill me, and go again to Rehoboam king of Judah.
>
> **12:28** Whereupon the king took counsel, and **made two calves of gold, and said unto them, It is too much for you to go up to Jerusalem: behold thy gods, O Israel, which brought thee up out of the land of Egypt. 12:29** And he set the one in Bethel, and the other put he in Dan.
>
> **12:30** And this thing became a sin: for the people went to worship before the one, even unto Dan. **12:31** And he made an house of high places, and made priests of the lowest of the people, which were not of the sons of Levi.

Jeroboam had no faith and was not willing to live by every Word of God, turning away from God and leading the people into following himself instead of following the Word of God: TO MAINTAIN CONTROL OVER THE BRETHREN!

The sin of Jeroboam the son of Nebat is the same sin that many leaders and elders have fallen into today!

They are afraid that if they teach the people to be faithful to God; that they will lose their power and control over the brethren! Why? Because they will not live by every Word of God themselves!

They teach loyalty to themselves, their false traditions and their groups and they ordain ministers based on personal loyalty rather than on any loyalty to God! Today's church organizations have fallen into gross idolatry and spiritual adultery with idols of men!

Hosea 4:14 I will not punish your daughters when they commit whoredom, nor your spouses when they commit adultery: for themselves are separated with whores, and they sacrifice with harlots: therefore the people that doth not understand shall fall.

God is asking why he should punish our spouses if they commit adultery against us; when we ourselves are adulterers against Christ.

All of us who exalt men, the false traditions of men and organizations above our espoused Husband are idolaters and spiritually adulterers; and we shall all be severely corrected if we do not repent and go worship him and to live by every Word that proceeds out of the mouth of God (Mat 4:4).

4:15 Though thou, Israel, play the harlot, yet let not Judah offend; and come not ye unto Gilgal, neither go ye up to Bethaven, nor swear, The LORD liveth.

In the next few years both physical Israel and physical Judah will be severely corrected one last time; and today's faithless Spiritual Ekklesia who follow idols of men and will not live by every Word of God, will be severely corrected along with them.

For we are all backsliders who claim to be godly. We pray and when we get up we follow idols of men and commit adultery against our espoused Husband.

4:16 For Israel slideth back as a backsliding heifer: now [once we are corrected and sincerely repent, God will feed us with his Word] the LORD will feed them as a lamb in a large place. **4:17** Ephraim is joined to idols: let him alone.

Like the leaders of physical Israel; most of today's leaders and elders of spiritual Israel are continually exalting idols above the Eternal and committing adultery against the Husband of our baptismal commitment. They love to demand that the brethren give, give, give to them, as they steal our crowns and lead us down the path to destruction like Balaam did to Israel.

4:18 Their drink [they have polluted the water of God's Spirit and Word] is sour: they have committed whoredom continually: her rulers with shame do love, Give ye [to them].

God has bound up physical and spiritual Israel in the wind to scatter them and their strength in the great correction of tribulation, in the hope that by afflicting the flesh he might bring us to sincere repentance and save the spirit.

4:19 The wind hath bound her up in her wings, and they shall be ashamed because of their sacrifices.

The leaders of physical and spiritual Israel love to receive a gift more than they love the Word of God and the commandments of our Husband; therefore God will remove those shepherds and appoint a new shepherd [the resurrected David over Israel, and Messiah over the whole earth] over his flock.

Our Mighty One will separate out the evil shepherds from the good shepherds and will raise up from death those who have proven faithful to live by his every Word; exalting them as his faithful priests and kings when he gathers Israel at his coming!

Jeremiah 23:1 Woe be unto the pastors that destroy and scatter the sheep of my pasture! saith the LORD. **23:2** Therefore thus saith the LORD God of Israel against the pastors that feed my people; Ye have scattered my flock, and driven them away, and have not visited them: behold, I will visit upon you the evil of your doings, saith the LORD.

23:3 And I will gather the remnant of my flock out of all countries whither I have driven them, and will bring them again to their folds; and they shall be fruitful and increase. **23:4** And I will set up shepherds over them which shall feed them: and they shall fear no more, nor be dismayed, neither shall they be lacking, saith the LORD. **23:5** Behold, the days come, saith the LORD, that I will raise unto David a righteous Branch, and a King shall reign and prosper, and shall execute judgment and justice in the earth.

23:6 In his days Judah shall be saved, and Israel shall dwell safely: and this is his name whereby he shall be called, THE LORD OUR RIGHTEOUSNESS.

Hosea 5

Most of the Levitical priests of God departed from God and became a snare leading physical Israel astray from the Eternal to follow idols.

Today most of the leaders and elders of the Ekklesia have departed from the Eternal and have become a snare, leading the called out of Spiritual Israel astray from the Eternal to follow idols of men.

Soon judgment will fall upon us and we will be rejected by the Eternal into great tribulation if we do not sincerely and quickly repent and become zealous and HOT to live by EVERY WORD of the Eternal.

Hosea 5:1 Hear ye this, O priests; and hearken, ye house of Israel; and give ye ear, O house of the king; for judgment is toward you, because ye have been a snare on Mizpah, and a net spread upon Tabor.

Those who revolt against any zeal to live by every Word of God, are going down to and are leading the brethren into A GREAT CORRECTION.

The Eternal will furiously rebuke the leaders and elders who lead the people astray from him to follow idols of men; for they bear the greater responsibility.

5:2 And the revolters are profound to make slaughter, though I have been a rebuker of them all.

Today the spirit of rebellion against the Eternal to go our own ways and follow our own idols fills physical AND spiritual Israel. Even when we claim to be worshiping God we insist on doing so by our own ways and not as the Eternal has commanded.

5:3 I know Ephraim, and Israel is not hid from me: for now, O Ephraim, thou committest whoredom, and Israel is defiled.

5:4 They will not frame their doings [repent and return] to turn unto their God: for the spirit of whoredoms is in the midst of them, and they have not known the LORD.

The sins of Israel and Judah are recorded for us so that we might learn from that history and avoid the same mistakes, yet we know from many scriptures that in the last days we will also be caught up in these same sins and we will also suffer great correction.

5:5 And the pride of Israel doth testify to his face: therefore shall Israel and Ephraim fall in their iniquity: Judah also shall fall with them.

In the final great correction, both Israel and Judah as well as the lax of Spiritual Israel will fall into great correction TOGETHER! This has NEVER happened before!

In ancient times Israel fell into captivity over 100 years before Judah, therefore this is a prophecy for the last days when BOTH Israel [physical AND spiritual] and the Jewish state WILL fall together; and Egypt will also be corrected in our time..

Almighty God will reject us (Rev 3:15), because we have rejected the knowledge that God has promised for these last days (Dan 12), and we insist on our own ways and false traditions, rejecting any zeal to live by every Word of God

5:6 They shall go with their flocks and with their herds to seek the LORD; but **they shall not find him; he hath withdrawn himself from them.**

Today the Ekklesia has leavened the Word of God with the false teachings of men.

5:7 They have dealt treacherously against the LORD: for they have begotten strange children [taught their children to be strangers to God, teaching them to follow false ways]: now shall a month devour them with their portions.

Mark 7:13 Making the word of God of none effect through your tradition, which ye have delivered: and many such like things do ye.

Because physical Israel and Judah have rejected their God, and because today's New Covenant called out have turned to idolatry; compromising with the Word of God for gain. Because of the overspreading of our abominations today's Physical and Spiritual Israel will be corrected together.

Hosea 5:8 Blow ye the cornet in Gibeah, and the trumpet in Ramah: cry aloud at Bethaven, after thee, O Benjamin.

5:9 Ephraim shall be desolate in the day of rebuke: among the tribes of Israel have I made known that which shall surely be.

5:10 The princes of Judah were like them that remove the bound [remove boundaries, to steal land]: therefore I will pour out my wrath upon them like water.

In this latter day Judah steals land by removing boundaries; this is speaking of what is going on in Palestine right now, but is more particularly speaking of what will come when the Settler Movement extremists reject the boundaries set by the coming peace deal. When they break the peace deal, the trumpets of war will sound and the tribulation will begin.

5:11 Ephraim is oppressed and broken in judgment, because he willingly walked after [against] the commandment [of God].

5:12 Therefore will I be unto Ephraim as a moth [to consume them, as a moth eats up wool], and to the house of Judah as rottenness.

5:13 When Ephraim saw his sickness, and Judah saw his wound, **then went Ephraim to the Assyrian, and sent to king Jareb** [literally, to plead with the ruler of Assyria]: **yet could he not heal you, nor cure you of your wound**.

Pleading with men and nations to help will not save us from our correction for our offenses against the Mighty One who inhabits eternity!

5:14 For I [Almighty God will correct the Judaeo, Anglo Saxon peoples and Spiritual Israel in furious rebuke] will be unto Ephraim as a lion, and as a young lion to the house of Judah: I, even I, will tear and go away; I will take away, and **none shall rescue him**.

This thing is from GOD, and it is HIS rebuke for OUR SINS! This is not some nasty NAZI attack, for Germany is our true friend who would save us if she could!

What is coming is GOD'S WRATH UPON A WICKED AND SINFUL PEOPLE!

Just as physical Israel failed to be an example of godliness under the Mosaic Covenant; WE have failed to be an example of godliness in the called out of today's Ekklesia! We have even failed to preach the Gospel of warning and repentance!

God will hide himself from our pleas for relief until we learn our lessons and we sincerely repent of our idolatries and spiritual adulteries against our espoused Husband, turning to HIM in wholehearted zeal to live by EVERY WORD of the Eternal God! Then he will rise up and deliver the sincerely repentant!

5:15 I will go and return to my place [God will remain in his place, and will not deliver us], **till they acknowledge their offence, and seek my face: in their affliction they will seek me early.**

Hosea 6

Because we have rejected him, God will soon go to his place and hide his face from us until we learn our lesson and sincerely repent, returning to him; then he shall rise up to deliver us beginning in the third year of our distress!

Hosea 6:1 Come, and let us return unto the LORD: for he hath torn, and he will heal us; he hath smitten, and he will bind us up.

6:2 After two days [years] will he revive us: in the third day [year] he will raise us up, and we shall live in his sight.

After two years and sometime into the third year, many will sincerely repent and God will begin to deliver us. The now rising New Federal Europe [King of the North, Babylon the Great] will attack the Asian nations. God will correct his people BOTH physical and spiritual Israel and he will then go out to correct the gentile nations, so that the whole world will be readied for the Kingdom of God.

After Christ comes and we have sincerely repented and begin to live by Every Word of God, God will rain his Holy Spirit on all flesh (Joel 2:28), then all shall understand and know godliness. The spring rains are a type of the giving of the Holy Spirit to the early harvest, and the fall rains are a type of the Holy Spirit raining down on the main harvest of humanity

6:3 Then shall we know, if we follow on to know the LORD: his going forth is prepared as the morning; and he shall come unto us as the rain, as the latter and former rain unto the earth.

When all Israel repents and the world is prepared, the Eternal will come like a refreshing rain to bring peace and righteousness to the earth.

God corrects those he loves:

> **Revelation 3:19** As many as I love, I rebuke and chasten: be zealous therefore, and repent.

Hosea 6:4 O Ephraim [the British peoples and nations], what shall I do unto thee? O Judah, what shall I do unto thee? for your goodness is as a morning cloud, and as the early dew it goeth away.

Physical Israel and Judah will yet become an example of godliness for all the earth; Spiritual Israel will yet become an example of godliness for the whole earth; which is the end purpose of the chastening of the Eternal

6:5 Therefore have I hewed them by the prophets; I have slain them by the words of my mouth: and [so that] thy judgments are [will become] as the light that goeth forth [as an example for all nations].

Oh, Israel [including both physical and spiritual Israel] beloved of God; you are like the goodness of the dew, but your goodness quickly fades just as the dew vanishes with the sun; therefore God must correct those who have gone astray so that they might be saved for eternity.

6:6 For I desired mercy, and not sacrifice; and the knowledge of God more than burnt offerings.

6:7 But they like men have transgressed the covenant: there have they dealt treacherously against me.

BOTH Mosaic Israel and the Spiritual Israel of Laodicea (Rev 3:15-22) have dealt treacherously with God our Husband in committing adultery against him with our idols.

6:8 Gilead [Israel] is a city of them that work iniquity, and is polluted with blood.

Most of the leaders and elders of today's Spiritual Ekklesia are full of lewdness for they are full of spiritual adultery against the Husband of our baptismal commitment.

Today's elders and spiritual leaders have become murders of the brethren by leading them into sinning against the Eternal, teaching them to commit spiritual idolatry and adultery just like Balaam taught the people to sin on the physical level. .

6:9 And as troops of robbers wait for a man, so the company of priests murder in the way by consent: for they commit lewdness.

Like physical Israel, the spiritual leaders of today's New Covenant called out are lewd adulterers against their Husband and are the way of death to those who would follow them.

We have sold ourselves to commit adultery against the Husband of our baptismal commitment, to exalt and to zealously follow idols of men in place of any zeal for living by Every Word of God.

6:10 I have seen an horrible thing in the house of Israel: there is the whoredom of Ephraim, Israel is defiled.

6:11 Also, O Judah, he hath set an harvest for thee, when I returned the captivity of my people.

Some of our leaders are not only spiritual adulterers but physical adulterers also. Some even openly living in adultery and letting others do so, via unlawful divorce and remarriage.

Hosea 7

Today the called out consider themselves righteous, thinking that they are God's people and that God will not hold them accountable for what they do.

They call the Sabbath holy and then routinely pollute it, claiming that they have the right to decide for themselves what is right and what is wrong; thereby exalting themselves above the Word of God, and above the author of that Word; Almighty God himself. When their papers on the Calendar are proven to be full of gross errors and falsehoods, they smile and say: "We have decided" as if they have the authority to sit in judgment of God's Word, to turn from it and to decide for themselves as Eve did in the garden. So that Romans 1:21 is fulfilled in us also.

> **Romans 1:21** Because that, when they knew God, they glorified him not as God, neither were thankful; but became vain in their imaginations, and their foolish heart was darkened.
>
> **1:22** Professing themselves to be wise, they became fools,

The sins and judgment of ancient Ephraim are a type of the sins and judgment of today's Spiritual Ekklesia.

Hosea 7:1 When I would have healed Israel, then the iniquity of Ephraim was discovered, and the wickedness of Samaria: for they commit falsehood [teach lies]; and the thief cometh in, and the troop of robbers spoileth without.

7:2 And **they consider not in their hearts that I remember all their wickedness**: now their own doings have beset them about; they are before my face.

7:3 They make the king glad with their wickedness, and the princes with their lies. **7:4** They are all adulterers, as an oven heated by the baker, who [We are like dough that does not rise after it is leavened; we are like dough that does not respond to the bakers work; we are worthless for the purpose which we have been called to.] ceaseth from raising after he hath kneaded the dough, until it be leavened.

Intoxication with wine is a symbol of being intoxicated with pride.

Today our nations, and the leaders and elders of the Spiritual Ekklesia have become intoxicated with pride in their idols of men and their own ways and false traditions, and they will not exalt the whole Word of God to zealously live by EVERY WORD of God.

7:5 In the day of our king the princes have made him sick with bottles of wine; he stretched out his hand with scorners.

7:6 For they have made ready their heart like an oven, whiles they lie in wait: their baker sleepeth all the night; in the morning it burneth as a flaming fire. **7:7** They are all hot as an oven, and have devoured their judges; all their kings [rulers and leaders of both physical and spiritual Israel] are fallen [away]: **there is none among them that calleth unto me** [in humble sincerity].

Before the fall of Samaria to Assyria the rulers of Ephraim were drunk with pride and none relied on God, they delighted in personal gain even by robbery, exalting themselves above all else and they are full of adulteries.

In the spiritual sense this is quite applicable to today's nations and the Spiritual Assemblies, whose leaders love the chief seats and love to exalt themselves leading the people into spiritual adultery against their espoused Husband: They compromise with God's Word in the hope of gaining a great following, and exalt their own ways and false traditions above the Word of God.

We are full of sin; from living in physical adultery through permissive divorce and remarriage, to Sabbath pollution; from personal politicking and power plays, to idolizing men, and the false traditions of men and organizations. Our elders tolerate sin without rebuke and pervert the Gospel of warning and repentance into a business model false gospel of having a part in a coming Kingdom of God without zealous obedience to the laws of that Kingdom.

Ephraim was and is like a pancake cooked on only one side and today's Spiritual Assemblies are no different. We are not wholehearted in our zeal for God but only halfhearted, paying lip-service to God while doing what we want. We have become a shallow pretense with no real substance because we have no zeal for living by the Word of God.

7:8 Ephraim, he hath mixed himself among the people; Ephraim [the British peoples] is a cake not turned.

As Ephraim has become weak by mixing himself with strange peoples, so the called out have become spiritually weak by mixing ourselves with those who have no zeal for godliness. By trying to mix the Word of God with our own ways and the false doctrines of the unconverted [like the Primacy of Peter] and by leavening the assemblies in tolerating willful self-justified sin we have polluted God's Word and made ourselves spiritually unclean.

7:9 Strangers have devoured his strength, and he knoweth it not: yea, gray hairs are here and there upon him, yet he knoweth not.

In the spiritual sense this means that today's Ekklesia has deliberately allowed itself to become filled with those who lack understanding and who are not committed to live by every Word of God, this for the sake of numbers and mammon; and they have dissipated our spiritual strength and relationship with God by leavening the body with sin. We are commanded by God to reject the heretic and the wicked from among us.

We are commended to remove willful sinners from our assemblies

> **Titus 3:10** A man that is an heretick after the first and second admonition reject;
>
> **1 Timothy 5:19** Against an elder receive not an accusation, but before two or three witnesses. **5:20** Them [the elders] that sin rebuke before all, that others also may fear.

For:

> **1 Corinthians 3:16** Know ye not that ye are the temple of God, and that the Spirit of God dwelleth in you? **3:17** If any man defile the temple of God, him shall God destroy; for the temple of God is holy, which temple ye are.

We are not to associate with willful self-justifying sinners in our assemblies.

> **1 Corinthians 5:11** But now I have written unto you not to keep company, if any man that is called a brother be a fornicator, or covetous, or an idolator, or a railer, or a drunkard, or an extortioner; **with such an one no not to eat.**

Brethren, it is because we have not obeyed the Word of our God to avoid polluting the congregations, that we are now half baked and have become a mixed people; mixing the holy with the profane.

And why? Because we have prostituted our loyalty to the sound doctrine of our Husband, Jesus Christ; for the supposed gain of numbers and mammon.

Hosea 7:10 And the pride of Israel testifieth to his face: and they do not return to the LORD their God, nor seek him for all this.

Why is Laodicea gone astray and will NOT repent? Because their pride is lifted up and they think they know it all!

No one, not even Jesus Christ and the scriptures can tell them anything. They twist the scriptures as they choose or simply ignore and reject them as applying to others what they should be applying all scripture to themselves.

> **Revelation 3:17** Because thou sayest, I am rich, and increased with goods, and have need of nothing; and knowest not that thou art wretched, and miserable, and poor, and blind, and naked:

Hosea 7:11 Ephraim also is like a silly dove without heart: they call to Egypt, they go to Assyria.

7:12 When they shall go, I will spread my net upon them; I will bring them down as the fowls of the heaven; I will chastise them, as their congregation hath heard.

Physical Israel depends upon her allies instead of upon God and the called out seek to avoid offending the mainstream today: Being more afraid of offending men, than of offending our God!

Those who have been called by God the Father and redeemed by the application of the sacrifice of Jesus Christ, speak evil of their Redeemer in claiming that he will tolerate and overlook sin, saying that they have a right to live contrary to the Word of God!

7:13 Woe unto them! for they have fled [departed from, run away from godliness] from me: destruction unto them! because they have transgressed against me: though **I have redeemed them**, yet they have spoken lies against me.

We mourn and call for deliverance from our troubles; but we will not turn to zealously live by every Word of God!

7:14 And they have not cried unto me with their [from the heart in sincerity] heart, when they howled upon their beds: they assemble themselves for corn [grain] and wine, and they rebel against me.

Though God has called and redeemed us, we have turned from him to follow idols of men and to live contrary to God's Word.

7:15 Though I have bound and strengthened their arms, yet do they imagine mischief against me.

We do not do what God intended us to do, which is to live by EVERY WORD of God; so that we might be a godly example for the nations and inherit life eternal.

7:16 They return, but not to the most High: they are like a deceitful bow [that does not hit the intended target]: their princes shall fall by the sword for the rage of their tongue: this shall be their derision in the land of Egypt.

This is about today's rebellious New Covenant Called Out who have been redeemed from among men and espoused to an Husband, The Lord of Hosts!

God strengthened and blessed us and we became proud and have lost sight of our God and instead we have become focused on our idols of men.

Hosea 8

God commands his watchmen to blast the warning like a trumpet; Crying, repent, repent; the enemy is at the gates the correction of the LORD is at hand!

I will not keep silent! I will warn the brethren with all the strength that the Eternal provides!

Because of our sins of idolatry, Sabbath breaking and rejecting godly knowledge and our spiritual adultery; our correction is at hand!

Hosea 8:1 Set the trumpet to thy mouth. He shall come as an eagle against the **house of the LORD**, because they have transgressed my covenant, and trespassed against my law.

In great tribulation spiritual and physical Israel will call out for deliverance but there will be NO deliverance any more until we have been thoroughly humbled and have sincerely repented and turned to live by EVERY WORD of God!

8:2 Israel shall cry unto me, My God, we know thee.

Because our Mighty One is against us, the enemy will pursue and overtake us, for the overspreading of all our abominations

8:3 Israel [physical and spiritual] hath cast off the thing that is good [We have rejected the good things of godliness.]: the enemy shall pursue him.

The nations of Israel are an instructional allegory of today's Ekklesia. We have ordained ungodly men and we love mammon more than we love God.

8:4 They have set up kings, but not by me: they have made princes, and I knew it not: of their silver and their gold have they made them idols, that they may be cut off.

Today we have exalted our idols of men and we do not follow the Holy One to live by every Word of God.

We follow idols of men, equating loyalty to them and their false traditions with loyalty to God himself. We follow such men into sin and away from the Husband of our baptismal commitment, instead of following them ONLY as they follow God the Father and Jesus Christ our Husband!

8:5 Thy calf, [idols] O Samaria [physical and spiritual Israel], hath cast thee off [Our idols of men cannot save us from the wrath of our offended Husband, against whom we have been adulterous.]; mine anger is kindled against them: how long will it be ere they attain to innocency [purity from sin]?

Almighty God destroyed the idols of the past and he will destroy the idols of today!

Our corporate church's will be destroyed along with all the unrepentant wicked shepherds who would lead the people to exalt idols of men above living by EVERY WORD of God.

8:6 For from Israel was it also: the workman made it [idols are made by men and shall perish]; therefore it is not God: but the calf of Samaria shall be broken in pieces.

Today our golden calf is our corporate churches!!! They are organizations of men made by men and are NOT God!!!

Almighty God is a jealous Husband and he will destroy our golden calf of corporate churches and turn his bride back to himself. In the soon coming tribulation our Lord will destroy the corporate churches and FORCE people to stand or fall spiritually, based on our zeal and fidelity to HIS WORD.

Almighty God will destroy our crutch and our cloak for our sins ["The elder said it was alright to do this" contrary to God's Word]; and FORCE us to stand like adults and place our Husband FIRST; or fail to do so and be counted unworthy of eternal life as a part in the bride.

We are like a wheat plant that has no stalk and cannot produce grain [spiritual fruit], and if we should have some natural good in us, it will perish. Strangers and enemies will swallow us up because we have not remained attached to the Vine of our Salvation, John 15. We have departed from any zeal to live by Every Word of God the Father and the Son to follow idols of men.

8:7 For they have sown the wind, and they shall reap the whirlwind: it hath no stalk; the bud shall yield no meal: if so be it yield, **the strangers shall swallow it up.**

8:8 Israel [both physical and apostate spiritual Israel] is swallowed up: now shall they be among the Gentiles as a vessel wherein is [God has no pleasure] no pleasure.

8:9 For they are gone up to Assyria, a wild ass alone by himself: Ephraim hath hired lovers

Ephraim represents the nations of Israel and they seek out allies of men which cannot save her; they have rejected turning to the God of Salvation, who ONLY can save; just as today's New Covenant brethren seek and follow idols of men and not God.

8:10 Yea, though they have hired among the nations, now will I gather them, and they shall sorrow a little for the burden of the king of princes.

Physical Israel will not be saved by her allies of men or through compromising with the enemy; and Spiritual Israel will not be saved by her idols of men when the Eternal corrects her. We shall BOTH be made to sorrow for all our abominations and brought to sincere repentance through that humbling.

8:11 Because Ephraim hath made many altars to sin, altars shall be unto him to sin.

8:12 I have written to him the great things of my law, but they were counted as a strange thing.

God does not accept us because we are full of sin.

8:13 They sacrifice flesh for the sacrifices of mine offerings, and eat it; but the LORD accepteth them not; now will he remember their iniquity, and visit their sins: they shall return to Egypt.

God does not accept our offerings and prayers to him because we are full of pride and unrepented sin; God has hidden his face from us because we have departed from his Word to commit adultery against the Husband of our baptismal commitment.

We of spiritual Israel, like physical Israel, have forgotten who has made us and we follow idols of men: While Judah trusts in her military strength which the Almighty will destroy with a wave of his hand for all their sins in idolizing the traditions of men above living by Every Word of God.

8:14 For Israel hath forgotten his Maker, and buildeth temples [to the idols in Samaria]; and Judah hath multiplied fenced cities: but I will send a fire upon his cities, and it shall devour the palaces thereof.

Today as in ancient Israel, neither our idols of men nor our idols of military might will save us from the wrath of a jealous Husband over his adulterous bride. We will not be saved because we belong to some group or race and consider ourselves the temple of God. Our deliverance comes through our sincere repentant ZEAL to live by every Word of God!

> **Jeremiah 7:1** The word that came to Jeremiah from the LORD, saying, **7:2** Stand in the gate of the LORD's house, and proclaim there this word, and say, Hear the word of the LORD, all ye of Judah, that enter in at these gates to worship the LORD. **7:3** Thus saith the LORD of hosts, the God of Israel, Amend your ways and your doings, and I will cause you to dwell in this place. **7:4 Trust ye not in lying words, saying, The temple of the LORD, The temple of the LORD, The temple of the LORD, are these**.
>
> **7:5** For if ye throughly amend your ways and your doings; if ye throughly execute judgment between a man and his neighbour; **7:6** If ye oppress not the stranger, the fatherless, and the widow, and shed not innocent blood in this place, neither walk after other gods to your hurt: **7:7** Then will I cause you to dwell in this place, in the land that I gave to your fathers, for ever and ever.
>
> **7:8** Behold, ye trust in lying words, that cannot profit. **7:9** Will ye steal, murder, and commit adultery, and swear falsely, and burn incense unto Baal, and walk after other gods whom ye know not; **7:10** And come and stand before me in this house, which is called by my name, and say, We are delivered to do all these abominations?

7:11 Is this house, which is called by my name, become a den of robbers in your eyes? Behold, even I have seen it, saith the LORD. **7:12 But go ye now unto my place which was in Shiloh, where I set my name at the first, and see what I did to it for the wickedness of my people Israel.**

Hosea 9

Because physical and spiritual Israel have sold themselves to idols; they will reap strong correction from God.

Hosea 9:1 Rejoice not, O Israel, for joy, as other people: for thou hast gone a whoring from thy God, thou hast loved a reward upon every cornfloor [threshing floor]. **9:2** The [threshing of harvest] floor and the winepress shall not feed them, and the new wine shall fail in her.

This is about the first captivity of Israel]aka Samaria] which began about 721 B.C. and is a type of the final tribulation now about to begin in our day.

9:3 They shall not dwell in the LORD's land [Palestine]; but Ephraim shall return to Egypt [spiritually a type of bondage], and they shall eat unclean things in Assyria.

Ancient Israel was taken captive to Assyria (2 Kings 17) c 721 B.C.

9:4 They shall not offer wine offerings to the LORD, neither shall they be pleasing unto him: their sacrifices shall be unto them as the bread of mourners; all that eat thereof shall be polluted: for their bread for their soul shall not come into the house of the LORD.

The coming correction of great tribulation

Brethren, it is far past time for the mourning and fasting of repentance and for the humbling of ourselves before our God in the hope that we might be delivered from the weakness and sin that besets us.

Let us wholeheartedly turn to our espoused spiritual Husband in passionate love, seeking his forgiveness; perhaps he will extend mercy before his anger grows hot and his correction comes upon us.

What will we do in the Feasts of the LORD during the time of our correction?

9:5 What will ye do in the solemn day, and in the day of the feast of the LORD?

9:6 For, lo, they are gone [the corporate churches will fail] because of destruction [during the tribulation]: Egypt [in this great tribulation Egypt will also be filled with great multitudes of dead] shall gather them up, Memphis shall bury them: the pleasant places for their silver, [The silver and gold will be taken as spoils and the store houses shall be empty and desolate.] nettles [the store houses will be filled with weeds and briers] shall possess them: thorns [deep sorrows] shall be in their tabernacles [tents, homes].

9:7 The days of visitation are come, the days of recompence are come; Israel shall know it: the [Today physical and spiritual Israel despise God's wisdom and consider God's true servants fools.] prophet is a fool, the spiritual man is [The true godly person is vexed by the wickedness in today's assemblies.] mad, for the multitude of thine iniquity, and the great hatred [of the wicked against the godly].

The sins and judgment of ancient Ephraim are a type of the sins and judgment of today's Spiritual Ekklesia.

9:8 The watchman of Ephraim was with my God: but the [false] prophet is a snare of a fowler in all his ways, and hatred in the house of his God.

The ancient watchman of Ephraim [a watchman from the British peoples] was a true man of God: but the false leaders hated the truth speakers who are zealous for the Eternal, because they wanted the people to follow them and not the Word of God; therefore such evil doers were despised and rejected by the Eternal God and removed from the land and today's Spiritual Ekklesia will also be strongly corrected (Rev 3:15-22).

9:9 They have deeply corrupted themselves, as in the days of Gibeah: therefore he will remember their iniquity, he will visit their sins.

The Watchman speaks the truth to the brethren and trumpets the true Gospel of warning and sincere repentance to live by every Word of God.

False prophets deceive the people and ensnare them into being lax for the practical application of God's Word; saying that they are delivered to pollute the Sabbath and to exalt men and the false traditions of men for the sake of organizational unity.

The false teachers say, "no correction will come upon us for we are the temple of the Lord" (Jer 7:4); they deceive the brethren into idolatry and then lull them to sleep with lullabies of how righteous they are.

As the Eternal in his anger turns away from us they promise safety and deliverance while they steal our crowns and lead us to our destruction.

Imagine yourself very hungry as you travel across a desolate place and you happened across some just ripe fresh grapes, or some first ripe figs, what a great delight; but after eating them you because sick because they turned bitter in your stomach. This is the experience of God with today's Spiritual Ekklesia.

9:10 I found Israel like grapes in the wilderness; I saw your fathers as the firstripe in the fig tree at her first time: but they went to Baalpeor [turned from God to their idols], and separated themselves unto that shame; and their abominations were according as they loved.

We were pleasant in our first passionate love when God the Father found us and called us out to be espoused to his Son; then later we played the spiritual whore falling into idolatry and spiritual adultery.

The glory of Ephraim and Israel will dissipate and the grand buildings and corporate assemblies of today's Spiritual Ekklesia will be destroyed.

9:11 As for Ephraim, their glory shall fly away like a bird, from the birth, and from the womb, and from the conception.

9:12 Though they bring up their children, yet will I bereave them, that there shall not be a man left: yea, woe also to them when I depart from them!

9:13 Ephraim, as I saw Tyrus, is planted in a pleasant place: but Ephraim shall bring forth his children to the murderer.

9:14 Give them, O LORD: what wilt thou give? give them a miscarrying womb and dry breasts.

Can one read this and not be reminded of how Jesus Christ [Hebrew: Yeshua Mashiach] drove the wicked out of the Temple?

Jesus did a similar thing before he gave up his Godhood to become flesh, when he gave ancient Israel over to the Assyrians and removed then from the land; later while in the flesh he drove the wicked out of God the Father's temple as an instructional example to today's Spiritual Ekklesia, that Jesus Christ will reject and cast out those who commit spiritual adultery against him by following idols of men.

9:15 All their wickedness is in Gilgal: for there I hated them: **for the wickedness of their doings I will drive them out of mine house, I will love them no more: all their princes are revolters.**

9:16 Ephraim is smitten, their root is dried up, they shall bear no fruit: yea, though they bring forth, yet will I slay even the beloved fruit of their womb.

9:17 My God will cast them away, because they did not hearken unto him: and they shall be wanderers among the nations.

Ephraim and Israel will be corrected with a great correction; their ancient captivity being but a a small foretaste of the great correction now at our door.

This warning also concerns the great correction of today's Spiritual Ekklesia and physical Israel for departing from any zeal to live by every Word of God to follow idols of men in spiritual adultery.

Hosea 10

Physical Israel is an example and instruction for the Spiritual Israel of the New Covenant called out.

Hosea 10:1 Israel is an empty vine, he bringeth forth fruit unto himself: according to the multitude of his fruit he hath increased the altars; according to the goodness of his land they have made goodly images.

Israel both physical and today's spiritual Israel, has not produced the fruit of godliness; instead they have used the fruit of the land [God's blessings] for idolatry.

10:2 Their heart is divided; now shall they be found faulty: he shall break down their altars, he shall spoil their images.

Today's Spiritual Ekklesia is divided [double minded, hypocritical] as they pay lip-service to God while they follow idols of men to do as they think right; instead of being zealous to live by what God teaches is right.

Our many corporate church organizations which we obey instead of living by God's Word are the altars of our idols of men which most of the brethren exalt above living by EVERY WORD of God today.

God will destroy all our organizational idols so that the brethren might be turned to a zeal for HIM alone. Many love their "church" more than they love God!

When we learn that total unity with God the Father and our espoused Husband Jesus Christ is the purpose for our calling, and when we achieve that unity through internalizing the mind, nature and Spirit of God through diligently learning and keeping of every Word of God: We will be acceptable as a part of the bride.

In tribulation we will learn that we are in severe affliction because we did not fear or love God enough to follow him with a whole heart.

10:3 For now they shall say, We have no king, because **we feared not the LORD;** what then should a king do to us?

When we made our baptismal commitment of espousal to God, to live by EVERY WORD of God; we made a commitment which we have not kept. Today's spiritually called out Ekklesia follow idols of men contrary to our commitment to live by EVERY WORD of God (Mat 4:4): And we are living in a continual state of spiritual adultery against our espoused Husband!

10:4 They have spoken words, **swearing falsely in making a covenant** [which we have not kept]: thus judgment springeth up as hemlock [our judgment (guilt and condemnation) is springing up everywhere like weeds in a field] in the furrows of the field.

Our false leaders will be removed to teach us to follow no leader except God the Father and the Lord of Hosts. Then we will turn to a zeal for God's Word and sound judgment will begin to spring up within us like a mighty fountain of godly righteousness.

10:5 The inhabitants of Samaria shall fear because of the calves of Bethaven [Today's Spiritual Ekklesia will learn to fear God when our spiritual idols of corporate church organizations and men are destroyed.]: for the people thereof shall mourn over it, and the priests thereof that rejoiced on it, for the glory thereof, because it is departed from it.

Just as ancient Israel was carried away in captivity to Assyria today we face severe correction because our Protector has abandoned us for our endless idolatry and spiritual adulteries.

Physical Israel will mourn in her affliction; and the spiritually called out brethren and elders who rejoiced in their corporate idols shall mourn when they are severely corrected.

10:6 It shall be also carried unto Assyria for a present to king Jareb: Ephraim shall receive shame, and Israel shall be ashamed of his own counsel. **10:7** As for Samaria [The ten tribes of the kingdom of Israel were taken away by the Assyrians 2 Kings 17.], her king is cut off as the foam upon the water.

All those who follow idols of men and refuse to live by EVERY WORD of God will be corrected: Then in the time of their affliction God will bring those who survive to repentance with HOPE!

Yes, when the peoples see the dead in Christ resurrected they will remember the words of God's servants that their Messiah is coming and that their deliverance is at hand! Then they will turn to accept and embrace HIM, and they will welcome him with a great rejoicing!

10:8 The high places also of Aven, the sin of Israel, shall be destroyed: the thorn and the thistle shall come up on their altars; and they shall say to the mountains, Cover us; and to the hills, Fall on us.

Our false gods will be taken away and we shall be turned back to our spiritual Husband.

10:9 O Israel, thou hast sinned from the days of Gibeah: there they stood: the battle in Gibeah against the children of iniquity did not overtake them.

10:10 It is in my desire that I should chastise them; and the people shall be gathered against them, when they shall bind themselves in their two furrows [The furrow of Israel and the furrow of Judah].

It is in God's mind to afflict us in order to correct us and turn us to live by every Word of God; so that he might save and deliver us.

10:11 And Ephraim is as an heifer that is taught, and loveth to tread out the corn [grain];

Ancient Ephraim [a type of modern Israel and Judah] loved to serve sin; but God will break us of that addiction and teach us to serve righteousness and to bring forth the fruits of righteousness.

. . . but I passed over upon her fair neck [God will deliver us from bondage to sin]: I will make Ephraim to ride; Judah shall plow, and Jacob shall break his clods.

10:12 Sow to yourselves in righteousness, reap in mercy; break up your fallow ground: for it is time to seek the LORD, till he come and rain righteousness upon you.

God commands us to repent and turn to him; to plow and sow righteousness in the sure hope of receiving mercy.

For we have sowed wickedness in departing from the Word of our God and we will be corrected if we do not quickly repent

10:13 Ye have plowed wickedness, ye have reaped iniquity; ye have eaten the fruit of lies: because thou didst trust in thy way [Today's Spiritual Ekklesia trust in our own ways and in our own wisdom and judgment and our own strength, instead of trusting in and living by the Word of God.]**, in the multitude of thy mighty men.**

Ancient Israel was defeated and removed from the land and today's nations of Israel and today's Spiritual Ekklesia will suffer severe correction.

10:14 Therefore shall a tumult arise among thy people, and all thy fortresses shall be spoiled, as Shalman spoiled Betharbel in the day of battle: the mother was dashed in pieces upon her children.

10:15 So shall Bethel do unto you **because of your great wickedness**: in a morning shall the king of Israel utterly be cut off.

Hosea 11

Israel was called out and delivered from Egypt, as a type of God calling people and delivering them out of bondage to Satan, sin and death.

Very many who were delivered out of Egypt turned away from their Deliverer to follow idols; just as very many of today's spiritually called out of bondage to sin, have departed from their Deliverer to follow idols of men and corporate entities.

Hosea 11:1 When Israel was a child, then I loved him, and called my son out of Egypt.

11:2 As they called them, so they went from them: they sacrificed unto Baalim, and burned incense to graven images.

God taught Ephraim [Israel] how to live righteously and Israel turned aside to idols; just as God has taught today's spiritually called out to live by every Word of God and we have departed from God to follow idols of men.

11:3 I taught Ephraim also to go, taking them by their arms; but they knew not that I healed them.

Ephraim as the head tribe of Israel is a type of the family of Jacob, which is the family of Israel and Judah. God loved Israel the wife of his covenant, delivering them from bondage in Egypt; and God passionately loves his beloved espoused bride spiritual Israel; delivering us from bondage to sin.

11:4 I drew them with cords of a man, with bands of love [Israel was delivered from bondage in Egypt with deep love, to be bound to the God Being who later gave up his Godhood to be made flesh.]: and I was to them as they that take off the yoke on their jaws [God delivered them from bondage, removing the yoke on them], and I laid meat unto them [fed them with the Word of God].

These things happened to physical Israel and they were recorded as a lesson for the Spiritual Ekklesia who have been called out from bondage to Satan, sin and death.

11:5 He [Israel] shall not return into the land of Egypt, and the Assyrian shall be his king, because they refused to return [they refused to repent and return to God].

Israel went into captivity by the Assyrians [modern Germany] c 721 B.C. In our time the nations of Israel will again be defeated; at this time by the final manifestation of Babylon, the soon coming New Europe which will include Germany.

11:6 And the sword shall abide on his cities, and shall consume his branches, and devour them, because of their own counsels.

Because they followed their own wicked ways and idols of men instead of following the Word of Go they were severely corrected. Today neither physical nor spiritual Israel exalts the Eternal to keep his Word.

During the coming 42 months of affliction, violence will abide in the nations of physical Israel; there will be riots over race and scarce food and necessities as desperate folks seek to survive.

The bulk of today's Spiritual Ekklesia will be corrected with the nations because we have also departed from living by every Word of God.

11:7 And my people are bent to backsliding from me: though they called them to the Most High, **none at all would exalt him.**

Like a loving father whose heart melts and goes out to his son that he loves, at the sincere repentance of a rebuked child: The heart of Almighty God will sorrow for us and his anger will vanish away and he will accept us when we sincerely repent.

11:8 How shall I give thee up, Ephraim? how shall I deliver thee, Israel? how shall I make thee as Admah? how shall I set thee as Zeboim? mine heart is turned within me, my repentings are kindled together.

11:9 I will not execute the fierceness of mine anger, I will not return to destroy Ephraim: for I am God, and not man; the Holy One in the midst of thee: and I will not enter into the city.

When God has humbled the people, he will come to deliver all humanity from bondage to Satan and sin. Then we shall all walk after [live by] every Word of God.

11:10 They shall walk after the LORD: he shall roar like a lion [to deliver the repentant at his coming]**:** when he shall roar, then the children shall tremble from the west.

The nations will tremble in fear at the coming of the LORD and they shall turn to help those that they have despoiled.

11:11 They shall tremble as a bird out of Egypt, and as a dove out of the land of Assyria: and I will place them in their houses, saith the LORD.

At that time c 721 B.C. Judah was still faithful. This is not so today and Judah will be afflicted with Israel, Hosea 5:5, during the 42 months of "Jacob's Trouble."

11:12 Ephraim compasseth me about with lies, and the house of Israel with deceit: but Judah yet ruleth with God, and is faithful with the saints.

Hosea 12

Did you ever try to grasp a handful of wind? It is pointless and so is our following idols of men and their errors while not being zealous to follow and live by every Word of God.

Today's spiritually called out, teach falsely and have no love of the truth; therefore because we have rejected a knowledge of the truth just like physical Israel has done we are being rejected by God the father and Jesus Christ (Rev 3:15-22) into great correction.

Hosea 12:1 Ephraim feedeth on wind, and followeth after the east wind [follows empty foolishness]: he daily increaseth lies and desolation; and they do make a covenant with the Assyrians, and oil is carried into Egypt.

In c 721 B.C. only the ten tribes of Israel were taken away by the Assyrians, but in this final tribulation both Israel and Judah shall fall together (Hos 5:5)

12:2 The LORD hath also a controversy with Judah, and will punish Jacob [God will correct all Israel including Judah in this latter day.] according to his ways; according to his doings will he recompense him.

God calls on the descendants of Jacob [all Israel and Judah, both physical and spiritual] to remember Jacob's zeal for and stubborn determination to serve God.

12:3 He took his brother by the heel in the womb, and by his strength [determination and zeal] he had power [was respected by God] with God:

12:4 Yea, he had power over the angel, and prevailed: he wept, and made supplication unto him: he found him in Bethel, and there he spake with us;

12:5 Even the LORD God of hosts; the LORD is his memorial.

God calls on the descendants of Jacob [both physical and spiritual Israel] to repent of our wicked deceitfulness and to serve God with a whole heart.

12:6 Therefore **turn thou to thy God: keep mercy and judgment and wait on thy God continually.**

Let the nations of Israel and the Nicolaitane elders of today's Spiritual Assemblies deeply and wholeheartedly repent of our deceitfulness and bullying.

12:7 He is a merchant, the **balances of deceit are in his hand: he loveth to oppress.**

We think that we are guiltless in our great pride; yet God will bring us down and humble us for our many sins.

12:8 And Ephraim said, Yet I am become rich, I have found me out substance: in all my labours they shall find none iniquity in me that were sin.

12:9 And I that am the LORD thy God from the land of Egypt will yet make thee to dwell in tabernacles, as in the days of the solemn feast.

God sent many prophets to warn ancient Israel of their coming captivity which came when they were taken by Assyria c 721 B.C.; and Israel rejected the prophets, the warnings and the call to repentance.

Just like ancient Israel, today physical and spiritual Israel reject the warnings of coming correction and the calls to repentance.

12:10 I have also spoken by the prophets, and I have multiplied visions, and used similitudes, by the ministry of the prophets.

Our sacrifices are meaningless because we do not repent of our wickedness in exalting the false teachings of men above any zeal to live by EVERY WORD of God.

What does it profit if the brethren fall on their knees and cry out that they repent, and then rise up to commit spiritual adultery against the Husband of their baptismal commitment by following idols of men?

12:11 Is there iniquity in Gilead [Israel]? surely they are vanity: they sacrifice bullocks in Gilgal; yea, their altars are as heaps in the furrows of the fields.

Just as Jacob was forced to flee because of his sin against Esau; surely in this latter day all Israel both physical and spiritual are full of sin and we will surely receive a severe correction for our sins.

12:12 And Jacob fled into the country of Syria, and Israel served for a wife, and for a wife he kept sheep.

God by the prophet Moses, led Israel out of physical Egypt, and by the prophet Jesus Christ the Lamb of God, God the Father delivered those whom God he calls out from bondage to sin; of which physical Egypt was a type.

12:13 And by a prophet the LORD brought Israel out of Egypt, and by a prophet was he preserved.

Yet, today's called out of Spiritual Ekklesia have provoked God, just as physical Israel has done; by following idols of men and teaching for doctrine the commandments of men (Mat 15:9).

12:14 Ephraim provoked him [God] to anger most bitterly: therefore shall he [Israel] leave his blood [require correction] upon him, and his reproach shall his LORD return unto him [our evil deeds will bring reproach and correction from God].

Hosea 13

When we tremble in humility before the Eternal and exalt him alone to live by his every Word, he will exalt us; but when we chose to abandon our zeal for godliness to follow idols of men, we shall be corrected and brought low.

Hosea 13:1 When Ephraim spake trembling [before God], he exalted himself in Israel; but when he offended in Baal [idolatry], he died.

The spiritual counterpart of idols of silver and gold; is pride and idols of men, false traditions, money and corporate organizations

13:2 And now they sin more and more, and have made them molten images of their silver, and **idols according to their own understanding,** all of it the work of the craftsmen: they say of them, Let the men that sacrifice kiss the calves.

Here on the coast we often wake up to a layer of cloud from the sea which we call marine fog, and as the sun rises up this cloud burns off and disappears. The wicked are like this marine fog, they exist for a moment and are gone. There is nothing lasting in idols or those who follow them.

13:3 Therefore they shall be as the morning cloud and as the early dew that passeth away, as the chaff that is driven with the whirlwind out of the floor, and as the smoke out of the chimney.

13:4 Yet **I am the LORD thy God from the land of Egypt, and thou shalt know no god but me: for there is no saviour beside me.**

13:5 I did know thee in the wilderness, in the land of great drought [in Egypt the land of no rain which requires irrigation].

God delivered physical Israel from bondage in Egypt to a rich land; and as they were blessed they were filled with pride and forgot the Eternal, turning from him to follow their own imaginations.

Just as God delivered Israel from bondage in Egypt; he delivers the Spiritual Ekklesia from bondage to sin and blessed them with spiritual riches and as they were blessed they were filled with pride and forgot the Eternal, turning from him to follow their own imaginations.

13:6 According to their pasture [according to the increase of their blessings], so were they filled; they were filled, and their heart was exalted [with pride and their own ways]; therefore have they forgotten me.

Therefore God the Almighty will withdraw his blessings from physical and spiritual Israel as he warned by Moses in Deuteronomy 28 and 30, and God will severely correct his people until they sincerely repent and wholeheartedly follow him to live by EVERY WORD of God.

13:7 Therefore I will be unto them as a lion: as a leopard by the way will I observe them:

13:8 I will meet them as a bear that is bereaved of her whelps, and will rend the caul [the covering of the heart, as a type of the covering of sin] of their heart, and there will I devour them like a lion: the wild beast shall tear them.

13:9 O Israel, thou hast destroyed thyself; but in me is thine help. 13:10 I will be thy king: where is any other that may save thee in all thy cities? and thy judges of whom thou saidst, Give me a king and princes? **13:11** I gave thee a king in mine anger, and took him away in my wrath.

13:12 The iniquity of Ephraim is bound up; his sin is hid.

Ephraim as the head and representative of all Israel and the Spiritual Ekklesia is full of sin, but he cannot see his sin. Today's Spiritual Ekklesia is blind to their sin which pride has hidden from his understanding (Rev 3:14-22).

A great affliction will come upon today's physical and spiritual Israel like the pains of a woman at the birth of a child. Israel will suffer dearly like a woman in labor, but like a child is born from the travail of its mother; a new Israel will be born who will be faithful to God in all her ways.

3:13 The sorrows of a travailing woman shall come upon him: he is an unwise son; for he should not stay long [Israel shall not suffer a long time in affliction, only 42 months (Rev 11:2)] in the place of the breaking forth of children.

God will deliver the repentant nations and God will also deliver the repentant of spiritual Israel from the grave in the resurrection to eternal life, and later he will deliver the dead in the main harvest to physical life and give them an opportunity to also be changed.

13:14 I will ransom them from the power of the grave; I will redeem them from death: O death, I will be thy plagues; O grave, I will be thy destruction: repentance shall be hid from mine eyes.

In the tribulation God will not deliver the sincerely repentant immediately, instead he will hide his eyes from our repentance to prove the sincerity of that repentance by requiring us to live by every Word of God in extreme conditions.

13:15 Though he be fruitful among his brethren, an east wind shall come, the wind of the LORD shall come up from the wilderness, and his spring shall become dry, and his fountain shall be dried up: he shall spoil the treasure of all pleasant vessels.

This being an allegory that God the Father and Jesus Christ will reject those who have rejected them (Rev 3:15), and will cast them out; drying up the fountain of God's Holy Spirit [which they have quenched] from those who have no zeal for godliness.

The Holy Spirit is the Spirit of Truth (John 14:17, John 15:26, John 16:13, 1 John 4:6), and most of today's assemblies have rejected truth for their own false ways.

13:16 Samaria shall become desolate; for she hath rebelled against her God: they shall fall by the sword: their infants shall be dashed in pieces, and their women with child shall be ripped up.

Hosea 14

God calls us to sincere wholehearted repentance

Hosea 14:1 O Israel, return unto the LORD thy God; for thou hast fallen by thine iniquity.

14:2 Take with you words, and turn to the LORD: say unto him, Take away all iniquity, and receive us graciously: so will we render the calves of our lips.

14:3 Asshur [Do not rely on allies and human helpers for safety, but trust in the Eternal.] shall not save us; we will not ride upon horses: neither will we say any more to the work of our hands, Ye are our gods: for in thee the fatherless findeth mercy.

Let us abandon all of our idolatry; both idols of stone and spiritual idols of men.

In this latter day; when we are afflicted we will repent and run to our Mighty One who alone can save. He will afflict our flesh to save our spirit, and he will heal us when we have learned our lesson and wholeheartedly turn to him.

After his coming the Eternal will greatly bless his people and bring them into the New Covenant of Jeremiah 31, and ultimately all nations and peoples will be grafted into New Covenant Israel.

14:4 I will heal their backsliding, I will love them freely: for mine anger is turned away from him. **14:5** I will be as the dew unto Israel: he shall grow as the lily, and cast forth his roots as Lebanon.

14:6 His branches shall spread, and his beauty shall be as the olive tree, and his smell as Lebanon. **14:7** They that dwell under his shadow shall return; they shall revive as the corn [grain], and grow as the vine: the scent thereof shall be as the wine of Lebanon.

When Christ comes a reunited Israel/Judah will return to the Land of Promise and will faithfully dwell in the shade of the Eternal and will live by every Word of God.

14:8 Ephraim [physical and spiritual Israel] **shall say, What have I to do any more with idols?** I have heard him, and observed him: I am like a green fir tree. From me is thy fruit found.

14:9 Who is wise, and he shall understand these things? prudent, and he shall know them? **for the ways of the LORD are right, and the just shall walk in them** [shall live by every Word of God]**: but the transgressors shall fall therein.**

The wicked will be corrected by God's righteous judgment.

Joel

Joel 1

Joel is about the fall of the ten tribes of Israel to Assyria which was an allegory of the now rapidly approaching great tribulation and the glorious coming of Messiah.

Joel 1:1 The word of the LORD that came to Joel the son of Pethuel.

1:2 Hear this, ye old men, and give ear, all ye inhabitants of the land. Hath this been in your days, or even in the days of your fathers?

1:3 Tell ye your children of it, and let your children tell their children, and their children another generation.

Great famine is coming due to crop pestilence and drought.

1:4 That which the palmerworm hath left hath the locust eaten; and that which the locust hath left hath the cankerworm eaten; and that which the cankerworm hath left hath the caterpiller eaten.

There will be no grapes for wine or grain for beer and those given to alcohol will have little during much of the tribulation. The same can be said for various narcotics and drugs as that supply will also dry up. This is a good thing as our people will be sobered up and forced to think of deeper much more meaningful things.

1:5 Awake, ye drunkards, and weep; and howl, all ye drinkers of wine, because of the new wine; for it is cut off from your mouth.

God tells us that many enemies will come up and over-flood Palestine [My land]. Jerusalem and Judah will be occupied of their enemies for the last 42 months before Messiah comes; while the other nations of Israel [primarily the Anglo Saxon countries] will collapse economically but will not necessarily occupied.

1:6 For a nation is **come up upon my land**, strong, and without number, whose teeth are the teeth of a lion, and he hath the cheek teeth of a great lion. **1:7** He hath laid my vine waste, and barked my fig tree: he hath made it clean bare, and cast it away; the branches thereof are made white.

God will allow others to take everything away from us in order to wake us up from our spiritual intoxication with pride.

This is an allegory that we in today's Spiritual Ekklesia have become drunk with pride and self- righteousness, we have turned from living by every Word of God unto corporate idols of our own devising; looking to idols of men as our moral authority instead of standing on the Word of God.

God tells on us to mourn for our sins as a young widow mourns in her widowhood; because our Husband has rejected us.

1:8 Lament like a virgin girded with sackcloth for the husband of her youth.

Physical Israel is told to lament and repent; and Spiritual Israel is to lament our sins, to sincerely repent and to wholeheartedly seek God the Father and Jesus Christ the Husband of our baptismal commitment.

1:9 The meat offering and the drink offering is cut off from the house of the LORD; the priests, the LORD's ministers, mourn.

Remember what the Meat [Unleavened Bread] Offering and the pouring out of the Drink [Wine] Offering symbolizes! These are symbols of the body of Christ broken for us, and the life blood of God become flesh as Jesus Christ poured out for the sincerely repentant.

Jesus, knowing that lambs could not be sacrificed on Passover after the destruction of the temple, and wanting to reveal what the Meat and Drink Offerings represented; explained the eating of the broken Unleavened Bread Offering and the drinking of the Wine in the Passover service.

In this age; the Spiritual Ekklesia is the House or Temple of the Lord!

> **2 Corinthians 6:16** . . . for ye are the temple of the living God; as God hath said, I will dwell in them, and walk in them; and I will be their God, and they shall be my people.

> **1 Corinthians 3:16** Know ye not that ye are the temple of God, and that the Spirit of God dwelleth in you? **3:17** If any man defile the temple of God [with sin], him shall God destroy; for the temple of God is holy, which temple ye are.

Today's Laodicea Ekklesia will be rejected and spewed out by Jesus Christ (Rev 3:15-22); and no longer covered by the blood of the New Covenant, because of their idolatry and spiritual adulteries and their rejection of living by every Word of God!

God will smash our corporate idols and take away the pleasant things of this world that we have compromised with his commandments to attain; so that we might know that our idols of men are NOT gods at all and that we should be zealous for the Husband of our baptismal commitment.

Because these corporate organizations teach people to exalt men as their idols and to follow the false traditions of men contrary to God's Word, our jealous Husband will destroy the corporate churches for turning the flock away from God and towards following idols of men. HE will smash our pride and destroy our idols, calling us to true sincere repentance.

Joel 1:10 The field is wasted, the land mourneth; for the corn [grain or seed] is wasted: the new wine is dried up, the oil languisheth [does not flow forth].

The great famine

Corn was discovered in the New World and was unknown elsewhere even in the middle ages, at that time the word "corn" simply meant a corn or a grain of something; for example corned beef is so called because of the corns of salt used to cure the meat.

1:11 Be ye ashamed, O ye husbandmen; howl, O ye vinedressers, for the wheat and for the barley; because the harvest of the field is perished. **1:12** The vine is dried up, and the fig tree languisheth; the pomegranate tree, the palm tree also, and the apple tree, even all the trees of the field, are withered: because joy is withered away from the sons of men.

Because our nations rebel against God, he will take away our foodstuffs to teach the people to hunger and thirst after God's Word (Mat 5:6).

1:13 Gird yourselves, and lament, ye priests: howl, ye ministers of the altar: come, **lie all night in sackcloth, ye ministers of my God: for the meat offering and the drink offering is withholden from the house of your God.**

The true shepherds are told to mourn their sins because the Atoning Sacrifice of Christ is withheld from his Called Out of Laodicea, the spiritual house of God: Because we have rejected our LORD for spiritual adulteries and idols of men, we have been rejected by our espoused Husband.

> **Revelation 3:14** And unto the angel of the church of the Laodiceans write; These things saith the Amen, the faithful and true witness, the beginning of the creation of God;
>
> **3:15** I know thy works, that thou art neither cold nor hot: I would thou wert cold or hot. **3:16** So then because thou art lukewarm, and neither cold nor hot, **I will spue thee out of my mouth**.

Yes, we are HOT for our own ways and for our corporate idols; and yes we are Cold to live by every Word of our God; such a mixture of hot and cold is called lukewarm. We pay lip-service to God and his Word as we compromise and make the Word of God of no effect by our false traditions.

Today is a time for sincere repentance in the hope that we might be spared the righteous correction of an offended God. Soon, if they will not repent now, very many will fall into severe correction to bring them to repentance.

Joel 1:14 Sanctify ye a fast, call a solemn assembly, gather the elders and all the inhabitants of the land into the house of the LORD your God, and cry unto the LORD,

Despite the various attempts to limit the Day of the Lord; the term applies to the entire period of God's correction, not merely to the seven last plagues, or the day of his coming. The Day [time] of God's correction of his people is at hand.

1:15 Alas for the day! for the day of the LORD is at hand, and as a destruction from the Almighty shall it come.

Our land will be plagued with great drought

1:16 Is not the meat [all food] cut off before our eyes, yea, joy and gladness from the house of our God?

1:17 The seed is rotten under their clods, the garners are laid desolate, the barns are broken down; for the corn [grain] is withered.

There is no more joy for the people: We have been wounded and broken as Hosea describes.

> **Hosea 6:1** Come, and let us return unto the Lord: for he hath torn, and he will heal us; he hath smitten, and he will bind us up.
>
> **6:2** After two days will he revive us: in the third day he will raise us up, and we shall live in his sight.
>
> **6:3** Then shall we know, if we follow on to know the Lord: his going forth is prepared as the morning; and he shall come unto us as the rain, as the latter and former rain unto the earth

Joel 1:18 How do the beasts groan! the herds of cattle are perplexed, because they have no pasture; yea, the flocks of sheep are made desolate.

Let us all therefore repent before our God; let us take hold of his Word and sincerely repent, pleading with him to cover our transgressions so that we might be reconciled to God.

1:19 O LORD, to thee will I cry: for the fire [severe drought brings fires] hath devoured the pastures of the wilderness, and **the flame hath burned all the trees** of the field.

1:20 The beasts of the field cry also unto thee: for the rivers of waters are dried up, and the fire hath devoured the pastures of the wilderness.

Joel 2

In the latter day the now rising New federal Europe will occupy Jerusalem for 42 months during which time half of the resident Jews will be deported.

Zechariah 14:1 Behold, the day of the Lord cometh, and thy spoil shall be divided in the midst of thee.

14:2 For I will gather all nations against Jerusalem to battle; and the city shall be taken, and the houses rifled, and the women ravished; and half of the city shall go forth into captivity, and the residue of the people shall not be cut off from the city.

Then the armies of Asia will come down to Jerusalem to confront the last redoubt of the false prophet and the king of the north. When that battle is joined Jesus Christ will intervene WITH his chosen resurrected saints.

14:3 Then shall the Lord go forth, and fight against those nations, as when he fought in the day of battle.

Joel 2:1 Blow ye the trumpet in Zion, and sound an alarm in my holy mountain: let all the inhabitants of the land tremble: for the day of the LORD cometh, for it is nigh at hand;

After Jerusalem has been occupied for over three years by the army of the New Europe and there is war between Europe and Asia; the Asian armies will sweep through the Middle East and surround the city, then Messiah the Christ will come with God's resurrected faithful.

2:2 A day of darkness and of gloominess, a day of clouds and of thick darkness, as the morning spread upon the mountains: a great people and a strong; there hath not been ever the like, neither shall be any more after it, even to the years of many generations.

2:3 A fire devoureth before them; and behind them a flame burneth: the land is as the garden of Eden before them, and behind them a desolate wilderness; yea, and nothing shall escape them.

2:4 The appearance of them is as the appearance of horses; and as horsemen, so shall they run. **2:5** Like the noise of chariots on the tops of mountains shall they leap, like the noise of a flame of fire that devoureth the stubble, as a strong people set in battle array. **2:6** Before their face the people shall be much pained: all faces shall gather blackness.

2:7 They shall run like mighty men; they shall climb the wall like men of war; and they shall march every one on his ways, and they shall not break their ranks: **2:8** Neither shall one thrust another; they shall walk every one in his path: and when they fall upon the sword, they shall not be wounded.

2:9 They shall run to and fro in the city; they shall run upon the wall, they shall climb up upon the houses; they shall enter in at the windows like a thief.

2:10 The earth shall quake before them; the heavens shall tremble: the sun and the moon shall be dark, and the stars shall withdraw their shining:

Then Messiah the Deliverer, the Christ will intervene to save the earth. He shall come with his resurrected saints to rule the earth in righteousness and teach the way to salvation to all humanity.

2:11 And the LORD shall utter his voice before his army: for his camp is very great: for he is strong that executeth his word: for the day of the LORD is great and very terrible; and who can abide it?

Repent for the Lord is strong to deliver, let all evil be destroyed and let all men repent before the Mighty One of New Covenant Spiritual Israel (Jer 31)! Sincerely repent and he will forgive and receive you!

Brethren, if we all sincerely repent and wholeheartedly turn to God the Father and our espoused Husband in passionate zeal to live by every Word of God; even now at this late hour he would rejoice in us and we would all be saved from his correction.

I call on all peoples to repent of their idolatries and spiritual adulteries and false human traditions, and to open up the Word of the Lord and study it with an open mind to diligently seek out the truth of God.

Remember how in today's Spiritual Ekklesia we call the Sabbath holy as we routinely pollute it, and many threw out the book of Nehemiah so that they could cling to their false traditions and continue to pollute the Sabbath by buying and selling?

Remember how men threw out the scriptures concerning the Sabbath, changing the Sabbath of God from the commanded seventh day to the first day of the week in rejection of God's Word for man's traditions.

Brethren, in the garden Satan presented clever arguments and persuaded the woman to disobey God and take the forbidden fruit. Did God care for fruit? No, this was a test of obedience!

The seventh day Sabbath is also a TEST; the command is a test to see if we will obey God or if we will do as we decide for ourselves. Changing the Sabbath to Sunday is supported by various reasons for doing so which reasons seem very good; but regardless of the human reasoning to justify this, doing this is rebellion against what God has commanded.

Exactly the same thing can be said about postponing God's Holy Days, clever arguments are presented for doing so; but regardless of the human reasoning to justify the move, doing this is rebellion against what God has commanded.

Today we are loyal to the traditions of men and NOT to the Word of God; even out-rightly rejecting those parts of God's Word that we do not want to obey. That is a shame and a disgrace, a blot on our conversion that must be removed.

All who do not repent will be severely corrected.

2:12 Therefore also now, **saith the LORD, turn ye even to me with all your heart, and with fasting, and with weeping, and with mourning:**

2:13 And rend your heart, and not your garments, and turn unto the LORD your God: for he is gracious and merciful, slow to anger, and of great kindness, and repenteth him of the evil.

2:14 Who knoweth if he will return and repent, and leave a blessing behind him; even a meat offering and a drink offering unto the LORD your God?

Fast the fast of sincere wholehearted repentance and turn to live by EVERY WORD of God.

2:15 Blow the trumpet in Zion, sanctify a fast, call a solemn assembly:

2:16 Gather the people, sanctify the congregation, assemble the elders, gather the children, and those that suck the breasts: let the bridegroom go forth of his [Let the bride and groom forsake their wedding night to repent before God.] chamber, and the bride out of her closet [forsake her wedding night to fast and repent before God].

2:17 Let the priests, the ministers of the LORD, weep [in repentance and prayer for deliverance] between the porch and the altar, and let them say, **Spare thy people, O LORD, and give not thine heritage to reproach, that the heathen should rule over them: wherefore should they say among the people, Where is their God?**

If we do these things and seek the Eternal with a sincere and whole heart, he will deliver us

2:18 Then will the LORD be jealous for his land, and pity his people.

Those who do not repent and turn to a genuine zeal for godliness will be cast into the severe correction of the 42 month trial of the great tribulation, so that through the affliction of the flesh, the spirit will be humbled to repentance and saved.

Then the Messiah will come to save all people beginning by resurrecting God's faithful and then delivering physical Israel, bringing them into a New Covenant with him (Jer 31:31), because they have been humbled and are repentant, ready to accept their Lord. Then all repentant humanity will be grafted into New Covenant Israel.

Then God will bless Israel and all nations who turn to him.

2:19 Yea, the LORD will answer and say unto his people, Behold, I will send you corn [grain, food], and wine, and oil, and ye shall be satisfied therewith: and I will no more make you a reproach among the heathen:

2:20 But I will remove far off from you the northern army [the armies of Asia which are attacking Jerusalem will be destroyed by Christ at his coming], and will drive him into a land barren and desolate, with his face toward the east sea, and his hinder part toward the utmost sea, and his stink shall come up, and his ill savour shall come up, because he hath done great things.

Christ will come with his resurrected chosen and they will destroy the invading armies and deliver Israel and Judah at Jerusalem.

Then the Kingdom of God will be established over all the earth, with David ruling a united Israel and each one of the twelve apostles ruling a tribe of Israel, and Jesus Christ ruling the whole world as King of kings and Lord of lords.

Then righteousness will break forth and cover the earth with peace like a garment; and God shall bless all those who love him enough to live by every Word of God and internalize the very nature of God becoming completely united with God!

2:21 Fear not, O land; be glad and rejoice: for the LORD will do great things. **2:22** Be not afraid, ye beasts of the field: for the pastures of the wilderness do spring, for the tree beareth her fruit, the fig tree and the vine do yield their strength.

2:23 Be glad then, ye children of Zion, and rejoice in the LORD your God: for he hath given you the former rain moderately, and he will cause to come down for you the rain, the former rain, and the latter rain in the first month.

2:24 And the floors shall be full of wheat, and the vats shall overflow with wine and oil. **2:25** And I will restore to you the years that the locust hath eaten, the cankerworm, and the caterpiller, and the palmerworm, my great army which I sent among you.

2:26 And ye shall eat in plenty, and be satisfied, and praise the name of the LORD your God, that hath dealt wondrously with you: and my people shall never be ashamed.

The people of God shall be doing the will of God and they will no longer be doing anything for which they should be ashamed. And all the earth shall KNOW that the Lord God is among them, and they shall keep all of his commandments without compromise, doing the will of God and living by EVERY WORD of God.

2:27 And ye shall know that I am in the midst of Israel, and that I am the LORD your God, and none else [there is no other God]**: and my people shall never be ashamed.**

If we live by every Word of God and internalize his very nature as expressed and defined by the whole Word of God; we shall NEVER be ashamed!

We shall be humbled and brought to sincere repentance and God will pour out his Spirit on ALL flesh, right after the day of the Lord, on the Feast of Pentecost!

Just as God poured out his Spirit in a small way on a few people on the Pentecost of 31 A.D.; he will pour out his Spirit in a much greater fulfillment in the near future.

> **Acts 2:15** For these are not drunken, as ye suppose, seeing it is but the third hour of the day. **2:16** But this is that which **was spoken by the prophet Joel**;
>
> **2:17** And it shall come to pass in the last days, saith God, I will pour out of my Spirit upon all flesh: and your sons and your daughters shall prophesy, and your young men shall see visions, and your old men shall dream dreams:

Joel 2:28 And it shall come to pass afterward [after Christ comes]**, that I will pour out my spirit upon all flesh;** and your sons and your daughters shall prophesy, your old men shall dream [inspired] dreams, your young men shall see visions:

2:29 And also upon the servants and upon the handmaids in those days will I pour out my spirit.

Christ's coming will be accompanied by these signs.

2:30 And I will shew wonders in the heavens and in the earth, blood, and fire, and pillars of smoke. **2:31** The sun shall be turned into darkness, and the moon into blood, before the great and terrible day of the LORD come.

Then after the armies who resist Christ are destroyed, Messiah will enter the city of Jerusalem from the Mount of Olives, just as he entered Jerusalem over nineteen hundred years ago to the rejoicing of all the people who will shout Hosanna [Save us] and accept him as their King; and when Pentecost comes God's Holy Spirit will be poured out on all flesh and all who call on him to save will be delivered!

2:32 And it shall come to pass, that whosoever shall call on the name of the LORD shall be delivered: for in mount Zion and in Jerusalem shall be deliverance, as the LORD hath said, and in the [surviving] remnant whom the LORD shall call.

God will call all of the surviving remnant of people to him and pour out his Spirit on all flesh.

Joel 3

The deliverance of physical Israel and Judah out of their captivity and their return to the land of Palestine.

Joel 3:1 For, behold, in those days, and in that time, when I shall bring again [take away] the captivity of Judah and Jerusalem,

As the New Europe attacks Asia in the third year and its leaders then flee to Jerusalem for their last stand, the nations of Asia will come up against the city

3:2 I will also gather all nations, and will bring them down into the valley of Jehoshaphat, and will plead with them there for my people and for my heritage Israel, whom they have scattered among the nations, and parted my land.

During the 42 months of the tribulation the Jewish state will be occupied and many Jews will be killed or removed from the land

3:3 And they have cast lots for my people; and have given [traded] a boy for an harlot, and sold a girl for wine, that they might drink.

Turkey, Lebanon, Syria, Jordan, the Arab states and the Palestinians will join with the New Europe and those occupying Judea as per Psalm 83.

3:4 Yea, and what have ye to do with me, O Tyre, and Zidon [Lebanon], and all the coasts of Palestine? will ye render me a recompence? and if ye recompense me, swiftly and speedily will I return your recompence upon your own head; **3:5** Because ye have taken my silver and my gold, and have carried into your temples my goodly pleasant things:

When the Jewish Settler Movement extremists break the coming peace deal, the Islamic nations of Psalm 83, except for Egypt, will sweep through the land after God removes his protection for the overspreading of sins.

The New Europe perhaps acting in the name of mercy will concentrate the Jews in ghettos for their safety and many will voluntarily leave or be deported from the land through Lebanese brokers and shipping companies.

Many Jews will be sold from Palestine to Greece and other nations in order to remove them from the land, but that project will not be completed before Christ comes and there will be a remnant of Judah still remaining in Palestine and Jerusalem.

3:6 The **children also of Judah and the children of Jerusalem have ye sold unto the Grecians, that ye might remove them far from their border.**

When Christ comes God will give the land to a reunited and deeply repentant Judah and Israel. The Palestinians will also be devastated by the Asian nations and those who survive will be subject to the resurrected king David and a united Israel.

3:7 Behold, **I will raise them out of the place whither ye have sold them, and will return your recompence upon your own head:**

Just as the Lebanese of Tyre and Sidon will remove many Jews from the land by selling them to other nations [probably as laborers in menial or dangerous jobs]; so God will give Lebanon to Israel who will sell many of them to remove them from the land.

3:8 And **I will sell your sons and your daughters** [the latter day descendants of Tyre and Sidon, Lebanon] **into the hand of the children of Judah, and they shall sell them to the Sabeans** [Sheba and Ophir, probably in India near modern Goa], to a people far off: for the LORD hath spoken it.

God calls forth all the nations of the earth and in particular the armies of Europe and Asia; to the battle of the day of the Lord's coming

3:9 Proclaim ye this among the Gentiles; Prepare war, wake up the mighty men, let all the men of war draw near; let them come up:

3:10 Beat your plowshares into swords and your pruninghooks into spears: let the weak say, I am strong. **3:11** Assemble yourselves, and come, all ye heathen, and gather yourselves together round about: thither cause thy mighty ones to come down, O LORD.

3:12 Let the heathen be wakened, and come up to the valley of Jehoshaphat: for there will I sit to judge all the heathen round about. **3:13** Put ye in the sickle, for the harvest is ripe: come, get you down; for the press is full, the fats overflow; for their wickedness is great.

3:14 Multitudes, multitudes in the valley of decision: for the day of the LORD is near in the valley of decision. **3:15** The sun and the moon shall be darkened, and the stars shall withdraw their shining.

Then Messiah the Christ will come with his resurrected faithful and will destroy the armies of wickedness and set up an eternal kingdom (Dan 2).

3:16 The LORD also shall roar out of Zion, and utter his voice from Jerusalem; and the heavens and the earth shall shake: but the LORD will be the hope of his people, and the strength of the children of Israel.

3:17 So shall ye know that I am the LORD your God dwelling in Zion, my holy mountain: then shall Jerusalem be holy, and there shall no strangers [foreign armies] pass through her any more.

After Christ comes no unconverted person will be allowed to enter the city of Jerusalem for all people will be converted into the New Covenant of espousal to Christ. The millennial kingdom and city are themselves analogies of the Eighth Day Feast representing man and God living in eternal peace and harmony as pictured by the New Jerusalem of Revelation 21.

While vast numbers of resurrected chosen land at points around the world to take over all local authority, Messiah the Christ will step onto the Mount of Olives with 144,000 [Rev 14] who will rule the earth from Jerusalem with him, and the mount will split in half making a way of escape for the people as he destroys the pursuing enemy.

> **Zechariah 14:3** Then shall the Lord go forth, and fight against those nations, as when he fought in the day of battle. **14:4** And his feet shall stand in that day upon the mount of Olives, which is before Jerusalem on the east, and the mount of Olives shall cleave in the midst thereof toward the east and toward the west, and there shall be a very great valley; and half of the mountain shall remove toward the north, and half of it toward the south.
>
> **14:5** And ye shall flee to the valley of the mountains; for the valley of the mountains shall reach unto Azal: yea, ye shall flee, like as ye fled from before the earthquake in the days of Uzziah king of Judah: and the Lord my God shall come, and all the saints with him.
>
> **Revelation 14:15** And another angel came out of the temple, crying with a loud voice to him that sat on the cloud, Thrust in thy sickle, and reap: for the time is come for thee to reap; for the harvest of the earth is ripe.
>
> **14:16** And he that sat on the cloud thrust in his sickle on the earth; and the earth was reaped. **14:17** And another angel came out of the temple which is in heaven, he also having a sharp sickle.

14:18 And another angel came out from the altar, which had power over fire; and cried with a loud cry to him that had the sharp sickle, saying, Thrust in thy sharp sickle, and gather the clusters of the vine of the earth; for her grapes are fully ripe.

14:19 And the angel thrust in his sickle into the earth, and gathered the vine of the earth, and cast it into the great winepress of the wrath of God.

14:20 And the winepress was trodden without the city, and blood came out of the winepress, even unto the horse bridles, by the space of a thousand and six hundred furlongs.

A furlong is an 8th of a mile.

This now speaks of the millennial Kingdom of God

Joel 3:18 And it shall come to pass in that day, that the mountains shall drop down new wine, and the hills shall flow with milk, and all the rivers of Judah shall flow with waters, and a fountain shall come forth out of the house of the LORD, and shall water the valley of Shittim.

3:19 Egypt shall be a desolation, and Edom shall be a desolate wilderness, for the violence against the children of Judah, because they have shed innocent blood in their land.

3:20 But Judah shall dwell for ever, and Jerusalem from generation to generation.

3:21 For I will cleanse their blood [guiltiness] that I have not [previously] cleansed: for the LORD [Messiah the Christ will dwell in Jerusalem] dwelleth in Zion.

The blood guilt of sin will be cleansed for all repentant people through the atoning sacrifice of the Lamb of God.

Joel 2:32 And it shall come to pass, that whosoever shall call on the name of the Lord shall be delivered: for in mount Zion and in Jerusalem shall be deliverance, as the Lord hath said, and in the remnant whom the Lord shall call.

AMOS

Amos 1

Amos 1:1 The words of Amos, who was among the herdmen of Tekoa, which he saw concerning Israel in the days of Uzziah king of Judah, and in the days of Jeroboam the son of Joash king of Israel, two years before the earthquake.

Amos was contemporary with Hosea, Jonah and Joel. These prophets warned Israel just before the ten tribes went into captivity c 721 B.C.; and that captivity was a foretaste of a future and greater latter day tribulation when Israel and Judah will fall together (Hos 5:5).

In this latter day BOTH physical Israel/Judah and the lax and complacent of Spiritual Israel, including professing Christianity; will be soundly corrected in the furnace of affliction.

That correction in the great tribulation is now at hand, which makes the words of these four prophets extremely significant to us at this time.

Amos prophesies against Israel, Judah and the surrounding nations, about the correction of God then and in the latter days.

1:2 And he said, The LORD will roar from Zion, and utter his voice from Jerusalem; and the habitations of the shepherds shall mourn, and the top of Carmel shall wither.

The great tribulation will begin from Zion and the Holy Place in Jerusalem, as Jesus Christ reminded us in Matthew 24:15-21.

God's Judgment on Syria

When Jewish extremists sabotage the coming Mideast peace deal, the Syrian regime will turn and rend the Jewish state along with Turkey, the Arab nations, Jordan and the Palestinians. Finally in the third year the new Europe will attack the nations of Asia which will absorb the attack and counterattack against Europe and her Middle East allies.

The armies of the major Asian nations will respond sweeping through the Middle East down to Jerusalem where the European political and military leaders are making their last stand. As they pass through the region on their way to Jerusalem the Asian armies will devastate Syria and many other nations.

1:3 Thus saith the LORD; For three transgressions of Damascus, and for four, I will not turn away the punishment thereof; because they have threshed [occupied and held captive with a rod of iron] Gilead [Israel and the Golan - Galilee region] with threshing instruments of iron:

The descendants of the ancient Syrian will be afflicted by the armies of Asia.

1:4 But I will send a fire into the house of Hazael, which shall devour the palaces of Benhadad.

1:5 I will break also the bar [defense] of Damascus, and cut off the inhabitant from the plain of Aven, and him that holdeth the sceptre from the house of Eden: and the people of Syria shall go into captivity unto Kir [all Syria from Kir (Moab, Jordan) to the Euphrates will be devastated] saith the LORD.

God's Judgment on Gaza [Modern Philistia]

When the Jewish state falls, the Gazan's [The modern descendants of the Philistines accompanied by hundreds of thousands of Palestinian refugees.] will join the fray, and will break out of their land to devastate the surrounding cities of Judah, giving the local Jews to Turkey to deport them from the land.

1:6 Thus saith the LORD; For three transgressions of Gaza, and for four, I will not turn away the punishment thereof; because they carried away captive the whole captivity, to deliver them up to Edom [Edom is modern Turkey]:

Then the armies of Asia will come up and over-flood Gaza and destroy them. The people of Gaza will be devastated and the cities of Gaza, Akron, Ashdod and Ashkelon will be given to a restored Israel.

1:7 But I will send a fire on the wall of Gaza, which shall devour the palaces thereof: **1:8** And I will cut off the inhabitant from Ashdod, and him that holdeth the sceptre from Ashkelon, and I will turn mine hand against Ekron: and the remnant of the Philistines shall perish, saith the Lord GOD.

> **Jeremiah 47:2** Thus saith the LORD; Behold, waters rise up out of the north [armies shall come from the north], and shall be an overflowing flood, and shall overflow the land, and all that is therein; the city, and them that dwell therein: then the men shall cry, and all the inhabitants of the land shall howl.
>
> **47:3** At the noise of the [armies] stamping of the hoofs of his strong horses, at the rushing of his chariots, and at the rumbling of his wheels, the fathers shall not look back to their children for

feebleness of hands [the mighty men will be made feeble because of great fear and terror];

47:4 Because of the day that cometh to spoil all the Philistines, and to cut off from Tyrus and Zidon [the Asian armies will also destroy the cities of Lebanon and every ally of the Psalm 83 confederation] every helper that remaineth: for **the LORD will spoil the Philistines, the remnant of the country of Caphtor [Gaza].**

47:5 Baldness [when the prophecy was given, it was the custom to shave off the hair in mourning] is come upon Gaza; Ashkelon is cut off with the remnant of their valley: how long wilt thou cut [it was also the custom when this prophecy was given, for people to cut themselves to appeal to their gods, see 1 Kings 18:28] thyself?

47:6 O thou sword of the LORD, how long will it be ere thou be quiet? put up thyself into thy scabbard, rest, and be still.

47:7 How can it be quiet, seeing the LORD hath given it a charge against Ashkelon, and against the sea shore [Gaza]? there hath he appointed it.

Zephaniah 2:4 For Gaza shall be forsaken, and Ashkelon a desolation: they shall drive out Ashdod at the noon day, and Ekron shall be rooted up.

2:5 Woe unto the inhabitants of the sea coast, the nation of the Cherethites [The Gazan's]! the word of the LORD is against you; O Canaan, the land of the Philistines [Gaza], I will even destroy thee, that there shall be no inhabitant.

2:6 And the sea coast shall be dwellings and cottages for shepherds, and folds for flocks.

2:7 And **the coast [of Gaza] shall be for the remnant of the house of Judah** [After Messiah comes]; they shall feed thereupon: in the houses of Ashkelon shall they lie down in the evening: for the LORD their God shall visit them, and turn away their captivity.

God's Judgment on Lebanon

Amos 1:9 Thus saith the LORD; For three transgressions of Tyrus, and for four, I will not turn away the punishment thereof; because they delivered up the whole captivity to Edom, and remembered not the brotherly covenant:

1:10 But I will send a fire on the wall of Tyrus, which shall devour the palaces thereof.

Lebanon will also be strongly corrected for joining the Psalm 83 alliance with Europe when the tribulation begins.

Lebanon will facilitate the removal of many Jews from Palestine over the 42 month tribulation and thereby reap the wrath of God.

1:11 Thus saith the LORD; For three transgressions of Edom [Turkey], and for four, I will not turn away the punishment thereof; because he did pursue his brother with the sword, and did cast off all pity, and his anger did tear perpetually, and he kept his wrath for ever:**1:12** But I will send a fire upon Teman, which shall devour the palaces of Bozrah.

Turkey will take the Jewish captives and treat them with the utmost cruelty.

God's Judgment on Modern Jordan
Ammon: Modern Jordan

1:13 Thus saith the LORD; For three transgressions of the children of Ammon, and for four, I will not turn away the punishment thereof; because they have ripped up the women with child of Gilead [Golan and the area of Reuben, Manasseh and Gad] that they might enlarge their border:

This happened in ancient times when Ammon helped the Assyrians and it will happen again as Ammon joins the nations of Psalm 83 to attack the modern Jewish state.

1:14 But I will kindle a fire in the wall of Rabbah, and it shall devour the palaces thereof, with shouting in the day of battle, with a tempest in the day of the whirlwind:

1:15 And their king shall go into captivity, he and his princes together, saith the LORD.

Ammon will also join with the King of the North seeking to take over the West Bank of Jordan that the children of Lot have lusted for, yet she shall fall to the men of Asia as they come up against the final seat of the political and religious leaders of the New Europe at Jerusalem.

Amos 2

God's Judgment on Moab: Also Modern Jordan

Amos writing in his time, writes of the wicked deeds of the ancient Moabites. In our modern day Moab is joined with Ammon as one nation [Jordan], which will ally with the New Europe and the nations of Psalm 83 against Judah.

Amos 2:1 Thus saith the LORD; For three transgressions of Moab, and for four, I will not turn away the punishment thereof; because he burned the bones of the king of Edom into lime:

2:2 But I will send a fire upon Moab, and it shall devour the palaces of Kirioth: and Moab shall die with tumult, with shouting, and with the sound of the trumpet:

2:3 And I will cut off the judge from the midst thereof, and will slay all the princes thereof with him, saith the LORD.

Because of the past sins of Moab and because they will join the Psalm 83 confederation in this latter day, they will be destroyed by the Asian nations moving towards Jerusalem.

God's Judgment on Judah

Today only a small percent of Jews are religious, and those who are religious are fixed on their traditions which they are zealous to keep, exalting them above the Word of God. Today Judah like the other nations is full of Sabbath breaking, adultery, homosexuality, robbery, lying, stealing and pride.

2:4 Thus saith the LORD; For three transgressions of **Judah,** and for four, I will not turn away the punishment thereof; because **they have despised the law of the LORD, and have not kept his commandments, and their lies caused them to err, after the which their fathers have walked: 2:5** But I will send a fire upon Judah, and it shall devour the palaces of Jerusalem.

Judah stands on its traditions and NOT on the Word of God. Modern Judaism is NOT the religion of Moses but is as apostate from Moses as today's Ekklesia and modern mainstream Christianity is apostate from Christ.

God's Judgment on the Nations of the Ten Tribes of Israel [Finland, Denmark, Ireland, Sweden, Norway, Belgium, the Netherlands, America,

South Africa and the British people of Britain, Canada, Australia and New Zealand].

2:6 Thus saith the LORD; For three transgressions of Israel, and for four, I will not turn away the punishment thereof; because they sold the righteous for silver, and the poor for a pair of shoes;

2:7 That pant after the dust of the earth on the head of the poor [they oppress the poor], and turn aside the way of the meek: and a man and his father will go in unto the same maid, to profane my holy name:

2:8 And they lay themselves down upon clothes laid to pledge by every altar, and they drink the wine of the condemned in the house of their god.

Because all Israel [including today's Spiritual Ekklesia] lusts for mammon, profit and advantage over others to such an extreme that they seem to lust to steal the dust on their heads; and have NOT dealt justly but deceitfully to rob them of their resources and wealth; Israel will be thrown into great tribulation along with Judah (Hosea 5:5).

2:9 Yet destroyed I the Amorite before them, whose height was like the height of the cedars, and he was strong as the oaks; yet I destroyed his fruit from above, and his roots from beneath.

2:10 Also I brought you up from the land of Egypt, and led you forty years through the wilderness, to possess the land of the Amorite. **2:11** And I raised up of your sons for prophets, and of your young men for Nazarites. Is it not even thus, O ye children of Israel? saith the LORD.

Has not God blessed us with mighty works and with physical and spiritual gifts and yet the nations of physical Israel along with spiritual Israel depart from the Word of God?

Today the people of physical and spiritual Israel seek to lead the zealous into sin and reject those who speak the truth to warn them.

2:12 But ye gave the Nazarites wine to drink [they seek to lead the righteous into sin]; and commanded the prophets, saying, Prophesy not.

Today physical Israel and the called out of the Spiritual Ekklesia are drunk with the wine of PRIDE and those teaching zeal to live by EVERY WORD of God are told to shut up!

2:13 Behold, I am pressed under you [we are a heavy burden to God for all our iniquities], as a cart is pressed that is full of sheaves.

God declares, you were my joy and now you have become a heavy burden to me. Therefore God will remove our blessings and remove the blessing of his protection and we shall be filled with a spirit of terror.

Deuteronomy 32:18 Of the Rock that begat thee thou art unmindful, and hast forgotten God that formed thee.

32:19 And when the LORD saw it, he abhorred them, because of the provoking of his sons, and of his daughters. **32:20** And he said, I will hide my face from them, I will see what their end shall be: for they are a very froward generation, children in whom is no faith.

32:21 They have moved me to jealousy with that which is not God; they have provoked me to anger with their vanities: and I will move them to jealousy with those which are not a people; I will provoke them to anger with a foolish nation. **32:22** For a fire is kindled in mine anger, and shall burn unto the lowest hell, and shall consume the earth with her increase, and set on fire the foundations of the mountains.

32:23 I will heap mischiefs upon them; I will spend mine arrows upon them. **32:24** They shall be burnt with hunger, and devoured with burning heat, and with bitter destruction: I will also send the teeth of beasts upon them, with the poison of serpents of the dust. **32:25** The sword without, and terror within, shall destroy both the young man and the virgin, the suckling also with the man of gray hairs.

Amos 2:14 Therefore the flight [the strength to run] shall perish from the swift, and the strong shall not strengthen his force, neither shall the mighty deliver himself:

2:15 Neither shall he stand that handleth the bow; and he that is swift of foot shall not deliver himself: neither shall he that rideth the horse deliver himself.

2:16 And he that is courageous among the mighty shall flee away naked [in terror] in that day [of God's correction], saith the LORD.

The might of Israel [mainly America, Judah and Britain] will not save him, and his strength and courage will flee away leaving him terrified and easily overcome. This is the doing of the Eternal to humble us and crush our pride, to bring us to sincere repentance and turn us to him.

Amos 3

A prophecy against all of Israel including Judah

Amos 3:1 Hear this word that the LORD hath spoken against you, O children of Israel, **against the whole family which I brought up from the land of Egypt**, saying,

3:2 You only have I known of all the families of the earth: therefore I will punish you for all your iniquities.

ALL the nations of today's Israel along with the lukewarm Spiritual Ekklesia; the Laodicean Church of God; will be severely corrected.

3:3 Can two walk together, except they be agreed?

How can God walk with us when we chose our own ways above his ways?

3:4 Will a lion roar in the forest, when he hath no prey? will a young lion cry out of his den, if he have taken nothing?

3:5 Can a bird fall in a snare upon the earth, where no gin [trap] is for him? shall one take up a snare from the earth, and have taken nothing at all?

3:6 Shall a trumpet be blown in the city, and the people not be afraid? shall there be evil [the affliction of correction] in a city, and the LORD hath not done it?

3:7 Surely the Lord GOD will do nothing, but he revealeth his secret unto his servants the prophets.

The evil [calamity, correction] comes from the Eternal because of our own idolatry and sin, yet a loving God will not send his correction without first warning the people.

3:8 The lion hath roared, who will not fear? the Lord GOD hath spoken, who can but prophesy?

Let Egypt and the people of Gaza [and all the nations] watch and see the mighty correction of the Eternal upon his wayward people; and be warned and tremble, and swiftly and wholeheartedly turn to God, lest a greater correction come upon them.

3:9 Publish in the palaces at Ashdod, and in the palaces in the land of Egypt, and say, Assemble yourselves upon the mountains of Samaria, and behold the great tumults in the midst thereof, and the oppressed in the midst thereof.

Physical Israel and Judah and those of today's called out Ekklesia do what we think is right according to our own ways, and we refuse to live by every Word of God the Father (Mat 4:4).

3:10 For they [Physical Israel and Judah and those of today's Spiritual Ekklesia] know not to do right, saith the LORD, who store up violence [against any zeal for godliness] and robbery in their palaces.

Physical Israel and Judah and those of today's Spiritual Ekklesia; have forgotten our zeal and passionate love for the Word of God the Father and the instructions of our Lord Husband; we have gone astray and rebelled against our Maker.

3:11 Therefore thus saith the Lord GOD; An adversary there shall be even round about the land; and he shall bring down thy strength from thee, and thy palaces shall be spoiled.

The land shall be corrected beginning at the physical temple mount and with the spiritual temple of the Lord, the Spiritual Ekklesia; because of the multitude of our idolatry's. Even now the people are being separated and measured out between the zealous and the lukewarm, so that the zealous may be spared by God as a man spares his son who loves him, while the rebellious are corrected.

> **Ezekiel 9:4** And the LORD said unto him, **Go through the midst of the city, through the midst of Jerusalem, and set a mark upon the foreheads of the men that sigh and that cry for all the abominations that be done in the midst thereof.**
>
> **9:5** And to the others he said in mine hearing, Go ye after him through the city, **and smite: let not your eye spare, neither have ye pity:**
>
> **9:6** Slay utterly old and young, both maids, and little children, and women: but come not near any man upon whom is the mark; and **begin at my sanctuary**. Then they began at the ancient men which were before the house.
>
> **9:7** And he said unto them, Defile the house, and fill the courts with the slain: go ye forth. And they went forth, and slew in the city.

Just as a man might try to rescue a lamb from a lion and find only pieces left, so only a remnant of physical Israel/Judah will remain and the vast majority of the Laodicean Ekklesia will perish in the flesh to prove the sincerity of their repentance.

Amos 3:12 Thus saith the LORD; As the shepherd taketh out of the mouth of the lion two legs, or a piece of an ear; so shall the children of Israel be taken out that dwell in Samaria in the corner of a bed, and in Damascus in a couch.

Only a few will be preserved alive from this terrible correction and very many of the Lord's elect will have to lay down their lives for him in this tribulation to prove their wholehearted repentance.

3:13 Hear ye, and testify in the house of Jacob [Israel and Judah; and spiritual Jacob], saith the Lord GOD, the God of hosts,

3:14 That in the day that I shall visit the transgressions of Israel upon him I will also visit the altars of Bethel [the golden calves that Jeroboam 1 set up]: and the horns of the altar shall be cut off, and fall to the ground.

God will destroy our idols and our altars to those idols, and he will crush our pride that we may be turned to him.

All the major corporate church groups will be destroyed and the called out Ekklesia will be forced to turn to and rely on God ALONE as our ONLY salvation.

Because we have made idols out of our organizations they will be destroyed, for the Lord our God is a jealous Husband; and he will destroy our lovers so that he may save us for himself alone! All of our great construction projects to honor idols of men will be destroyed.

3:15 And I will smite the winter house with the summer house; and the houses of ivory shall perish, and the great houses shall have an end, saith the LORD.

ALL our pleasant things and the worldly possessions that we have lusted for and delighted in and for which we have compromised with God's Word to obtain; shall be taken from us and destroyed so that we may learn to delight in the Lord our God and to live by every Word of God.

We will be afflicted until we learn and KNOW; that the only thing of lasting importance is our relationship with the Mighty God!

Amos 4

The leaders of the nations of Israel and Judah and the leaders and elders of today's Ekklesia who seek to destroy any zeal to live by every Word of God are likened to the strong bulls of the herd who dominate and seek their own advantage.

Amos 4:1 Hear this word, ye kine [cattle, bulls] of Bashan, that are in the mountain of Samaria, **which oppress the poor, which crush the needy,** which say to their masters [whose leaders intoxicate them with the strong drink of pride], Bring, and let us drink.

The day of affliction is at hand when God will take us like fish caught on a hook and draw us into great correction.

4:2 The Lord GOD hath sworn by his holiness, that, lo, the days shall come upon you, that he will **take you** [the Israel of c 721 B.C.] **away with hooks, and your posterity** [the Israel and Judah and the Spiritual Ekklesia of today] **with fishhooks.**

Breaches will be made in our defenses and our people [especially today's Judah] will be removed through the breaches as water flows through the breaches in a dam

4:3 And ye shall go out at the breaches, every cow [People will leave the land like cows which wander from their field through the breaches in a fence.] at that which is before her; and ye shall cast them into the palace, saith the LORD.

God reminds the people of the warnings and the past corrections he has sent; and still we have not repented and turned to him. Therefore he declares that a major correction will come upon us that will destroy our pride and turn the nations of Israel and the whole world to him.

God has removed many of our blessings already and today's Spiritual Ekklesia has responded by fighting with each other and coveting physical things instead of diligently seeking the spiritual things of God.

Today's Ekklesia is like a group of little children who fight each other as their house burns down around them, ignoring the warnings from their Father to obey him, or he will spank them.

Jeroboam set up his golden calves in Bethel and Dan (1 Kings 12:29 - 1 Kings 13:10), and led Israel to sacrifice to idols there. He established the feast of the eighth month [of which today's remnant is Thanksgiving] to replace God's Feast of the seventh month.

The people sacrificed to idols and made their meat [grain, unleavened bread] offerings with leaven. The unleavened bread offerings are to be unleavened as a type of Messiah the Bread of Life and the pure Word of God.

4:4 Come to Bethel, and transgress; at Gilgal multiply transgression; and bring your sacrifices every morning, and your tithes after three years:

4:5 And offer a sacrifice of thanksgiving with leaven, and proclaim and publish the free offerings: for this liketh you, O ye children of Israel, saith the Lord GOD.

Go ahead and remain in your sins and I will correct you, saith the Eternal.

4:6 And I also have given you cleanness of teeth [God will also give us famine because we commit idolatry with idols of men and false traditions.] in all your cities, and want of bread in all your places: yet have ye not returned unto me, saith the LORD.

Scarcity of physical rain is an allegory of God withholding the spiritual rain of God's Spirit in the called out who apostatize to follow idols of men; for God's Spirit is the Spirit of Truth and if we reject truth we are rejecting God's Spirit.

Brethren, God's Spirit is truth, therefore those with God's Spirit will love the truth. Godly men who are full of God's Spirit will quickly turn and accept what is true. It is ungodly wickedness to refuse truth and to be willing to close ones eyes to truth and even to lie to cleave to falsehood.

God is testing the people to see who is godly and has God's love for truth and to see who is evil and rejects truth.

By their love of truth or the lack thereof, we can discern who is godly and who is not.

How do you want to be judged by God?

> **John 14:17** Even **the Spirit of truth**; whom the world cannot receive, because it seeth him not, neither knoweth him: but ye know him; for he dwelleth with you, and shall be in you.

John 15:26 But when the Comforter is come, whom I will send unto you from the Father, **even the Spirit of truth, which proceedeth from the Father**, he shall testify of me:

Amos 4:7 And also I have withholden the rain from you, when there were yet three months to the harvest: and I caused it to rain upon one city, and caused it not to rain upon another city: one piece was rained upon, and the piece whereupon it rained not withered.

Today's drought is only the very early beginning warning; soon the drought will become so severe in the tribulation [when it is possible that no rain at all will come to our peoples], so that the thirsty will be forced to migrate for lack of water.

4:8 So two or three cities wandered unto one city, to drink water; but they were not satisfied: yet have ye not returned unto me, saith the LORD.

In the days of ancient Israel the people gathered together for the available water, today men build pipelines, dams and canals. Yet for the same sins: God is beginning to withhold the blessing of rain and dew in due season. In the tribulation much of that infrastructure will fail and there will be much thirst, famine and starvation.

4:9 I have smitten you with blasting and mildew [fungal infestations and disease of our crops]: when your gardens and your vineyards and your fig trees and your olive trees increased, [when our plants actually produce fruit, pests will eat up the produce] the palmerworm devoured them: yet have ye not returned unto me, saith the LORD.

Disease and insects afflict our crops and we rely on ever more dangerous and deadly chemicals that are now destroying the health of the population.

God has afflicted us with war and disease in a small warning, and our affliction will increase dramatically in the coming time of trouble, so that the stench of death will abound.

4:10 I have sent among you the pestilence [disease especially that carried by rodents] after the manner of Egypt: your young men have I slain with the sword, and have taken away your horses [our mobility will fail]; and I have made the stink [of disease and death] of your camps to come up unto your nostrils: yet have ye not returned unto me, saith the LORD.

We have been subjected to diseases like cancer and heart attacks as well as much else, until the costs of our medical services sap the economy and strength of the nation; and we have fallen into many wars, most of our own choosing, in order to seize the wealth of others.

4:11 I have overthrown some of you, as God overthrew Sodom and Gomorrah, and ye were as a firebrand plucked out of the burning: yet have ye not returned unto me, saith the LORD.

Some of our cities suffered massive destruction in wars like WW 2, and we did not learn to turn to God, but leaned even more to our own means.

4:12 Therefore thus will I do unto thee, O Israel: and because I will do this unto thee, **prepare to meet thy God** [prepare to die]**, O Israel. 4:13** For, lo, he that formeth the mountains, and createth the wind, and declareth unto man what is his thought, that maketh the morning darkness, and treadeth upon the high places of the earth, The LORD, The God of hosts, is his name.

Amos 5

Amos 5:1 Hear ye this word which I take up against you, even a lamentation, O house of Israel.

This is the correction of the latter day tribulation which is very close at hand.

5:2 The virgin of Israel is fallen; she shall no more rise: she is forsaken upon her land; there is none to raise her up.

God here speaks of only ten percent of ancient Israel surviving the drought and terrible onslaught of Assyria, and only and only a small remnant of Israel/Judah will survive the wars, famine, thirst, starvation and disease that is about to come upon us in our time.

5:3 For thus saith the Lord GOD; **The city that went out by a thousand shall leave an hundred, and that which went forth by an hundred shall leave ten**, to the house of Israel.

Therefore quickly repent, oh idolatrous Spiritual Ekklesia, while God may be found of you: for your punishment will be of a similar manner. God will afflict our flesh so that he may humble us and save our spirit.

5:4 For **thus saith the LORD unto the house of Israel, Seek ye me, and ye shall live:**

5:5 But seek not [the calf idols of] Bethel [Be diligently zealous to follow and live by every Word of God and do not follow idols of men. Do not put your trust in fortifications and cities and the strength of men, but put your trust in the Eternal God!], nor enter into Gilgal, and pass not to Beersheba: for Gilgal shall surely go into captivity, and Bethel shall come to nought.

5:6 Seek the LORD, and ye shall live; [Sincerely repent and be diligently zealous to live by EVERY WORD of God.] lest he break out like fire in the house of Joseph [both physical and today's apostate spiritual Israel], and devour it, and there be none to quench it in Bethel.

Our idols of men will not save us.

It is WE who must seek God the Father, for if the spiritually called out will not turn to zealously live by every Word of God and our salt of passionate zeal for godliness has lost its savor; how can anyone be saved at all?

5:7 Ye who turn judgment to wormwood [we who have perverted godly judgment into the bitterness of injustice], and leave [turn away from] off righteousness [godliness] in the earth,

5:8 Seek him that maketh the seven stars and Orion, and turneth the shadow of death into the morning [God can turn death into the bright morning of life.], and maketh the day dark with night: that calleth for the waters of the sea, and poureth them out upon the face of the earth: The LORD is his name:

5:9 That strengtheneth the spoiled against the strong, so that the spoiled shall come against the fortress.

We, the Ekklesia of God, who have turned from the Word of God, forgetting sound judgment and turning good into evil: Shall not our God correct his faithless bride before he corrects the nations?

5:10 They [the wicked hate those who warn them] **hate him that rebuketh in the gate, and they abhor him that speaketh uprightly.**

Those who despise correction from God's Word: Will God not recompense your rejection of him?

5:11 Forasmuch therefore as your treading is upon the poor, and ye take from him burdens [seize his necessities of life] of wheat: ye have built houses of hewn stone, but ye shall not dwell in them; ye have planted pleasant vineyards, but ye shall not drink wine of them.

God will take away what we have gained through oppressing others.

5:12 For I know your manifold transgressions and your mighty sins: they afflict the just, they take a bribe, and they turn aside the poor in the gate from their right [denying justice].

Many elders work for mammon and not for love of God. They take to themselves the best of everything and feed not the flock with the goodness of the Bread of Life; which is the whole Word of God. Jesus Christ is the Bread of Life, and the Word of God defines his very mind, spirit and nature.

When we compromise with any part of God's Word we reject the Author of that Word!

Therefore God will break up our idols and remove our sinful gains.

5:13 Therefore the prudent shall keep silence in that time; for it is an evil time.

The abused brethren keep silent lest they be subjected to further abuse.

Let us quickly and sincerely repent and:

5:14 Seek good, and not evil, that ye may live: and so the LORD, the God of hosts, shall be with you, as ye have spoken.

5:15 Hate the evil, and love the good, and establish judgment in the gate: it may be that the LORD God of hosts will be gracious unto the remnant of Joseph.

If we repent and learn to love every Word of God which Word defines God, and do what is good in God's sight; and learn to hate and be repulsed by any compromise with that good Word, and begin to live by every Word of God, then we shall become acceptable to the Eternal God.

However, if we will not sincerely repent and seek to live by every Word of God we will be severely corrected.

5:16 Therefore the LORD, the God of hosts, the LORD, saith thus; Wailing shall be in all streets; and they shall say in all the highways, Alas! alas! and they shall call the husbandman to mourning, and such as are skilful of lamentation to wailing.

5:17 And in all vineyards shall be wailing: for I will pass through thee, saith the LORD.

5:18 Woe unto you that desire the day of the LORD! to what end is it for you[the unrepentant sinner referenced in v 16-17 above]**? the day of the LORD is darkness, and not light** [God will inflict justice on the wicked].

Here it is revealed that this is a dual prophecy for that day and for this latter day as well: And the warning is to the sinner and the unrepentant in today's Ekklesia who are not zealous for every Word of God yet who desire the coming of our Lord, proudly thinking themselves righteous.

> **Matthew 7:21** Not every one that saith unto me, Lord, Lord, shall enter into the kingdom of heaven; but he that doeth the will of my Father which is in heaven.

7:22 Many will say to me in that day, Lord, Lord, have we not prophesied in thy name? and in thy name have cast out devils? and in thy name done many wonderful works?

7:23 And then will I profess unto them, I never knew you: depart from me, ye that work iniquity.

Those who think themselves godly as they follow idols of men and refuse to live by every Word of God, will not be resurrected to spirit by Jesus Christ as they suppose.

Amos 5:19 As if a man did flee from a lion, and a bear met him; or went into the house, and leaned his hand on the wall, and a serpent bit him.

Christ's coming will be a huge disappointment for those who are righteous in their own eyes and are not zealous for the righteousness of living by every Word of God.

5:20 Shall not the day of the LORD be darkness, and not light? even very dark, and no brightness in it?

God despises the Sabbaths and Festivals observed by much of today's Spiritual Ekklesia; because we use them to deceive ourselves into thinking that we are godly when we are full of sin.

5:21 I hate, I despise your feast days, and I will not smell [we have no sweet perfume of dedicated service to God] in your solemn assemblies.

Today God does not accept us or our offerings and God does not accept our Sabbaths and Feasts; because we idolize men and pollute God's Sabbaths and Feasts.

5:22 Though ye offer me burnt offerings and your meat [unleavened bread] offerings, I will not accept them: neither will I regard the peace offerings of your fat beasts.

God even rejects our music and songs of praise because they are hypocritical, for we sing his praises and we have no zeal to live by his Word; preferring to follow our idols of men and rejecting truth to cleave to false teachings.

5:23 Take thou away from me the noise of thy songs; for I will not hear the melody of thy viols.

God despises the Festivals that we observe in his name, because we are NOT righteous in his sight.

We walk all over God's Word and justifying our sins, saying that we are his temple and he loves us and will overlook our sins. In so saying we condemn ourselves for we acknowledge the we are his temple as we pollute that temple with sin.

Such persons God will destroy.

> **1 Corinthians 3:17 If any man defile the temple of God, him shall God destroy; for the temple of God is holy, which temple ye are.**

God wants us to do justice and to make godly judgments and he wants us to live righteously, living by every Word of God.

Amos 5:24 But let judgment run down as waters, and righteousness as a mighty stream.

Today spiritual Israel offers sacrifices of praise and offerings to God and we pretend to keep his Sabbaths and Festivals; while we follow our idols of men and we commit spiritual adultery against the Mighty One of our baptismal commitment.

5:25 Have ye offered unto me sacrifices and offerings in the wilderness forty years, O house of Israel?

5:26 But ye have borne the tabernacle of your Moloch and Chiun **your images, the star of your god, which ye made to yourselves.**

Our idols are our false traditions of men, human leaders and the corporate organizations that we have exalted and allowed to come between us and a passionate zeal to live by every Word of God.

5:27 Therefore will I cause you to go into captivity beyond Damascus, saith the LORD, whose name is The God of hosts.

Amos 6

Woe to those who are at ease, full of pride and trusting in there own ways; and are not living by every Word of God.

Amos 6:1 Woe to them that are at ease in Zion, and trust in the mountain of Samaria, which are named chief of the nations, to whom the house of Israel came!

6:2 Pass ye unto Calneh, and see; and from thence go ye to Hamath the great: then go down to Gath of the Philistines: be they better than these kingdoms? or their border greater than your border?

Our people are violent and think that no evil will befall them for our wicked deeds. Just as the nation is violent, so too the Ekklesia does violence against those who are zealous for God; condemning those who reject idols of men to live by every Word of God.

6:3 Ye that put far away the evil day, and cause the seat of violence to come near;

6:4 That lie upon beds of ivory, and stretch themselves upon their couches, and eat the lambs out of the flock, and the calves out of the midst of the stall;

6:5 That chant to the sound of the viol, and invent to themselves instruments of musick, like David;

6:6 That drink wine in bowls [using bowls in place of glasses for the great amount that they drink], and anoint themselves with the chief ointments: but they are not grieved for the affliction of Joseph.

Today's spiritual leaders have gone the way of the physical leaders in feeding themselves physical things and not seeking to live by every Word of God nor feeding the flock the spiritual things of God.

The day of our correction [which we want to believe will never come upon us], is now close at hand. God will withdraw his blessings and where there was plenty, very little will remain.

6:7 Therefore now shall they go captive with the first that go captive, and the banquet of them that stretched themselves shall be removed.

6:8 The Lord GOD hath sworn by himself, saith the LORD the God of hosts, I abhor the excellency of Jacob, and hate his palaces [pride in ourselves]**: therefore will I deliver up the city with all that is therein.**

Today's nations of Israel will be corrected and the Laodicean Spiritual Ekklesia which departs from zeal to live by every Word of God will also be corrected, and such organizations and all the grand monuments to false traditions, pride and ego will be destroyed and brought down to nothing.

6:9 And it shall come to pass, if there remain ten men in one house, that they shall die.

6:10 And a man's uncle shall take him up, and he that burneth him, to bring out the bones out of the house, and shall say unto him that is by the sides of the house, Is there yet any with thee? and he shall say, No. Then shall he say, Hold thy tongue: for we may not make mention of the name of the LORD.

In our afflictions and sorrows we will leave off glorying in our self-righteousness, for we will be made to understand that we have defiled ourselves with pride, idolatry and much sin and that we are suffering God's wrath.

6:11 For, behold, the LORD commandeth, and he will smite the great house [the great corporate churches] with breaches, and the little house [small church groups] with clefts.

The houses [families and corporations] shall be brought down. Can we plough rocks? God will make our land like solid rock so that it will produce nothing.

> **Leviticus 26:14** But if ye will not hearken unto me, and will not do all these commandments; **26:15** And if ye shall despise my statutes, or if your soul abhor my judgments, so that ye will not do all my commandments, but that ye break my covenant:

26:16 I also will do this unto you; I will even appoint over you terror, consumption, and the burning ague, that shall consume the eyes, and cause sorrow of heart: and ye shall sow your seed in vain, for your enemies shall eat it.

26:17 And I will set my face against you, and ye shall be slain before your enemies: they that hate you shall reign over you; and ye shall flee when none pursueth you.

26:18 And if ye will not yet for all this hearken unto me, then I will punish you seven times more for your sins. **26:19** And I will break the pride of your power; and I will make your heaven as iron, and your earth as brass: **26:20** And your strength shall be spent in vain: for your land shall not yield her increase, neither shall the trees of the land yield their fruits.

Amos 6:12 Shall horses run upon the rock? will one plow there with oxen? for ye have turned judgment into gall [bitterness], and the fruit of righteousness into hemlock [poison, death]:

6:13 Ye which rejoice in a thing of nought, which say, Have we not taken to us horns [conquered nations] by our own strength?

We say that we have victory by our own strength.

6:14 But, behold, I will raise up against you a nation, O house of Israel, saith the LORD the God of hosts; and they shall afflict you from the entering in of Hemath [from the Euphrates to the Nile] unto the river of the wilderness.

In those days God raised up Assyria and the ten tribes of Israel were removed from the land of promise; God will also greatly correct us once again in this latter day.

Very soon now our glorying will be turned into shame and we will realize that we have gloried in a thing of no value when we gloried in our buildings, our corporate assemblies, our false traditions, our own strength and in our idols of men.

These things are all vanity and nothing at all, perishing in their time. We and our leaders will all likewise perish if we forsake any part of the Word of our God.

Only the Eternal and his Word stand forever!

Amos 7

God tells Amos that he will send a plague of grasshoppers to eat up the main harvest of ancient Israel and Amos begs God to relent.

Amos 7:1 Thus hath the Lord GOD shewed unto me; and, behold, he formed grasshoppers in the beginning of the shooting up of the latter growth [the early growth of the main fall harvest was to be eaten by the grasshoppers]; and, lo, it was the latter growth [the growing main fall harvest] after the king's [harvest] mowings.

7:2 And it came to pass, that when they had made an end of eating the grass of the land, then I said, O Lord GOD, forgive, I beseech thee: by whom shall Jacob arise? for he is small.

Then Amos cried out to God begging God not to send this grasshopper plague and God relented.

7:3 The LORD repented for this: It shall not be, saith the LORD.

Then God said that he would destroy ancient Samaria by fire from heaven like Sodom, and again Amos cried out for deliverance and God relented.

7:4 Thus hath the Lord GOD shewed unto me: and, behold, the Lord GOD called to contend by fire, and it devoured the great deep, and did eat up a part. **7:5** Then said I, O Lord GOD, cease, I beseech thee: by whom shall Jacob arise? for he is small. **7:6** The LORD repented for this: This also shall not be, saith the Lord GOD.

Then God determined to abandon ancient Israel to Assyria for all their sins against him.

7:7 Thus he shewed me: and, behold, the LORD stood upon a wall made by a plumbline, with a plumbline in his hand.

God then declares that he will measure Israel and give them to the enemy [the Assyrians].

7:8 And the LORD said unto me, Amos, what seest thou? And I said, A plumbline. Then said the LORD, Behold, I will set a plumbline in the midst of my people Israel: I will not again pass by them any more:

7:9 And **the high places of Isaac shall be desolate, and the sanctuaries of Israel shall be laid waste; and I will rise against the house of Jeroboam** [the ten tribes of Israel] **with the sword** [of Assyria].

Finally God declared that he would abandon the ancient ten tribes of Israel to the sword of Assyria.

7:10 Then Amaziah the priest of Bethel [the priest of the golden calf idols] sent to Jeroboam king of Israel, saying, Amos hath conspired against thee in the midst of the house of Israel: the land is not able to bear all his words. **7:11** For thus Amos saith, Jeroboam [Jeroboam 2] shall die by the sword, and Israel shall surely be led away captive out of their own land.

The priest of the idols then told Amos to go prophesy elsewhere and to leave the ancient ten tribes of Israel alone.

7:12 Also Amaziah said unto Amos, O thou seer, go, flee thee away into the land of Judah, and there eat bread, and prophesy there: **7:13** But prophesy not again any more at Bethel: for it is the king's chapel, and it is the king's court.

Amos responded by saying that he does not speak his own words and speaks only what God has called him to speak; indicating that he Amos has no choice in what is spoken or to whom.

7:14 Then answered Amos, and said to Amaziah, I was no prophet, neither was I a prophet's son; but I was an herdman, and a gatherer of sycomore fruit [figs]:

7:15 And the LORD took me as I followed the flock, and **the LORD said unto me, Go, prophesy unto my people Israel.**

The apostate religious leader then pretested against Amos, and called on him to keep silent and flee the land. Amos responded that he must declare the message that God has told him to declare.

Amos then declared the fate of the religious leaders who would stop godly mouths from speaking the warning from God.

Today most leaders and elders of the Ekklesia say the same thing: saying, "Keep silent and do not warn the people, do not tell us we are sinning and that we will be corrected for we are God's church."

I say: Surely God will remove his blessings and protection from us for our idolizing and exalting of men and false traditions above the Word of God! Today, we, like ancient Israel, are full of idolatry and we will receive a very severe correction!

7:16 Now therefore hear thou the word of the LORD: Thou sayest, Prophesy not against Israel, and drop not thy word against the house of Isaac. **7:17** Therefore thus saith the LORD [God declared his judgment to this priest of the golden calves who rebuked Amos] Thy wife shall be an harlot in the city, and thy sons and thy daughters shall fall by the sword, and thy land shall be divided by line; and thou shalt die in a polluted land: and Israel shall surely go into captivity forth of his land.

History

The captivities began in approximately 740 BC (or 733/2 BC according to other sources).

And the God of Israel stirred up the spirit of Pul king of Assyria, and the spirit of Tilgathpilneser king of Assyria, and he carried them away, even the Reubenites, and the Gadites, and the half tribe of Manasseh [who dwelled east of the Jordan], and brought them unto Halah, and Habor, and Hara, and to the river Gozan, unto this day. (1 Chronicles 5:26)

In the days of Pekah king of Israel came Tiglathpileser king of Assyria, and he took Ijon, and Abelbethmaachah, and Janoah, and Kedesh, and Hazor, and Gilead, and Galilee, all the land of Naphtali, and carried them captive to Assyria. (2 Kings 15:29)

In 722 BC, nearly ten to twenty years after the initial deportations, the ruling city of the Northern Kingdom of Israel, Samaria, was finally taken by Sargon II after a three-year siege started by Shalmaneser V.

Against him came up Shalmaneser king of Assyria; and Hoshea became his servant, and gave him presents.

And the king of Assyria found conspiracy in Hoshea: for he had sent messengers to So king of Egypt, and brought no present [tribute] to the king of Assyria, as he had done year by year: therefore the king of Assyria shut him up, and bound him in prison. Then the king of Assyria came up throughout all the land, and went up to Samaria, and besieged it three years.

In the ninth year of Hoshea the king of Assyria took Samaria, and carried Israel away into Assyria, and placed them in Halah and in Habor by the river of Gozan, and in the cities of the Medes. (2 Kings 17:3–6) And the king of Assyria did carry away Israel unto Assyria and put them in Halah and in Habor by the river of Gozan, and in the cities of the Medes: because they obeyed not the voice of the LORD their God, but transgressed his covenant, and all that Moses the servant of the LORD commanded and would not hear them, nor do them. (2 Kings 18:11–12).

During the many years from the initial apostasy of Jeroboam God had sent many prophets continuously warning the ten tribes to sincerely repent of their idolatry and return to God.

During those years God continued to call many in Israel and there were many faithful among the overwhelmingly ungodly in the ten tribes. For example Elijah felt so alone that God had to assure him that there remained seven thousand godly in Israel.

After hearing the words of God's servants and seeing the rise of Assyria, many godly faithful did flee down into Judah. This influx of godly from the ten tribes contributed to the ability of several good kings of Judah to make reforms in the areas that they controlled, for example Hezekiah (2 Chronicles 30).

It should be remembered that since Rehoboam lost all the tribes except Judah and Benjamin, the kings of Judah had always coveted a restoration of their monarchy over the northern kingdom of Israel.

Therefore when Assyria depopulated the land of Samaria of the ten tribes and began to bring in people from the Euphrates valley to occupy the land, Judah rushed in and seized what they could of the adjacent land of Samaria.

Historically from that time onward there was friction between the Samaritans and the Jews. The Jews thinking that the ten tribes were restored to them because some of the ten tribes had fled to Judah and the remainder had been deported and presumed lost; while the Samaritans could rightly claim that God had removed the ten tribes and given them the land. This conflict of claims would have strong consequences right up to today.

Amos 8

Amos 8:1 Thus hath the Lord GOD shewed unto me: and behold a basket of summer fruit.

Today's Spiritual Ekklesia is like the ripened fruit, ready to fall or be picked.

8:2 And he said, Amos, what seest thou? And I said, A basket of summer fruit. Then said the LORD unto me, The end is come upon my people of Israel; I will not again pass by them any more.

This basket of Summer Fruit pictures Israel at the end of this age, at the latter day. Notice below that the temple was in Judah and NOT in Israel, therefore this is a prophecy about the latter days including both Judah and Israel.

In this latter day the "Time of Jacob's Trouble" will come upon all Israel and Judah, and also upon the unrepentant Laodicean Spiritual Ekklesia. The bodies will pile up in great calamity, as we suffer in order to bring us to see that our own power, pride and glory are as nothing; they perish in a day and are gone like a wilted flower.

Why do you think that God did what he did to the king Nebuchadnezzar in sending him madness? Was Nebuchadnezzar doing anything that other kings throughout the ages have not done? Why single him out?

It was for our instruction and for our advantage, so that we could also learn the lesson; that it is the Eternal who is God Indeed!

Will we look on what we have built and say in our heart: look what I have built. Do we look at men and say: Look what these great men have built, surely God was with them? Do we rely on our own false traditions and idols of men INSTEAD of relying upon the Word of Almighty God?

8:3 And the songs of the temple shall be howlings [the music of joy will become laments of sorrow and suffering] in that day, saith the Lord GOD: there shall be many dead bodies in every place; they shall cast them forth with silence.

There will be so many dead that people will be exhausted with weeping and the dead will be buried without mourning or crying.

Our nations and the assemblies of today's Spiritual Ekklesia, which greedily extract all that they can from even the needy and which respect neither new moon nor Sabbath will be severely corrected with a terrible correction.

8:4 Hear this, O ye that swallow up the needy, even to make the poor of the land to fail,

Today we call the Sabbath holy as we pollute it, and most reject God's command to worship him on the New Moons. No, the New Moons are not holy days on which no work of any kind should be done like High Days and Sabbaths; but they are appointed times for worshiping God like the Wave Offering day, the middle Feast days and the Passover day.

8:5 Saying, When will the new moon be gone [having our minds on carnal pursuits and wishing that the worship was over], that we may sell corn ? and the sabbath, that we may set forth wheat, making the ephah small, and the shekel great, and falsifying the balances by deceit?

8:6 That we may buy the poor for silver, and the needy for a pair of shoes; yea, and sell the refuse of the wheat?

8:7 The LORD hath sworn by the excellency of Jacob, Surely I will never forget any of their works.

God will not forget [overlook] our sins as some wicked men teach; but God will surely correct us and make us quake in fearful horror, humble us and bring us to sincerely repent of our idolatries.

8:8 Shall not the land tremble for this, and every one mourn that dwelleth therein? and it shall rise up wholly as a flood; and it shall be cast out and drowned, as by the flood of Egypt.

When we have been corrected with sword, famine, disease and captivity, with great suffering and dying: We shall sincerely repent and seek out the LORD God to do his will and to live by every Word of God without compromise.

We will learn that the physical is only vanity and that the things that truly matter are the things of God. Then we will turn away from the vanity of carnality and begin to internalize the very nature, mind and Spirit of God, through a diligent seeking of him and living by every Word of God.

It is then that we will seek UNITY WITH OUR FATHER in sincerity and truth; and we shall be united with God as the children of the Most High!

Before that can happen, we must either sincerely repent or be corrected in tribulation, and be humbled and our great pride must be crushed.

8:9 And it shall come to pass in that day, saith the Lord GOD, that **I will cause the sun to go down at noon, . . .**

The sun set ends the day and so we speak of the end of something as the sun setting on that thing. For example we might say that the sun set on the empire; meaning that the empire has ended. We also know that the sun is said to be at the peak of its height at noon. The above statement is a poetic allegory that our glory will perish [set] at its peak.

Once Islamic Extremism is defeated and regional governments have been changed, our power will be at its peak and from there it will quickly fail and collapse. Our sun will set at midday as it were.

. . . and I will darken the earth in the clear day:

Just as God sent Israel into the hand of the Assyrians in c 721 B.C. God is not a respecter of persons and will also send strong correction on today's Spiritual Ekklesia when we follow idols of men and sin against our LORD.

8:10 And I will turn your feasts into mourning, and all your songs into lamentation; and I will bring up sackcloth [mourning] upon all loins, and baldness upon every head [in those days they shaved their heads in mourning, this is about mourning]; and **I will make it as the mourning of** [for] **an only son**, and the end thereof as a bitter day.

8:11 Behold, the days come, saith the Lord GOD, that I will send a famine in the land, not a famine of bread, nor a thirst for water, but of hearing the words of the LORD:

8:12 And they shall wander from sea to sea, and from the north even to the east, they shall run to and fro to seek the word of the LORD, and shall not find it.

Famine means scarcity, not complete absence; and today there is a great scarcity a great famine of the truth of the Word of God.

Because we reject truth and zeal for godliness to follow idols of men and to teach our own false traditions and ways; because we exalt idols of men and their false teachings and we do NOT teach the brethren to live by EVERY WORD of GOD; and because we do NOT preach the Gospel of warning and repentance that we are commanded to preach: We will be severely corrected.

Because of these sins God will remove from us the means to teach our errors and the Word of truth will be taught by the Two Sent Ones.

No more mass magazine distribution, no more funds or means for TV or radio, possibly a failure of electrical power and the internet in various areas in the devastated nations of Israel. Only by the power of God will the truth be taught. By God's power these two will be a center of media focus and the truth will be made known to the nations.

In Israelite nations [and ultimately in every nation] there will be no escape from the wrath of God for all our abominations; and those who sincerely repent will surely be killed by the wicked: God will require that we give our lives for him to prove our repentance is true and not just a temporary remorse before sliding back into idolatry again.

Brethren, NOW is our last chance to sincerely repent of our idolatry and spiritual adultery, to turn from idolizing men, false traditions and the institutions of men and to embrace the Eternal and his very nature and ways through diligently living by every Word of God, before we are corrected in the furnace of affliction as per Revelation 3:14-22.

During our correction we will be made to thirst for water so that we can learn to thirst after the Living Waters of Salvation; which is to live by EVERY WORD of GOD!

All those who idolize men and exalt the words of men above Living by Every Word of GOD, will perish unless they sincerely repent! YES that means today's corporate Ekklesia as well as the general public!

8:13 In that day shall the fair virgins and young men faint for thirst.

8:14 They that swear by the sin of Samaria [all idolaters will repent or perish], and say, Thy god, O Dan [the golden calf], liveth; and, The manner [idolatry] of Beersheba liveth; even they shall fall, and never rise up again.

Amos 9

God will surely bring great affliction on today's called out for all our idolatries and spiritual adultery against the Husband of our baptismal commitment, and for all the sins that our great pride has caused us to fall into.

There will be no escape, it does not matter if we prepare ourselves physically and hoard food etc. we shall surely be afflicted so that God might humble us to sincere repentance and save the spirit.

We cannot escape from our correction except by sincere repentance and living by every Word of God BEFORE that correction comes. Once it commences it will last for 42 months, and even if we repent during that time we will surely remain in affliction [or die] until Messiah comes.

Amos 9:1 I saw the LORD standing upon the altar: and he said, Smite the lintel of the door [of the temple including the latter day spiritual temple], that the posts may shake: and cut [fall on them] them in the head, all of them [those who sin and justify their sins]; and I will slay the last of them with the sword: he that fleeth of them shall not flee away [escape], and he that escapeth of them shall not be delivered.

Those who escape the sword of violence will suffer in other ways, by disease, starvation, natural disasters and plagues.

9:2 Though they dig into hell [dig holes and caves to hide in], thence shall mine hand take them; though they [try to hide in the high mountains] climb up to heaven, thence will I bring them down:

9:3 And though they hide themselves in the top of [Mount] Carmel, I will search and take them out thence; and though they be hid from my sight in the bottom of the sea, thence will I command the serpent, and he shall bite them:

9:4 And though they go into captivity before their enemies, thence will I command the sword, and it shall slay them: and I will set mine eyes upon them for evil, and not for good.

The Greatness and Might of God

9:5 And the Lord GOD of hosts is he that toucheth the land, and it shall melt, and all that dwell therein shall mourn: and it shall rise up wholly like a flood; and shall be drowned, as by the flood of Egypt.

9:6 It is he that buildeth his stories in the heaven, and hath founded his troop [people] in the earth; he that calleth for the waters of the sea, and poureth them out upon the face of the earth: The LORD is his name.

Just as God delivered the Ethiopians from the Egyptians and delivered other nations from their oppressors, God delivered Israel from Egypt also; for God is Mighty and Able to deliver!

Just as God is ABLE to deliver out of the hand of men, he is also ABLE to deliver the sinner INTO the hand of men for our correction.

9:7 Are ye not as children of the Ethiopians unto me, O children of Israel? saith the LORD. Have not I brought up Israel out of the land of Egypt? and the Philistines from Caphtor, and the Syrians from Kir?

9:8 Behold, the eyes of the Lord GOD are upon the [God sees and will correct any sinful people, including the sinners in the assemblies of today's called out] sinful kingdom, and I will destroy it from off the face of the earth; saving that I will not utterly destroy the house of Jacob, saith the LORD.

Did not God call us out of the Egypt of this world? and do we not seek to remain worldly in many things, just like ancient Israel sought to return to Egypt?

9:9 For, lo, I will command, and I will sift the house of Israel among all nations, like as corn is sifted in a sieve, yet shall not the least grain fall upon the earth.

9:10 All the sinners of my people shall die by the sword, which say, The evil shall not overtake nor prevent us.

The spiritually called out who sin against our LORD say this very thing!

Attending some corporate organized "church" will not deliver us from the wrath of God, if we will not zealously live by EVERY WORD of GOD!

Claiming that we are God's people will not save us if we idolize men and do not live by EVERY WORD of our GOD!

Finally when we have been torn and wounded by the agents of the Great God, we will sincerely repent; and our Lord will resurrect those who have been faithful to him, raising up David to once again rule the families of Israel.

9:11 In that day will I raise up the tabernacle of David that is fallen [the life of David will be restored and he shall be king over a united Israel/Judah], and close up the breaches [the breach between Israel and Judah will be healed and they shall be united under the house of David once again] thereof; and I will raise up his ruins, and I will build it as in the days of old:

9:12 That they may possess the remnant of Edom [after Messiah comes a repentant Turkey will serve king David of Israel], and of all the heathen, which are called by my name [the nations will also sincerely repent and shall be called by the name of the Lord], saith the LORD that doeth this.

The breach between Israel and her God will also be healed; and a New Covenant shall be made with Israel (Jer 31:31).

After the resurrection at Christ's coming most of those who remain alive and their descendants will sincerely repent and enter into a New Covenant (Jer 31).

Hosea speaks of the New Covenant after Christ comes this way:

> **Hosea 2:18** And in that day will I make a covenant for them with the beasts of the field and with the fowls of heaven, and with the creeping things of the ground: and I will break the bow and the sword and the battle out of the earth, and will make them to lie down safely [God's Spirit will be poured out on all flesh, Joel 2:28].
>
> **2:19 And I will betroth thee [in a New Covenant] unto me for ever; yea, I will betroth thee unto me in righteousness, and in judgment, and in lovingkindness, and in mercies.**

2:20 I will even betroth thee unto me in faithfulness: and thou shalt know the LORD.

Ezekiel puts it this way:

Ezekiel 36:24 For I will take you from among the heathen, and gather you out of all countries, and will bring you into your own land.

36:25 Then will I sprinkle clean water upon you, and ye shall be clean: from all your filthiness, and from all your idols, will I cleanse you.

36:26 A new heart also will I give you, and a new spirit will I put within you: and I will take away the stony heart out of your flesh, and I will give you an heart of flesh.

36:27 And **I will put my spirit within you, and cause you to walk in my statutes, and ye shall keep my judgments, and do them**.

36:28 And ye shall dwell in the land that I gave to your fathers; and ye shall be my people, and I will be your God.

Jeremiah writes:

Jeremiah 31:31 Behold, the days come, saith the Lord, that I will make a new covenant with the house of Israel, and with the house of Judah:

31:32 Not according to the covenant that I made with their fathers in the day that I took them by the hand to bring them out of the land of Egypt; which my covenant they brake, although I was an husband unto them, saith the Lord:

31:33 But this shall be the covenant that I will make with the house of Israel; After those days, saith the Lord, I will put my law in their inward parts, and write it in their hearts; and will be their God, and they shall be my people.

31:34 And they shall teach no more every man his neighbour, and every man his brother, saying, Know the Lord: for they shall all know me, from the least of them unto the greatest of them, saith the Lord: for I will forgive their iniquity, and I will remember their sin no more.

During the millennial Kingdom of God, the world will be blessed and rest at peace in the presence of the Creator. Then after 1,000 years Satan must be released for a short time before he is finally removed forever.

Amos 9:13 Behold, the days [of great prosperity] come, saith the LORD, that the plowman shall overtake the reaper, and the treader of grapes him that soweth seed; and the mountains shall drop sweet wine, and all the hills shall melt.

9:14 And I will bring again the [deliver from] captivity of my people of Israel, and they shall build the waste cities, and inhabit them; and they shall plant vineyards, and drink the wine thereof; they shall also make gardens, and eat the fruit of them.

9:15 And I will plant them upon their land, and they shall no more be pulled up out of their land which I have given them, saith the LORD thy God.

Obadiah

Obadiah

INTRODUCTION: The coming regional war in the Middle East will reset regional realities bringing a genuine dialogue for peace and finally a real peace deal. When peace is declared (1 Thess 5:3) the extremist Jewish Settler Movement will work to sabotage that deal, possibly including staging an attack on the Roman Pope when he visits the temple mount in Jerusalem.

This will bring on the occupation of Jerusalem and Judea by the Europeans in the name of stopping the bloodshed and securing peace, which will be applauded by the surrounding Islamic nations including Turkey which desires to once again lead the Islamic world.

The Psalm 83 nations including Turkey will control Judea and thrust as many Jews as possible from off the land.

God has warned throughout the Fifth Book of Moses that possession of the Promised Land is totally dependent on the inhabitants living by every Word of God. Since modern Jews in Judea do NOT do so and the land of full of abominations, they will see one final captivity.

The Book of Obadiah is a warning to Turkey that if they ally with the New Europe and afflict Judah; they will also be destroyed in their turn.

The New Europe will go forth to attack Asia during the third year of the occupation of Judea, and the Asian nations will respond against Europe and overrun the Middle East to attack Jerusalem, where the Europeans leaders have fled to in order to make their last stand.

Daniel 11:40 And at the time of the end shall the king of the south [Judah/Egypt] push at him: and the king of the north [the New Europe] shall come against him like a whirlwind, with chariots, and with horsemen, and with many ships; and he shall enter into the countries, and shall overflow and pass over.

11:41 He shall enter also into the glorious land [Palestine], and many countries shall be overthrown: but these shall escape out of his hand, even [his allies] Edom [Turkey], and Moab, and the chief of the children of Ammon [Moab and Ammon are modern Jordan].

11:42 He shall stretch forth his hand also upon the countries: and the land of Egypt shall not escape.

11:43 But he shall have power over the treasures of gold and of silver, and over all the precious things of Egypt: and the Libyans and the Ethiopians shall be at his steps [shall serve the New Europe] .

11:44 But tidings out of the east and out of the north [Russia and China] shall trouble him: therefore he shall go forth [in the third year of the occupation of Jerusalem] with great fury to destroy, and utterly to make away many.

11:45 And he shall [the rulers of the New Europe will then flee to Jerusalem for their last stand] plant the tabernacles of his palace between the seas in the glorious holy mountain; yet he shall come to his end, and none shall help him.

Obadiah 1:1 The vision of Obadiah. Thus saith the Lord GOD concerning Edom [Modern Turkey]; We have heard a rumour from the LORD, and an ambassador is sent among the heathen [the nations of Asia], Arise ye, and let us rise up against her in battle.

Edom is modern Turkey; who will be in league with the New Europe and the nations surrounding modern Judea [except for Egypt] against Judah (Psalm 83).

1:2 Behold, I have made thee small among the heathen: thou art greatly despised.

1:3 The pride of thine heart hath deceived thee, thou that dwellest in the clefts of the rock, whose habitation is high [those who live in the mountains of modern Turkey]; that saith in his heart, Who shall bring me down to the ground?

1:4 Though thou exalt thyself as the eagle, and though thou set thy nest among the stars, thence will I bring thee down, saith the LORD.

After the New Europe conquers Judea, the Turks will think in their heart that as an ally of the New Europe they are safe from all possible enemies and that they will never fall in their mountainous land.

1:5 If thieves came to thee, if robbers by night, (how art thou cut off!) would they not have stolen till they had enough? if the grape gatherers [reapers] came to thee, would they not leave some grapes?

1:6 How are the things of Esau [Esau is Edom, modern Turkey] searched out! how are his hidden things sought up!

1:7 All the men of thy confederacy have brought thee even to the border: the men that were at peace with thee have deceived thee, and prevailed against thee; that they eat thy bread have laid a wound under thee: there is none understanding in him.

Turkey's allies cannot save her and cannot defend her against the massive armies of Asia.

Germany, Austria and Hungary [Assur] will be a part of the New Europe and the following nations will be allied with the New Europe.

Turkey shall ally themselves with the New Europe and their other allies.

> **Psalm 83:1** Keep not thou silence, O God: hold not thy peace, and be not still, O God.
>
> **83:2** For, lo, thine enemies make a tumult: and they that hate thee have lifted up the head. **83:3** They have taken crafty counsel against thy people, and consulted against thy hidden ones.
>
> **83:4** They have said, Come, and let us cut them off from being a nation; that the name of Israel may be no more in remembrance. **83:5** For they have consulted together with one consent: they are confederate against thee:
>
> **83:6** The tabernacles of Edom [Turkey], and the Ishmaelites [true Arabs, sons of Ishmael; sons of Abraham and Agar]; of Moab [northern Jordan today], and the Hagarenes [Arabs who are sons of

Agar by a different husband than Abraham, and also not the sons of Ishmael];

83:7 Geba [Lebanon], and Ammon [southern Jordan today], and Amalek [a tribe of the Turks]; the Philistines [Gaza] with the inhabitants of Tyre;

83:8 Assur [Germany, Austria, Hungary] also is joined with them: they have holpen the children of Lot [will help modern Jordan; Ammon and Moab]. Selah.

Obadiah 1:8 Shall I not in that day, saith the LORD, even destroy the wise men out of Edom [Turkey], and understanding out of the mount of Esau [Turkey]

1:9 And thy mighty men, O Teman [Esau, Turkey], shall be dismayed, to the end that every one of the mount of Esau may be cut off by slaughter.

Turkey will fall for he shall be given over to the nations of the East for his perfidy against his brother Jacob [Judah and all the modern Israelite nations]. The mighty men of war of Turkey will be destroyed by the coming Russian/Chinese/Asian counter attack into the Middle East during and after the third year of the captivity of Judah.

Jerusalem will be trodden down of the Gentles for forty-two months (Rev 11) and then Messiah the Christ will come with all his saints; to bring in righteousness and to rule the whole earth.

1:10 For thy violence against thy brother Jacob shame shall cover thee, and thou shalt be cut off for ever.

Turkey will be cut off from being an independent nation by the destruction of the invasion from Asia.

1:11 In the day that thou stoodest on the other side, in the day that the strangers carried away captive his [Judah's] forces, and foreigners entered into his [Judah's] gates, and cast lots upon Jerusalem, even thou wast as one of them [one of the enemies of Judah] .

1:12 But thou shouldest not have looked on the day of thy brother in the day that he became a stranger; neither shouldest thou have rejoiced over the children of Judah in the day of their destruction; neither shouldest thou have spoken proudly in the day of distress.

When the New Europe conquers modern Judah; Turkey will rejoice and take part in dividing the spoils taken from his brother Judah.

1:13 Thou shouldest not have entered into the gate of my people in the day of their calamity; yea, thou shouldest not have looked on their affliction in the day of their calamity, nor have laid hands on their substance in the day of their calamity;

1:14 Neither shouldest thou have stood in the crossway, to cut off those of his that did escape; neither shouldest thou have delivered up those of his that did remain in the day of distress.

Turkey will take part in despoiling Judah,

1:15 For the day of the LORD is near upon all the heathen: as thou hast done, it shall be done unto thee: thy reward shall return upon thine own head.

1:16 For as ye have drunk upon my holy mountain, so shall all the heathen drink continually, yea, they shall drink, and they shall swallow down, and they shall be as though they had not been.

In the third year of the occupation of Judea, the New Europe will go to make war with Russia, China and the Shanghai Cooperation Organization and they will respond by defeating Europe and then invading Turkey and the Middle East, massing outside Jerusalem where the leaders of Europe will have fled to make their last stand.

When Messiah the Christ comes he will give the land of modern Turkey to Jacob [a newly reunited Israel/Judah under the resurrected king David].

1:17 But upon mount Zion shall be deliverance, and there shall be holiness; and the house of Jacob shall possess their possessions.

Messiah will come to deliver all Israel and he will destroy all those arrayed against her.

1:18 And the house of Jacob [Israel] shall be a fire, and the house of Joseph [Ephraim (the British peoples) and Manasseh (the Anglo Saxon Americans)] a flame, and the house of Esau [Turkey] for stubble, and they shall kindle in them, and devour them; and there shall not be any remaining of the house of Esau; for the LORD hath spoken it.

1:19 And they of the south [Judah] shall possess the mount of Esau [Turkey]; and they of the plain [Judah will possess Gaza] the Philistines [Gaza]: and they [Israel] shall possess the fields of Ephraim, and the fields of Samaria: and Benjamin shall possess Gilead.

The land of Benjamin is around Jerusalem in the south, but Christ will give them a place in Gilead [Golan]. Originally the region of Gilead was allotted by Moses to the tribes of Gad, Reuben, and the eastern half of Manasseh (Deuteronomy 3:13; Numbers 32:40).

In that day the reunited nations of Israel and Judah under the resurrected king David will be given Turkey, Jordan, Gaza and Syria for vassal states by the Eternal.

The removal of the Jews from much of the land north of Jerusalem by the New Europe and the Psalm 83 alliance, will clear that land for the ingathering of the ten tribes to their land of Samaria.

A great number of Palestinians [the modern descendants of the ancient Samaritans who converted to Islam] who came from Mesopotamia (2 Kings 17:23-34) will also be slaughtered by the Asian armies and the remnant will be subject to Israel.

Today Judah considers the Palestinians as Canaanites because most of them converted to Islam during the spread of that religion.

Palestinians are not Canaanites! They are Samaritans who converted to Islam or Catholicism.

The Canaanites of today live in Lebanon and their remnant will be relocated to the land of the Sabeans [modern India near Goa] after Christ comes (Joel 3:4-8).

1:20 And the captivity of this host of the children of Israel shall possess that of the Canaanites [Lebanon], even unto Zarephath [Sidon]; and the captivity of Jerusalem, which is in Sepharad [removed to Spain], shall possess the cities of the south.

1:21 And saviours [the resurrected chosen] shall come up on mount Zion to judge the mount of Esau; and the kingdom shall be the LORD's.

The Kingdom of God will be established by Messiah the Christ, and he shall rule over the whole earth.

Jonah

Jonah 1

The Book of Jonah is set during the reign of Jeroboam II (786–746 BC), when other prophets like Hosea were predicting the fall of the ten tribes of Israel to the Assyrians; which prophecies of an Assyrian attack explain Jonah's animosity towards Nineveh the capital of Assyria.

The Assyrian wave of captivities began in approximately 740 BC (or 733/2 BC according to other sources) only a few years after the mission of Jonah to Nineveh.

And the God of Israel stirred up the spirit of Pul king of Assyria, and the spirit of Tilgathpilneser king of Assyria, and he carried them away, even the Reubenites, and the Gadites, and the half tribe of Manasseh, and brought them unto Halah, and Habor, and Hara, and to the river Gozan, unto this day. (1 Chronicles 5:26)

Far more than a history of a reluctant prophet and the citizens of Nineveh Jonah is an allegorical prophecy about the burial and resurrection of Jesus Christ and points to God's mercy to all nations when Christ comes.

Jonah was a contemporary of Hosea, Joel and Amos, giving the lie to the teaching that God only works through one man at a time.

The book starts off with the reluctance of Jonah to preach repentance to Assyria because of the prophecies of Assyria concerning their future treatment of Israel. The book then proceeds with Jonah's burial at sea, repentance and resurrection from the deep and his warning to Nineveh, which results in the repentance of Nineveh.

Then comes a new understanding of the need to forgive all the terrors and hatreds of the past and welcome all nations into the Family of God.

Verse 1 to 16 sets the stage for the main analogy; which is the burial and resurrection of Christ.

Jonah 1:1 Now the word of the LORD came unto Jonah the son of Amittai, saying, **1:2** Arise, go to Nineveh, that great city, and cry against it; for their wickedness is come up before me.

Nineveh is here an allegorical example of all unconverted people.

1:3 But Jonah rose up to flee unto Tarshish from the presence of the LORD, and went down to Joppa [today a sister city of Tel Aviv]; and he found a ship going to Tarshish: so he paid the fare thereof, and went down into it, to go with them unto Tarshish from the presence of the LORD.

Jonah refused to obey God and preach the message of warning and repentance to Nineveh the capital of Assyria.

1:4 But the LORD sent out a great wind into the sea, and there was a mighty tempest in the sea, so that the ship was like to be broken. **1:5** Then the mariners were afraid, and cried every man unto his god, and cast forth the wares that were in the ship into the sea, to lighten it of them. But Jonah was gone down into the sides of the ship; and he lay, and was fast asleep.

The length of time of the storm is not stated and it could have lasted for a few or for many days.

1:6 So the shipmaster came to him, and said unto him, What meanest thou, O sleeper? arise, call upon thy God, if so be that God will think upon us, that we perish not.

Jonah is then urged to repent and call upon God.

1:7 And they said every one to his fellow, Come, and let us cast lots, that we may know for whose cause this evil is upon us. So they cast lots, and the lot fell upon Jonah. **1:8** Then said they unto him, Tell us, we pray thee, for whose cause this evil is upon us; What is thine occupation? and whence comest thou? what is thy country? and of what people art thou?

1:9 And he said unto them, I am an Hebrew; and I fear the LORD, the God of heaven, which hath made the sea and the dry land.

Then it is revealed that this evil came on them because the servant of God rebelled against his Maker.

1:10 Then were the men exceedingly afraid, and said unto him. Why hast thou done this? For the men knew that he fled from the presence of the LORD, because he had told them.

1:11 Then said they unto him, What shall we do unto thee, that the sea may be calm unto us? for the sea wrought, and was tempestuous.

1:12 And he said unto them, Take me up, and cast me forth into the sea; so shall the sea be calm unto you: for I know that for my sake this great tempest is upon you.

Jonah then acknowledged his guilt and bids the men to save themselves by casting him into the sea.

1:13 Nevertheless the men rowed hard to bring it to the land; but they could not: for the sea wrought, and was tempestuous against them.

1:14 Wherefore they cried unto the LORD, and said, We beseech thee, O LORD, we beseech thee, let us not perish for this man's life, and lay not upon us innocent blood: for thou, O LORD, hast done as it pleased thee.

1:15 So they look up Jonah, and cast him forth into the sea: and the sea ceased from her raging.

1:16 Then the men feared the LORD exceedingly, and offered a sacrifice unto the LORD, and made vows.

These men, not wanting to send Jonah to certain death and worked to save themselves including Jonah, until finally they had to obey the voice of the prophet.

1:17 Now the LORD had prepared a great fish to swallow up Jonah. And Jonah was in the belly of the fish three days and three nights.

This great fish was not a whale nor was it a regular fish; it was a special creature created by God for a special purpose. Logically it would have had a special pocket which would have supported Jonah's life. The secondary stomachs of ruminants and the crops of birds come to mind as examples of similar arrangements, although access to air was also provided to sustain Jonah.

Jonah 2

Jonah 2:1 Then Jonah prayed unto the LORD his God out of the fish's belly, **2:2** And said, I cried by reason of mine affliction unto the LORD, and he heard me; out of the belly of hell [the grave] cried I, and thou heardest my voice.

Jonah cries out in repentance to God, likening his situation to being in the grave. This is an allegory of the sins of the world being imputed to Christ; and as Jonah was buried in the deep for three days and nights because of sin, Christ was buried for three days and nights in the earth for the sins of the world.

See our article on the three days and three nights in the grave of Christ.

> **Matthew 12:38** Then certain of the scribes and of the Pharisees answered, saying, Master, we would see a sign from thee.
>
> **12:39** But he answered and said unto them, An evil and adulterous generation seeketh after a sign; and there shall no sign be given to it, **but the sign of the prophet Jonas: 12:40 For as Jonas was three days and three nights in the whale's belly; so shall the Son of man be three days and three nights in the heart of the earth.**
>
> **12:41** The men of Nineveh shall rise in judgment with this generation, and shall condemn it: because they repented at the preaching of Jonas; and, behold, a greater than Jonas is here.

Jonah 2:3 For thou hadst cast me into the deep, in the midst of the seas; and the floods compassed me about: all thy billows and thy waves passed over me. **2:4** Then I said, I am cast out of thy sight; yet I will look again toward thy holy temple.

Jonah cried out in repentance, just as nearly all men will cry out in repentance [at their appointed time] and be saved through the application of the atoning sacrifice of Jesus Christ and his bearing of the sins of the sincerely repentant who commit to "go and sin no more."

Jonah was cast out of God's sight because of his sin of rebellion, and God the Father could not look upon Jesus when he was bearing the sins of the world; which is an example that sin separates us from God.

> **Matthew 27:46** And about the ninth hour Jesus cried with a loud voice, saying, Eli, Eli, lama sabachthani? that is to say, My God, my God, why hast thou forsaken me?

Jonah 2:5 The waters compassed me about, even to the soul: the depth closed me round about, the weeds were wrapped about my head. **2:6** I went down to the bottoms of the mountains; the earth with her bars was about me for ever: yet hast thou brought up my life from corruption, O LORD my God. **2:7 When my soul fainted within me I remembered the LORD:** and my prayer came in unto thee, into thine holy temple.

This is a prophecy of the repentance of all men in their due time.

2:8 They that observe lying vanities forsake their own mercy.

Those who refuse to repent are rejecting God's saving mercy.

2:9 But I will sacrifice unto thee with the voice of thanksgiving; I will pay that that I have vowed. **Salvation is of the LORD.**

This speaks of the resurrection of Christ and through his atoning sacrifice, the salvation of all sincerely repentant humanity.

2:10 And the LORD spake unto the fish, and it vomited out Jonah upon the dry land.

Jonah was in type also an example of the resurrection, being resurrected from burial in the sea. This is a prophecy and picture of the resurrection of Christ after three days and nights buried in the earth. They was not parts of days and nights but three full days and three full nights.

This is not speaking about Christ being dead for three days and three nights but about him actually being buried in the earth for three full days and three full nights.

Jesus died at 3 PM on Passover Wednesday 31 A.D. and was buried before sunset and the First High Holy Day of the Feast of Unleavened Bread. He was then resurrected just after the sun had set ending the Saturday Sabbath at the same time that the high priest harvested the Wave Sheaf.

Therefore Jesus was resurrected on a Sunday just after the sun had set to end the Saturday Sabbath and begin a Sunday. Then the next morning after the Morning Daily Sacrifice, Jesus ascended to be accepted by God the Father and returned to the earth just as the high priest lifted up the Wave Offering to God and brought it back down to the earth.

Jonah 3

Jonah 3:1 And the word of the LORD came unto Jonah the second time, saying, **3:2** Arise, go unto Nineveh, that great city, and preach unto it the preaching that I bid thee.

Jonah was only in the fish for three days and three nights, and a fish could not have traversed the Mediterranean Sea and then gone around Africa and up to Nineveh in three days!

Jonah could have been cast ashore on the coast at any place, including on the Palestine or Syrian coast; at which time God told him once again to go to Nineveh and he would then have traveled there.

This concept that Jonah may have been cast up at the gates of Nineveh is a fairy tale. The fact that Jonah could well have traveled for a long time to reach Nineveh after being cast up by the fish is contained in the phrase: "So Jonah arose, and went unto Nineveh," which does not say how many days journey it took to reach the city. It was only AFTER Jonah had reached the city, that he traveled another full day into the heart of the city!

3:3 So Jonah arose, and went unto Nineveh, according to the word of the LORD. Now Nineveh was an exceeding great city of three days' journey [across].

3:4 And Jonah began to **enter into the city a day's journey**, and he cried, and said, Yet forty days, and Nineveh shall be overthrown.

After his resurrection from the sea, Jonah traveled to Nineveh and the length of time of that journey in not revealed; then AFTER arriving at the city Jonah journeyed a day into the city and began to preach the Word of God.

When he returns with his faithful resurrected chosen Jesus Christ and his bride will preach the same Gospel of Warning and Repentance to the whole world. What the called out are instructed to do now, will be done in its fullness after the resurrection of the chosen to spirit!

> **Matthew 28:18** And Jesus came and spake unto them, saying, All power is given unto me in heaven and in earth.
>
> **28:19** Go ye therefore, and teach all nations, baptizing them in the name of the Father, and of the Son, and of the Holy Ghost: **28:20** Teaching them to observe all things whatsoever I have commanded you: and, lo, I am with you alway, even unto the end of the world. Amen.

Jonah 3:5 So the people of Nineveh believed God, and proclaimed a fast, and put on sackcloth, from the greatest of them even to the least of them. **3:6** For word came unto the king of Nineveh, and he arose from his throne, and he laid his robe from him, and covered him with sackcloth, and sat in ashes.

3:7 And he caused it to be proclaimed and published through Nineveh by the decree of the king and his nobles, saying, Let neither man nor beast, herd nor flock, taste any thing: let them not feed, nor drink water: **3:8** But let man and beast be covered with sackcloth, and cry mightily unto God: yea, let them turn every one from his evil way, and from the violence that is in their hands. **3:9** Who can tell if God will turn and repent, and turn away from his fierce anger, that we perish not?

3:10 And God saw their works, that they turned from their evil way; and God repented of the evil, that he had said that he would do unto them; and he did it not.

This great city the capital of Assyria was a typical example of all sinners repenting at the preaching of the Gospel of warning and repentance after the coming of Christ when all humanity if called to God. The repentance of Nineveh is a picture of how all nations will ultimately repent and become grafted into the New Covenant.

Jonah 4

A lesson in forgiveness and mercy

Jonah 4:1 But it displeased Jonah exceedingly, and he was very angry.

Jonah had a problem, he did not want these Assyrians to repent; he wanted God to destroy them. This is typical of the attitude of people today who tend to bear grudges and have trouble forgiving one another over the sufferings of the past.

4:2 And he prayed unto the LORD, and said, I pray thee, O LORD, was not this my saying, when I was yet in my country? Therefore I fled before unto Tarshish: for I knew that thou art a gracious God, and merciful, slow to anger, and of great kindness, and repentest thee of the evil. **4:3** Therefore now, O LORD, take, I beseech thee, my life from me; for it is better for me to die than to live.

Jonah was so angry and hateful that he wanted to die so as not to have to live in a world containing the repentant Assyrians. Why? Because the prophets knew that the ancient Israel of that day would be conquered and removed from their land by Assyria [remember that Jonah was contemporary to Hosea, Amos and Joel]! God therefore gave Jonah an object lesson to bring him to repent of his anger and hatred.

4:4 Then said the LORD, Doest thou well to be angry?

4:5 So Jonah went out of the city, and sat on the east side of the city, and there made him a booth, and sat under it in the shadow, till he might see what would become of the city.

4:6 And the LORD God prepared a gourd [vine, bush], and made it to come up over Jonah, that it might be a shadow over his head, to deliver him from his grief. So Jonah was exceeding glad of the gourd.

4:7 But God prepared a worm when the morning rose the next day, and it smote the gourd that it withered.

4:8 And it came to pass, when the sun did arise, that God prepared a vehement east wind; and the sun beat upon the head of Jonah, that he fainted, and wished in himself to die, and said, It is better for me to die than to live.

4:9 And God said to Jonah, Doest thou well to be angry for the gourd? And he said, I do well to be angry, even unto death.

4:10 Then said the LORD, Thou hast had pity on the gourd, for the which thou hast not laboured, neither madest it grow; which came up in a night, and perished in a night:

4:11 And should not I spare Nineveh, that great city, wherein are more then sixscore thousand persons that cannot discern between their right hand and their left hand; and also much cattle?

God then revealed his great mercy towards humanity; teaching Jonah a lesson in humility and mercy and revealing how mercy will be shown to ALL sincerely repentant humanity at their appointed time.

This is especially a lesson for the survivors of today's great tribulation: When Christ comes and sets things right we must all forgive our enemies to bring in a New World Order of peace and prosperity in the Kingdom of God!

~ 150 ~

Micah

Micah 1

The Book of Micah is the sixth of the twelve minor prophets. It records the sayings of Micah, Mikayahu, meaning "Who is like Yahweh?", an 8th century B.C. prophet from the village of Moresheth [near Bethlehem] in Judah The book has three major divisions, chapters 1-2, 3-5 and 6-7, each introduced by the word "Hear," with a pattern of alternating announcements of warning and correction, and expressions of hope within each division.

Micah 1:1 The word of the LORD that came to Micah the Morasthite in the days of Jotham, Ahaz, and Hezekiah, kings of Judah, which he saw concerning Samaria and Jerusalem. Judgment against Samaria [Israel] and Judea [Judah]

1:2 Hear, all ye people; hearken, O earth, and all that therein is: and let the Lord GOD be witness against you, the LORD from his holy temple.

1:3 For, behold, the LORD cometh forth out of his place, and will come down, and tread upon the high places of the earth. **1:4** And the mountains shall be molten under him, and the valleys shall be cleft, as wax before the fire, and as the waters that are poured down a steep place.

1:5 For the transgression of Jacob [Israel and Judah; BOTH physical AND spiritual] is all this, and for the sins of the house of Israel. What is the transgression of Jacob? is it not Samaria [the idol calves of Samaria]? and what are the high places of Judah? are they not [Judah trusted in Jerusalem and in the temple; thinking that God would not correct them because they called themselves God's people as they sinned] Jerusalem?

1:6 Therefore I will make Samaria [Israel] as an heap [ruin] of the field, and as plantings of a vineyard: and I will pour down the stones thereof into the valley, and I will discover the foundations thereof.

Remember that this is written for ancient Israel and for us today being dual; we must take it to heart and acknowledge our own wrong doings.

This is a double dual, and by that I mean that it refers to all physical Israel in those days and also in the latter days, and it is also dual in that it refers to BOTH physical and spiritual Israel.

1:7 And all the graven images thereof shall be beaten to pieces, and all the hires thereof shall be burned with the fire, and all the idols thereof will I lay desolate: for she gathered it of the hire of an harlot [gained their wealth through disloyalty to God] , and they shall return to the hire of an harlot.

God will destroy ALL of the idols of today's Spiritual Ekklesia and of the nations of Israel and Judah first, and then he will go on to destroy all of the idols in this world;

God will destroy BOTH our physical idols like our wealth, buildings and possessions, and also our spiritual idols like false teachings and organizations and idols of men that do not live by every Word of God with enthusiastic zeal. An idol is anything that comes between the people and God.

1:8 Therefore I will wail and howl, I will go stripped and naked [In our correction we will mourn greatly]: I will make a wailing like the dragons [we will wail in our mourning like a howling wolf or coyote], and mourning as the owls.

God's true prophets and followers will mourn over the coming correction upon his people and upon the nations.

1:9 For her wound is incurable; for it [correction] is come unto Judah; he [it] is come unto the gate of my people, even to Jerusalem.

The correction will come to Jerusalem and the correction will also begin at the temple of God's called out; let the reader understand.

> **Revelation 11:1** And there was given me a reed like unto a rod: and the angel stood, saying, Rise, and measure the temple of God, and the altar, and them that worship therein.

God will measure out the true worshipers of God, the true temple of the Spirit; for they are beloved of God; but the outer courtyard will not be measured for it represents those are those who will be corrected.

Brethren, this is speaking about measuring out the true temple of God's Spirit, God's pillars; so that they will not be taken into the severe correction along with the faithless. They are to be separated from the lukewarm Laodicean types who are represented by the Outer Courtyard, still a part of the Temple but lukewarm for living by every Word of God.

11:2 But the court which is without the temple leave out, and measure it not; for it is given unto the Gentiles: and the holy city shall they tread under foot forty and two months.

Today God is marking out and separating the faithful from the faithless, the zealous to live by every Word of God from those who follow the false ways of their idols of men.

Ezekiel 9:4 And the Lord said unto him, Go through the midst of the city, through the midst of Jerusalem, and set a mark upon the foreheads [placing God's Spirit in the minds] of the men that sigh and that cry for all the abominations that be done in the midst thereof.

9:5 And to the others he said in mine hearing, Go ye after him through the city, and smite: let not your eye spare, neither have ye pity:

9:6 Slay utterly old and young, both maids, and little children, and women: but come not near any man upon whom is the mark; and **begin at my sanctuary** [God's sanctuary is the place where God dwells; His called out people]. Then they began at the ancient men [correction begins with so called, wise men of the Ekklesia] which were before the house.

9:7 And he said unto them, Defile the house, and fill the courts with the slain: go ye forth. And they went forth, and slew in the city.

9:8 And it came to pass, while they were slaying them, and I was left, that I fell upon my face, and cried, and said, Ah Lord God! wilt thou destroy all the residue of Israel in thy pouring out of thy fury upon Jerusalem?

9:9 Then said he unto me, The iniquity of the house of Israel and Judah is exceeding great, and the land is full of blood, and the city full of perverseness: for they say, The Lord hath forsaken the earth, and the Lord seeth not.

9:10 And as for me also, mine eye shall not spare, neither will I have pity, but I will recompense their way upon their head.

Brethren, this is coming on our lands because of the overspreading of our abominations, and it is coming on today's Spiritual Ekklesia for their idolatry and lack of zeal to live by every Word of God as they exalt their idols of men and false traditions above the Word of God.

The true faithful are being measured out, so that the pillars can be spared while the Laodicean's receive their correction.

Micah 1:10 Declare ye it not at Gath, weep ye not at all: in the house of Aphrah roll thyself in the dust. **1:11** Pass ye away, thou inhabitant of Saphir, having thy shame naked: the inhabitant of Zaanan came not forth in the mourning of Bethezel; he shall receive of you his standing.

1:12 For the inhabitant of Maroth waited carefully [anxiously] for good [deliverance]: but evil came down from the LORD unto the gate of Jerusalem.

Correction will begin at Jerusalem and at the House of God; his spiritually called out who are his Spiritual Temple today.

1:13 O thou inhabitant of Lachish, bind the chariot to the swift beast: she is the beginning of the sin to the daughter of Zion: for the transgressions of Israel [idolatry] were found in thee. **1:14** Therefore shalt thou give presents to Moreshethgath: the houses of Achzib shall be a lie to the kings of Israel.

A short promise of Messiah to provide hope for the saints and for the people of Israel.

1:15 Yet will I bring an heir unto thee, O inhabitant of Mareshah [a city near Bethlehem]: he shall come unto Adullam the glory of Israel.

1:16 Make thee bald [shave the head in mourning], and poll [cut our hair in mourning over our children] thee for thy delicate children; enlarge thy baldness [make ourselves bald like the bald eagle in our mourning to repentance] as the eagle; for they are gone into captivity from thee.

Micah 2

Micah 2:1 Woe to them that devise iniquity, and work evil upon their beds [who lay awake at night imagining doing evil things]! when the morning is light, they practise it [and in the morning they do the evil they have planned in the night], because it is in the power of their hand.

Woe unto the wicked who lay awake at night thinking about how to gain personal advantage.

2:2 And they covet fields, and take them by violence; and houses, and take them away: so they oppress a man and his house, even a man and his heritage.

2:3 Therefore thus saith the LORD; Behold, against this family [Israel/Judah and today's Spiritual Ekklesia] do I devise an evil [the affliction of severe correction], from which ye shall not remove your necks [we will not be delivered]; neither shall ye go haughtily [be full of arrogant pride]: for this time [of rebuke is come] is evil.

2:4 In that day shall one take up a parable against you, and lament with a doleful lamentation, and say, We be utterly spoiled: he hath changed the portion of my people [from blessings to cursing's]: how hath he removed it from me! turning away he hath divided our fields. **2:5** Therefore thou shalt have none [no godly left] that shall cast a cord by lot in the congregation of the LORD.

Today the Ekklesia do not want to hear the truth. Oh we listen to prophecies of trial and tribulation but we have absolutely the wrong take on these things, believing that they will come upon others and not on ourselves. We judge ourselves righteous while we are full of pride, idolatry of men and sin; being totally blind to our spiritual condition because we WILL NOT SEE (Rev 3:16).

Today the vast majority of the Ekklesia declare: "speak nothing bad about us, for we are righteous in our own eyes." When told the truth we immediately shut out what God thinks of us, preferring to live in a world of self-delusion following our idols of men in our social club assemblies; rather than sincerely repenting of our sins to turn and live by every Word of God.

2:6 Prophesy ye not, say they to them that prophesy: they shall not prophesy to them, that they shall not take shame.

The false prophet's who say that the time is delayed, will be destroyed along with the people and the nations that they have deceived.

God's warnings are for our good so that we will repent and depart from our evil ways and find peace and refuge in him during the time of correction.

2:7 O thou that art named the house of Jacob [physical Israel, and the Spiritual Ekklesia], is the spirit of the LORD straitened [limited or restrained]? are these his doings? **do not my words do good to him that walketh uprightly?**

The wicked dominate the godly; they will surely be corrected.

2:8 Even of late my people is risen up as an enemy: ye pull off the robe with the garment from them that pass by securely as men averse from war.

The wicked have taken the Word of God away from the people and have destroyed the spiritual strength of God's people by teaching people to depart from the Word of God.

2:9 The women of my people have ye cast out from their pleasant houses; from their children have ye taken away my glory for ever.

The many elders and leaders who pollute God's spiritual temple [turning God's people (temple, sanctuary) away from him and teaching the brethren to idolize men and false traditions] with idolatries and who cast out the righteous: will be rejected from the presence of God.

> **Revelation 3:15** I know thy works, that thou art neither cold nor hot: I would thou wert cold or hot. **3:16** So then because thou art lukewarm, and neither cold nor hot, I will spue thee out of my mouth.

The wicked of ancient Israel are told that they must depart from the land by the hand of Assyria. Similarly today's wicked will be severely corrected.

Micah 2:10 Arise ye, and depart [the wicked of ancient Israel]; for this is not your rest: because it is polluted, it shall destroy you, even with a sore destruction.

The people desire to hear the smooth things of the false prophets who teach that we are righteous and no harm will befall us. We seek prophets who lie to us and intoxicate us with pride by their false words

2:11 If a man walking in the spirit and falsehood do lie, saying, I will prophesy unto thee of wine and of strong drink; he shall even be the prophet of this people.

The people seek leaders who tell them smooth things and prophecy of near term good. Who deceive the brethren with their feigned love as they pervert the Word of God.

Yet, after our correction, Messiah will surely gather the sincerely repentant remnant which is left and lead them to good.

2:12 I will surely assemble, O Jacob, all of thee; **I will surely gather the remnant of Israel**; I will put them together as the sheep of Bozrah, as the flock in the midst of their fold: they shall make great noise by reason of the multitude of men.

2:13 The breaker is come up before them: they have broken up, and have passed through the gate, and are gone out by it: and their king shall pass before them, and the LORD on the head of them.

Micah 3

Micah cried out against the leaders and elders of the people of God

Micah 3:1 And I said, Hear, I pray you, O heads [leaders] of Jacob [physical and spiritual Israel], and ye princes of the house of Israel; Is it [should you not know] not for you to know judgment?

Most of today's leaders and elders of the called out despise the good things of God and reject them for their own ways, making merchandise of the brethren and taking more than is right.

3:2 Who hate the good, and love the evil; who pluck off their skin from off them, and their flesh from off their bones; **3:3** Who also eat the flesh of my people, and flay their skin from off them; and they break their bones, and chop them in pieces, as for the pot, and as flesh within the caldron.

The national leaders who break the people with taxes, and the elders who demand far more than they should in offerings and who cause the people to follow themselves as idols, will be punished.

Because of their sins, when they cry out to God in their correction he will not listen to them.

3:4 Then shall they cry unto the LORD, but he will not hear them: he will even hide his face from them at that time, as they have behaved themselves ill in their doings.

Those who tell the brethren that no correction will come upon them and that safety lies in loyalty to men are speaking lies in the name of the Lord; calling themselves leaders and elders of God when the Eternal has not sent them: they are opposing God and they shall surely fall. These people are not with God and God does not inspire those who lead the people astray to follow idols of men.

Brethren, Paul tells us that when peace is declared the trial will begin (1 Thes 5:3), and when the miracle working man of sin goes to the temple mount, Jesus Christ tells us that the tribulation will immediately begin (Mat 24:15). Yet these false teachers will not believe.

3:5 Thus saith the LORD concerning the prophets that make my people err, that bite with their teeth, and cry, Peace; and he that putteth not into their mouths, they even prepare war against him [they resist God and fight against God].

3:6 Therefore night shall be unto you, that ye shall not have a vision; and it shall be dark unto you, that ye shall not divine; and the sun shall go down over the prophets, and the day shall be dark over them.

When tribulation and affliction comes these false teachers will be ashamed as real events prove them to be false, and all will KNOW that they have been false teachers.

3:7 Then shall the seers be ashamed, and the diviners confounded: yea, they shall all cover their lips; for there is no answer of God.

The false religious teachers who say that there will be time after a peace agreement before the tribulation begins, will be made desolate by the Eternal for their false words which have led many astray; and they will be ashamed when their words fail and their correction comes.

The true man of God is full of power to declare the truth to the brethren. he obeys the Word of the LORD and warns of the coming correction for the sins of the Ekklesia and the sins of the nations.

> **Isaiah 58:1** Cry aloud, spare not, lift up thy voice like a **trumpet**, and shew my people their transgression, and the house of Jacob their sins.

Micah 3:8 But **truly I am full of power by the spirit of the LORD, and of judgment, and of might, to declare unto Jacob his transgression, and to Israel his sin.**

3:9 Hear this, I pray you, ye heads of the house of Jacob, and princes of the house of Israel, that abhor judgment, and pervert all equity.

3:10 They build up Zion with blood, and Jerusalem with iniquity.

Today's religions, including the spiritually called out Ekklesia, are built upon the iniquity of idolizing men and their false teachings and traditions, instead of relying on the Word of Almighty God.

3:11 The heads thereof judge for reward [take bribes], and the priests thereof teach [they will teach whatever the people want, for money] for hire, and the prophets thereof divine [they will foretell whatever the people want to hear for money] for money: yet will they lean [yet they claim to be God's chosen leaders] upon the LORD, and [call themselves godly as they teach the brethren to depart from the truth and to follow every false way] say, Is not the LORD among us? none evil can come upon us.

All these evils are done by today's religious leaders and most of the leaders and elders in today's Spiritual Ekklesia; and then they say "we are God's people, no harm shall befall us."

3:12 Therefore shall Zion for your sake be plowed as a field, and Jerusalem shall become heaps, and the mountain of the house as the high places of the forest.

Our false leaders and elders who teach the brethren to sin and the people which they deceive to follow them, will be plowed under and brought to ruin until they learn that the Eternal is God.

Micah 4

The prophecy now shifts to the coming Kingdom of God

Micah 4:1 But in the last days it shall come to pass, that the mountain [government] of the house of the LORD shall be established in the top of the mountains [all the earth's governments], and it shall be exalted above the hills [smaller local governments]; and people shall flow unto it.

4:2 And **many nations shall come, and say, Come, and let us go up to the mountain of the LORD, and to the house of the God of Jacob; and he will teach us of his ways, and we will walk in his paths: for the law shall go forth of Zion, and the word of the LORD from Jerusalem.**

At that time Messiah the Christ will come with all his chosen resurrected saints and they will build the Ezekiel Temple on the Holy Mount at Jerusalem, and Jerusalem shall be the capital of all nations and all the peoples of the entire earth.

All the nations of the earth will look to Jerusalem and to the House of God [the Ezekiel Temple] there; and they will worship God the Father and live by every Word of God and godly righteousness will be spread abroad through the whole earth from Jerusalem by the King of kings, Jesus Christ.

4:3 And he shall judge among many people, and rebuke strong nations afar off; and they shall beat their swords into plowshares, and their spears into pruninghooks: nation shall not lift up a sword against nation, neither shall they learn war any more.

War and violence and the breaking of any part of God's Word will be destroyed out of the earth and Satan will be banished for one thousand years in a millennial Sabbath of rest for humanity with their Creator.

4:4 But they shall sit every man under his vine and under his fig tree; and none shall make them afraid: for the mouth of the LORD of hosts hath spoken it.

All people will live securely in safety and none shall be afraid of any violence against themselves, or their property.

4:5 For **all people will walk every one in the name of his God, and we will walk in the name of the LORD our God for ever and ever.**

May God speed that day!

> **Joel 2:28** And it shall come to pass afterward, that **I will pour out my spirit upon all flesh**; and your sons and your daughters shall prophesy, your old men shall dream dreams, your young men shall see visions: **2:29** And also upon the servants and upon the handmaids in those days will I pour out my spirit.

Micah 4:6 In that day, saith the LORD, will I assemble her [Israel] that halteth [had balked at serving God], and I will gather her that is driven out [in correction for not living by EVERY WORD of God], and her that I have afflicted;

4:7 And I will make her that halted [shied away from serving God] a remnant, and her that was cast far off [Those who were corrected and afflicted by God for balking like a stubborn mule at serving him, will be delivered and will become a strong nation.] a strong nation: and the LORD shall reign over them in mount Zion from henceforth, even for ever.

The remnant of Israel and Judah will both be brought back to Palestine and shall become a strong united kingdom under the resurrected David their king, and the resurrected David will rule over a united Israel under the authority of the King of Kings, Jesus Christ the Creator and Savior of humanity, who shall rule over all the earth.

4:8 And thou, O tower of the flock, the strong hold of the daughter of Zion, unto thee shall it come, even the first dominion; the kingdom shall come to the daughter of Jerusalem.

To the daughter of Jerusalem; the latter day Jerusalem; shall the King of kings come.

The Time of Jacob's Trouble

4:9 Now why dost thou cry out aloud? is there no king in thee? is thy counsellor perished? for pangs [The correction of tribulation and affliction will humble the nations and a new world of joy and peace will be born.] have taken thee as a woman in travail.

4:10 Be in pain, and labour to bring forth, O daughter [latter day physical and spiritual Israel] of Zion, like a woman in travail: for now shalt thou go forth out of the city, and thou shalt dwell in the field, and thou shalt go even to Babylon [the New Europe]; there shalt thou be delivered; there the LORD shall redeem thee from the hand of thine enemies.

We will be corrected in great tribulation for our many sins; yet when we are humbled and sincerely repentant in our captivity: We SHALL be delivered and a new world of righteousness will be born!

4:11 Now also many nations are gathered against thee, that say, Let her be defiled, and let our eye look upon Zion.

4:12 But they know not the thoughts of the LORD, neither understand they his counsel: for he shall gather them as the sheaves into the floor.

The armies of Europe and of Asia will be gathered at Jerusalem by the hand of the Lord, and he will thresh them like wheat.

4:13 Arise and thresh, O daughter of Zion: for I will make thine horn iron, and I will make thy hoofs brass: and thou shalt beat in pieces many people: and I will consecrate their gain unto the LORD, and their substance unto the Lord of the whole earth.

The Eternal will come with his resurrected saints and Judah will also fight at Jerusalem.

> **Zechariah 14:13** And it shall come to pass in that day, that a great tumult from the Lord shall be among them; and they [the wicked who resist Christ at his coming] shall lay hold every one on the hand of his neighbour, and his hand shall rise up against the hand of his neighbour.
>
> **14:14** And Judah also shall fight at Jerusalem; and the wealth of all the heathen round about shall be gathered together, gold, and silver, and apparel, in great abundance.

Micah 5

A Prophecy of Messiah

Micah 5:1 Now gather thyself in troops, O daughter [The Roman army crucified Christ, but he did not remain dead] of troops: he hath laid siege against us: **they shall smite the judge of Israel with a rod upon the cheek.**

A prophecy that Messiah would be born in Bethlehem

5:2 But thou, Bethlehem Ephratah, though thou be little among the thousands of Judah, yet **out of thee shall he come forth unto me that is to be ruler in Israel; whose goings forth have been from of old, from everlasting.**

The Creator who existed from everlasting gave up his godhood to be made flesh, and Micah prophesies that Israel and Judah will be saved in the latter day by the coming of the resurrected Christ.

5:3 Therefore will he give them [Judah / Israel] up, until the time that she [physical Israel/Judah] which travaileth hath brought forth: then the remnant of his brethren [Israel/Judah will be reunited] shall return unto the children of Israel.

Jesus Christ will give up the bulk of Israel and Judah until the time of their correction and repentance comes; then the Deliverer Redeemer will come and Judah will be reunited with Israel and enter a New Covenant with the Eternal, (Jer 31:31).

5:4 And he [Messiah] shall stand and feed in the strength of the LORD [YHVH, in this case God the Father], in the majesty of the name of the LORD his God; and they [Israel shall be saved] shall abide: **for now shall he**[Messiah the Christ] **be great unto the ends of the earth** [Christ shall rule all nations] .

When Christ comes he will act in the name and by the authority of God the Father, and he shall rule to the very ends of the earth. Then the nations that had corrected us will also be corrected and humbled so that all nations can be grafted into spiritual Israel.

5:5 And this man [Messiah shall come to deliver and bring peace] shall be the peace, when the Assyrian shall come into our land: and when he [The Assyrian, as a type of the modern soon coming New Europe.] shall tread in our palaces, then shall we raise against him seven shepherds, and eight principal men.

5:6 And they shall waste the land of Assyria with the sword, and the land of Nimrod in the entrances thereof: thus shall he deliver us from the Assyrian, when he cometh into our land, and when he treadeth within our borders.

When Christ comes, he will defeat the destroyer of his heritage. I do not know what these seven shepherds and eight principle men are, but they will crush the land of Assyria when Christ comes.

Then those of Israel who remain will be sincerely repentant and they shall embrace the Eternal, they shall be unstoppable by the power of God.

5:7 And the remnant of Jacob shall be in the midst of many people as a dew from the LORD, as the showers upon the grass, that tarrieth not for man, nor waiteth for the sons of men.

5:8 And the remnant of Jacob shall be among the Gentiles in the midst of many people as a lion among the beasts of the forest, as a young lion among the flocks of sheep: who, if he go through, both treadeth down, and teareth in pieces, and none can deliver.

In the day that Christ comes many of Israel will have been scattered throughout the nations, yet they shall be delivered. Then all who oppose God and his people will be overcome.

5:9 Thine hand shall be lifted up upon thine adversaries, and all thine enemies shall be cut off.

In the 42 months of our correction, God will destroy our idols, including our corporate churches, and our false prophets and false teachers who exalt themselves and their false traditions above the Word of God.

5:10 And it shall come to pass in that day, saith the LORD [to his enemies], that I will cut off thy horses out of the midst of thee, and I will destroy thy chariots [God will destroy the armies and weapons of those who oppose Christ]:

When Christ comes he will destroy all wickedness and rebellion against God from off the face of the earth

5:11 And I will cut off the cities of thy land, and throw down all thy strong holds:

5:12 And I will cut off witchcrafts [rebellion against God] out of thine hand; and thou shalt have no more soothsayers [false teachers]:

5:13 Thy graven images [all idolatry] also will I cut off, and thy standing images out of the midst of thee; and thou shalt no more worship the work of thine hands.

5:14 And I will pluck up thy groves [false places of worship] out of the midst of thee: so will I destroy thy cities.

5:15 And I will execute vengeance in anger and fury upon the heathen [The term heathen refers to the rebellious against God, who exalt their idols above the Eternal as is done in today's Spiritual Ekklesia], such as they have not heard.

Micah 6

The Eternal's controversy with the nations of today

Micah 6:1 Hear ye now what the LORD saith; Arise, contend thou before the mountains [governments, nations], and let the hills [small nations and provinces] hear thy voice.

6:2 Hear ye, O mountains, the LORD's controversy, and ye strong foundations of the earth: for the LORD hath a controversy with his people, and he will plead with Israel.

The Eternal will plead with his people by strong correction, before all the governments and peoples of the earth.

God asks us why we have turned aside from him to follow idols?

6:3 O my people, what have I done unto thee? and wherein have I wearied thee? testify against me.

6:4 For I brought thee up out of the land of Egypt, and redeemed thee out of the house of servants [bondage, servitude]; and I sent before thee Moses, Aaron, and Miriam.

6:5 O my people, remember now what Balak king of Moab consulted, and what Balaam the son of Beor answered him [Remember how Balaam taught Balak that God had blessed Israel and that Israel should be tempted to sin so that God would turn on them.] from Shittim unto Gilgal; that ye may know the righteousness of the LORD.

God reveals his good works and blessings towards his people and then asks for faithfulness to his commandments which are for our own good in return.

God wants humility, justice and mercy without sin, rather than sacrifice for sin. God wants us to do no sin at all so that sacrifice for sin is no longer needed!

6:6 Wherewith shall I come before the LORD, and bow myself before the high God? shall I come before him with burnt offerings, with calves of a year old?

6:7 Will the LORD be pleased with thousands of rams, or with ten thousands of rivers of oil? shall I give my firstborn for my transgression, the fruit of my body for the sin of my soul?

6:8 He hath shewed thee, O man, what is good; and what doth the LORD require of thee, but to do justly, and to love mercy, and to walk humbly with thy God?

6:9 The LORD's voice crieth unto the city, and the man of wisdom shall see thy name: hear ye the rod, and who hath appointed it.

The warnings have gone out, who will take them to heart and turn his face to the Eternal in true wholehearted repentance and zeal to live by every Word of God?

If we will not repent now; then let us hear and respond to the rod of God's loving correction with sincere repentance when our time of correction comes.

If we remain wicked to deceive and defraud, we will surely be afflicted.

6:10 Are there yet the treasures of wickedness in the house of the wicked, and the scant measure that is abominable?

6:11 Shall I count them pure with the wicked balances, and with the bag of deceitful weights?

6:12 For the rich men thereof are full of violence, and the inhabitants thereof have spoken lies, and their tongue is deceitful in their mouth.

Will God hold those who cheat and steal, who are violent and seek personal advantage; guiltless?

Here is the curse upon the wicked who commit idolatry, exalting idols and traditions of men above the Word of God and persecuting those who are zealous to live by EVERY WORD of God.

God will smite and correct us until we sincerely and wholeheartedly repent.

6:13 Therefore also will I make thee sick in smiting thee, in making thee desolate because of thy sins.

6:14 Thou shalt eat, but not be satisfied; and thy casting down shall be in the midst of thee; and thou shalt take hold, but shalt not deliver; and that which thou deliverest will I give up to the sword.

6:15 Thou shalt sow, but thou shalt not reap; thou shalt tread the olives, but thou shalt not anoint thee with oil; and sweet wine, but shalt not drink wine.

Like our forefathers, today our nations are full of idolatry and sin; and like the priesthood of Aaron who led the people astray, most leaders and elders of today's Spiritual Ekklesia also lead the brethren astray: For they teach the brethren to follow idols of men and to turn aside from any zeal to live by the whole Word of God.

6:16 For the statutes of Omri [idolatry] are kept, and all the works of the house of Ahab [idolatry and adultery], and ye [the spiritual leaders and elders of today's Ekklesia] walk in their counsels [to do wickedness and provoke the Eternal]; that I should make thee a desolation, and the inhabitants thereof an hissing: therefore ye shall bear the reproach of my people.

Those who bow to idols of men, organizations and false traditions, and who commit the same sins as ancient Samaria; will not be judged guiltless.

Micah 7

God spoke through Micah, lamenting that there is nothing to harvest. This an allegory that there are no longer any large clusters of righteous godly people remaining in the called out Ekklesia; only scattered individuals here and there. God says that the field has no spiritual first fruits barley to harvest; only a grain here and a handful there, who are zealous to live by EVERY WORD of God.

Micah 7:1 Woe is me! for I am as when they have [when someone else has taken the harvest] gathered the summer fruits, as the grapegleanings of the vintage: there is no cluster to eat: my soul desired the firstripe fruit.

The true pillars of God are one here and another there, and there are no big clusters of first fruits, for the majority have fallen away into idolizing men and false traditions and organizations above the Word of God and they will not turn away from their errors without severe correction.

God speaks in a generality here because of the extremely rarity of zealous godly persons; even among the spiritually called out.

7:2 The good man is perished out of the earth: and there is none upright among men [except for the extremely rare faithful individual]: they all lie in wait for blood; they hunt every man his brother with a net. **7:3** That they may do evil with both hands earnestly, the prince asketh, and the judge asketh for a reward; and the great man, he uttereth his mischievous desire: so they wrap it up.

Our leaders take bribes and seek reward and personal advantage, respecting persons in their judgments and exalting their own ways and false traditions over the Word of God.

7:4 The best of them is as a brier: the most upright is sharper than a thorn hedge: the day of thy watchmen and thy visitation cometh; now shall be their perplexity.

The day of our calamity is at hand; who will take it to heart and turn to God?

7:5 Trust ye not in a friend, put ye not confidence in a guide [an elder]: keep the doors of thy mouth from her that lieth in thy bosom.

People are afraid to speak their minds in today's Spiritual Ekklesia, and this fear is widespread in our nations today where political correctness rules.

Faithfulness to and zeal for God will bring the enmity of the people and of today's brethren. Today the corporate assemblies will tolerate just about any sin, but they will not tolerate a zeal to wholeheartedly live by every Word of God as Jesus Christ commanded (Mat 4:4).

This prophecy was quoted by Christ

> **Matthew 10:35** For I am come to set a man at variance against his father, and the **daughter** against her mother, and the **daughter** in law against her mother in law.

Micah 7:6 For the son dishonoureth the father, the daughter riseth up against her mother, the daughter in law against her mother in law; a man's enemies are the men of his own house.

Few can be trusted, which trial drives the godly to draw ever closer to God!

7:7 Therefore I will look unto the LORD; I will wait for the God of my salvation: my God will hear me.

The righteous godly person says. "I will seek the Eternal all my days; and my feet shall not depart from his ways."

Godly people are not afraid of anything, not even death itself; for they KNOW that God will deliver them!

7:8 Rejoice not against me, O mine enemy: when I fall, I shall arise; when I sit in darkness, the LORD shall be a light unto me.

Let us accept the merciful correction of our Greatly Beloved Father

7:9 I will bear the indignation of the LORD, because I have sinned against him, until he plead my cause, and execute judgment for me: he will bring me forth to the light, and I shall behold his righteousness.

The godly accept God's correction and sincerely repent, then God will forgive and save them.

7:10 Then she that is mine enemy shall see it, and shame shall cover her which said unto me, Where is the LORD thy God? mine eyes shall behold her: now shall she be trodden down as the mire of the streets.

Those who despise the wholeheartedly zealous for God today, will be corrected and will come to understand and repent of that attitude.

God will deliver those whom he loves after he has corrected their errors and they have returned unto him. His correction is a manifestation of his great love in that he desired to save us from our wickedness by humbling us so that we might turn to him and remain faithful for eternity.

When Messiah the Christ comes he will build Jerusalem and the Ezekiel Temple, and all nations shall flow unto God.

7:11 In the day that thy walls are to be built, in that day shall the decree [of correction] be far removed.

7:12 In that day also he shall come even to thee from Assyria, and from the fortified cities, and from the fortress even to the river, and from sea to sea, and from mountain to mountain.

All nations, from the Assyrians [Germany, Austria and Hungary] to the Egyptians, shall turn to the Eternal after Christ comes.

7:13 Notwithstanding the land shall be desolate [shall be desolated for the 42 month tribulation, in order to correct us from our wickedness] because of them that dwell therein, for the [wicked] fruit of their doings.

Our land will be made desolate because of our own evil; until the time that we honestly repent and turn from our wicked ways. When those who were made desolate will sincerely repent and turn to God and they shall be delivered.

7:14 Feed thy people with thy rod, the flock of thine heritage, which dwell solitarily in the wood, in the midst of Carmel: let them feed in [the fruitful lands of] Bashan [the Golan area] and Gilead [east of Galilee], as in the days of old.

When Messiah the Christ comes he will deliver with mighty deeds

7:15 According to the days of thy coming out of the land of Egypt will I shew unto him marvellous things.

As the days of deliverance from Egypt; Messiah will deliver his people when he comes and the nations will fear dreadfully and seek out the Eternal to be their God.

7:16 The nations shall see and be confounded at all their might [of God and Israel]: they shall lay their hand upon their mouth, their ears shall be deaf [in shock that those who had been made desolate are delivered and risen back up by the might of God].

7:17 They shall lick the dust like a serpent, they shall move out of their holes like worms of the earth: **they shall be afraid of the LORD our God, and shall fear because of thee**.

The nations of the world will be astonished at the deliverance of the Eternal, when Christ comes with his saints to execute judgment and to deliver humanity from Satan.

After our correction we will be humbled and we will repent to follow the LORD our DELIVERER! Then God will forgive all our wickedness in his tender loving mercy!

May God speed that day!

7:18 Who is a God like unto thee, that pardoneth iniquity, and passeth by the transgression of the remnant of his heritage? he retaineth not his anger for ever, because he delighteth in mercy.

7:19 He will turn again, he will have compassion upon us; he will subdue our iniquities; and thou wilt cast all their sins into the depths of the sea.

7:20 Thou wilt perform the truth to Jacob, and the mercy to Abraham, which thou hast sworn unto our fathers from the days of old.

Nahum

Introduction:

Nineveh was the capital of the Assyrian Empire and this prophecy is against Nineveh and Assyria [modern Germany, Austria and Hungary] and the latter day Babylon, the coming New Europe and its leader, called a beast in scripture. Just as the head controls the whole body so the capital city controls and therefore represents the whole nation. Therefore the prophecy of Nineveh is about all of Assyria, some of which was fulfilled in the past and some of which is to be fulfilled in the near future.

> **Daniel 8:23** And in the latter time of their kingdom, when the transgressors are come to the full, a king of fierce countenance, and understanding dark sentences [the occult (spiritualism and witchcraft) and also highly technical things], shall stand up.
>
> **8:24** And his power shall be mighty, but not by his own power [his power will come from fallen spirits and the occult]: and he shall destroy wonderfully [to an awesome degree], and shall prosper, and practise, and shall destroy the mighty and the holy people.
>
> **8:25** And through his policy also he shall cause craft to prosper in his hand; and he shall magnify himself in his heart [great pride], and **by peace**(1 Thess 5:3) shall destroy many: he shall also stand up against the Prince of princes [Messiah the Christ when he comes];

but he shall be broken without hand [By Messiah the Christ when he comes (Dan 2)].

The prophecy is about latter day Germanic peoples as the descendants of Nineveh and Assyria, who will be the chief nations of the New Europe which is the feet of the image of Babylon the Great of Daniel 2.

Assyria is not only Germany but also the nations of Austria and Hungary.

To this day Europeans call Germany "Allemagne" or some derivative and the Alemanni were the chief tribe of Assyria.

Hungary, Hun-Gary [Hun-Land], is the land given to the Huns by the Romans to keep them out of Rome.

While Germany had its own "king" until after the revolution ending WW 1; The Austro-Hungarian [both of whom are also Assyrian] Empire was the Holy Roman Empire, and it is entirely possible that a descendant of that line would be the evil political leader of the New Europe referenced by Nahum and referred to in Revelation as the Beast ruling the soon coming New Federal Europe.

It is certainly clear that Germany, Austria, Hungary and France will be the core of the New Europe; possibly joined by the overwhelmingly Catholic countries of Italy, Spain, Poland, the Czech Republic, the Slovak Republic and Portugal.

The prophecy begins with the Might, and Glory of the Eternal; and then chastises the latter day leader of Assyria for his affront against God and God's people, concluding with God's correction of all of Assyria [Austro-Hungary and Germany] as representing the Babylon of the New Europe; for their pride and for their over zealousness in correcting Israel and the called out of God's people.

In the third year of the correction of Israel this New Europe will go out to attack the nations of Asia who will counterattack destroying the New Europe including the German nations, then Israel will be delivered by the Almighty.

> **Isaiah 10:12** Wherefore it shall come to pass, that when the Lord hath performed his whole work upon mount Zion and on Jerusalem, **I will punish the fruit of the stout heart of the king of Assyria, and the glory of his high looks.**
>
> **10:13 For he saith, By the strength of my hand I have done it, and by my wisdom; for I am prudent: and I have removed the**

bounds of the people, and have robbed their treasures, and I have put down the inhabitants like a valiant man:

10:14 And my hand hath found as a nest the riches of the people: and as one gathereth eggs that are left, have I gathered all the earth; and there was none that moved the wing, or opened the mouth, or peeped.

God used Assyria to humble the nations, and not acknowledging that they will become filled with pride in what they see as their own achievements.

10:15 Shall the axe boast itself against him that heweth therewith? or shall the saw magnify itself against him that shaketh it? as if the rod should shake itself against them that lift it up, or as if the staff should lift up itself, as if it were no wood.

10:16 Therefore shall the Lord, the Lord of hosts, send among his fat ones leanness; and under his glory he shall kindle a burning like the burning of a fire.

10:17 And the light of Israel shall be for a fire, and his Holy One for a flame: and it shall burn and devour his thorns and his briers in one day; **10:18** And shall consume the glory of his forest [symbolic of armies; the trees being men and all the trees together being a forest or army], and of his fruitful field, both soul [spirit, the false religion] and body [the physical government]: and they shall be as when a standard-bearer fainteth [the standard or flag is the symbol of the national government and when the flag falls it is indicative that the government has fallen].

The men of Europe and Asia who survive and remain shall be so small in number that a child could count them.

10:18 And shall consume the glory of his forest [his mighty men], and of his fruitful field, both soul and body: and they shall be as when a standard-bearer fainteth.

10:19 And the rest of the trees [his armies of men] of his forest shall be few, that a child may write [count] them.

10:20 And it shall come to pass in that day, that the remnant of Israel, and such as are escaped of the house of Jacob, shall no more again stay upon [serve] him that smote them; but shall stay upon [serve] the Lord, the Holy One of Israel, in truth.

This is after the resurrection of the repentant, zealous and chosen; and in the Kingdom of God when all flesh shall repent and God's Spirit shall be poured out on all flesh (Joel 2:28).

> **10:21** The remnant shall return, even the remnant of Jacob, unto the mighty God.

The correction from God for spiritual Israel in tribulation will result in contrite repentance, and the correction of Christ on the nations of physical Israel including America and the British peoples will turn the people to God. God's correction will bring an overflowing of repentance and righteous zeal for the Holy Commandments and every Word of God the Father and the Son!

A remnant of physical Israel and Judah will be left and they SHALL return to the Word of their God!

Nahum 1

Nahum 1:1 The burden of Nineveh [The capital represents all of Assyria (the Austro Hungarian German people) and their descendants]. The book of the vision of Nahum the Elkoshite.

A warning against those who would attack those that God has called out of bondage in ancient physical Egypt, or those who are called out of bondage to Satan and sin.

1:2 God is jealous, and the LORD revengeth; the LORD revengeth, and is furious; the LORD will take vengeance on his adversaries, and he reserveth wrath for his enemies.

The latter day Germanic nation's leading the New Europe will do the will of God in correcting us for our wickedness, but they will then be lifted up with pride thinking that they had done this by their own wisdom and strength. They will overdo and take pleasure in the correction of God's people, and being full of sin themselves will be corrected by the nations of Asia.

The Eternal is Mighty and we would do well to quickly and sincerely repent before him, for he will correct all the wicked.

1:3 The LORD is slow to anger, and great in power, and will not at all acquit the wicked: the LORD hath his way in the whirlwind and in the storm, and the clouds are the dust of his feet.

1:4 He rebuketh the sea, and maketh it dry, and drieth up all the rivers: Bashan languisheth, and Carmel, and the flower of Lebanon languisheth. **1:5** The mountains quake at him, and the hills melt, and the earth is burned at his presence, yea, the world, and all that dwell therein.

1:6 Who can stand before his indignation? and who can abide in the fierceness of his anger? his fury is poured out like fire, and the rocks are thrown down by him.

As the LORD is strong to rebuke and correct the wicked; he is also Mighty to save his faithful who live by his EVERY WORD!

1:7 The LORD is good, a strong hold in the day of trouble; and he knoweth them that trust in him.

Those who put their trust in God and faithfully live by every Word of God without compromise will never be disappointed by his love, mercy and ultimate deliverance; those who are against him and his beloved will certainly feel his wrath.

1:8 But with an overrunning flood he will make an utter end of the place thereof, and darkness shall pursue his enemies.

God will not allow the New Europe to make an utter and full end of physical and spiritual Israel! No not at all! God will bring us to sincere repentance for our idolatries and the Almighty will then deliver those who turn to HIM!

1:9 What do ye imagine against the LORD? [Do you imagine that God will permit you (the New Europe) to totally destroy the nations of Israel?] he will make an utter end: [God will make an end of affliction, delivering his people once they have been humbled to contrition and he will never again afflict them to this degree] affliction shall not rise up the second time.

When the New Europe is rich and satisfied and full of prosperity, drunken with pride; in the third year they will be devoured like dry stubble by the armies of Asia.

> **Daniel 11:44** But tidings out of the east and out of the north shall trouble him: therefore he shall go forth with great fury to destroy, and utterly to make away many.

Nahum 1:10 For while they be folden together as thorns, and while they are drunken [with pride] as drunkards, they shall be devoured as stubble fully dry.

1:11 There is one come out of thee [a ruler will yet rise up out of Assyria, the Germanic peoples; possibly an Austro Hungarian], that imagineth evil against the LORD, a wicked counsellor.

A wicked leader who despises God's Word for his own ways and is deeply into the occult will rise up to rule the New Europe and he will rise above Judah and many other nations.

1:12 Thus saith the LORD; Though they [physical and spiritual Israel/Judah] be quiet [at peace], and likewise many [though they be very strong] yet thus shall they be cut down, when he [this wicked leader of the New Europe] shall pass through [correct Israel/Judah and many nations]. Though I have afflicted thee, I will afflict thee no more. [God promises us that when we have been humbled and are sincerely repentant he will deliver us.]

Once we are humbled to contrition and are sincerely repentant, the yoke of this oppressor will be broken.

1:13 For now will I break his yoke from off thee, and will burst thy bonds in sunder.

The judgment of this wicked political leader, is that he will be destroyed along with his idols.

> **Revelation 19:19** And I saw the beast, and the kings of the earth, and their armies, gathered together to make war against him that sat on the horse, and against his army. **19:20** And the beast was taken, and with him the false prophet that wrought miracles before him, with which he deceived them that had received the mark of the beast, and them that worshipped his image. These both were cast alive into a lake of fire burning with brimstone.

Nahum 1:14 And the LORD hath given a commandment concerning thee, that no more of thy name be sown: out of the house of thy gods will I cut off the graven image and the molten image: I will make thy grave; for thou art vile.

The Eternal will cut off this political leader and the final false prophet and his false religion; Messiah the Christ and will destroy them. Then peace will come with the destruction of wickedness and the nations will observe the Solemn Feasts of the LORD in Jerusalem with Judah.

1:15 Behold upon the mountains the feet of him that bringeth good tidings, that publisheth peace! O Judah, keep thy solemn feasts, perform thy vows: for the wicked shall no more pass through thee; he is utterly cut off.

Nahum 2

The Asian armies will come up against Assyria [the head of the New Europe] because the correction of Israel is completed and is at an end. Now it is Assyria's turn to be corrected for their witchcraft's [occult spiritualism] and great pride. The armies of Asia will surround Jerusalem where this wicked leader has taken refuge with his religious leader.

The destruction of Nineveh was a type of the latter day defeat of Assyria (the New Europe) at Jerusalem.

Nahum 2:1 He that dasheth in pieces is come up before thy face: keep the munition, watch the way, make thy loins strong, fortify thy power mightily.

God had used the New Europe to correct Israel and many countries, and now it is the turn of Assyria and the New Europe to be corrected.

2:2 For the LORD hath turned away the excellency of Jacob, as the excellency of Israel: for the emptiers have emptied them out, and marred their vine branches.

The armies of Asia will surround Jerusalem where the last army of the New Europe is entrenched.

2:3 The shield of his mighty men is made red [with blood], the valiant men are in scarlet [covered in blood]: the chariots [vehicles] shall be with flaming torches in the day of his preparation, and the fir trees [mighty men] shall be terribly shaken.

2:4 The chariots [modern military vehicles] shall rage in the streets, they shall justle one against another in the broad ways: they shall seem like torches, they shall run [speedily] like the lightnings.

These prophesied things give us the reason behind Jonah's hatred of Nineveh [Assyria], yet Jonah was forced to act out an allegorical prophecy that after the coming of Christ, the Word of God will go even to Nineveh [the Assyrians] and they will repent just like the ancient city did.

2:5 He shall recount his worthies: they shall stumble in their walk; they shall make haste to the wall thereof, and the defence shall be prepared.

2:6 The gates of the rivers [the waters of ancient Nineveh will fail] shall be opened, and the palace shall be dissolved.

2:7 And Huzzab [meaning "established," refers to the Assyrian army] shall be led away captive, she shall be brought up, and her maids shall lead her as with the voice of doves, tabering upon their breasts [in mourning].

2:8 But Nineveh is of old like a pool of water: yet they shall flee away. Stand, stand, shall they cry; but none shall look back.

Messiah the Christ will come and he will destroy the armies who resist him delivering a repentant Judah. Then Judah will flee by the Mount of Olives while their men rise up against the enemy within the city and take a great spoil (Zech 14:14).

2:9 Take ye the spoil of silver, take the spoil of gold: for there is none end of the store and glory out of all the pleasant furniture.

Then Israel will despoil their oppressors and empty them of their good things for God is against them.

2:10 She is empty, and void, and waste: and the heart melteth, and the knees smite together, and much pain is in all loins, and the faces of them all gather blackness.

2:11 Where is the dwelling of the lions [the mighty men who devoured Israel/Judah shall be destroyed], and the feedingplace of the young lions, where the lion, even the old lion, walked, and the lion's whelp, and none made them afraid?

2:12 The lion did tear in pieces enough for his whelps, and strangled for his lionesses, and filled his holes with prey, and his dens with ravin.

2:13 Behold, I am against thee, saith the LORD of hosts, and I will burn her chariots in the smoke, and the sword shall devour thy young lions [mighty men]: and I will cut off thy prey from the earth, and the voice of thy messengers shall no more be heard.

Nahum 3

Judgment on Nineveh the capital of Assyria [today, Austria, Hungary and Germany will become the head of the now rising New Europe]. The head represents the whole body and the capital city represents the whole nation.

Nahum 3:1 Woe to the bloody city [Nineveh the capital of Assyria is a type of the soon coming New Europe]! it is all full of lies and robbery; the prey departeth not;

3:2 The noise of a whip, and the noise of the rattling of the wheels, and of the pransing horses, and of the jumping chariots.

The Assyrian and his empire has killed, torn and devoured like a lion, therefore the sword of the Eternal shall correct him.

3:3 The horseman lifteth up both the bright sword and the glittering spear: and there is a multitude of slain, and a great number of carcases; and there is none end of their corpses; they stumble upon their corpses:

The leader of the soon coming New Europe will be deep into the occult along with the false prophet.

3:4 Because of the multitude of the whoredoms of the wellfavoured harlot, the mistress of witchcrafts, that selleth nations through her whoredoms, and families through her witchcrafts. **3:5** Behold, I am against thee, saith the LORD of hosts; and I will discover thy skirts upon thy face, and I will shew the nations thy nakedness [the wickedness will be revealed], and the kingdoms thy shame.

God corrects all the wicked in his own time.

3:6 And I will cast abominable filth upon thee, and make thee vile, and will set thee as a gazingstock. **3:7** And it shall come to pass, that all they that look upon thee shall flee from thee, and say, Nineveh is laid waste: who will bemoan her? whence shall I seek comforters for thee?

3:8 Art thou better than populous No, that was situate among the rivers, that had the waters round about it, whose rampart was the sea, and her wall was from the sea? **3:9** Ethiopia and Egypt were her strength, and it was infinite; Put and Lubim were thy helpers. **3:10** Yet was she carried away, she went into captivity: her young children also were dashed in pieces at the top of all the streets: and they cast lots for her honourable men, and all her great men were bound in chains.

3:11 Thou also shalt be drunken [with pride]: thou shalt be hid, thou also shalt seek strength [seek help] because of the enemy. **3:12** All thy strong holds shall be like fig trees with the firstripe figs: if they be shaken, they shall even fall into the mouth of the eater. **3:13** Behold, thy people in the midst of thee are [become like helpless] women: the gates of thy land shall be set wide open unto thine enemies: the fire shall devour thy bars.

3:14 Draw thee waters for the siege, fortify thy strong holds: go into clay, and tread the morter, make strong the brickkiln [build strong defenses]. **3:15** There shall the fire devour thee; the sword shall cut thee off, it shall eat thee up like the cankerworm: make thyself many as the cankerworm, make thyself many as the locusts.

3:16 Thou hast multiplied thy merchants above the stars of heaven: the cankerworm spoileth, and fleeth away. **3:17** Thy crowned are as the locusts [in numbers], and thy captains [are as many as the grasshoppers] as the great grasshoppers, which camp in the hedges in the cold day, but when the sun ariseth they flee away, and their place is not known where they are.

3:18 Thy shepherds slumber, O king of Assyria: thy nobles shall dwell in the dust: thy people is scattered upon the mountains, and no man gathereth them.

3:19 There is no healing of thy bruise; thy wound is grievous: all that hear the bruit of thee shall clap the hands [in rejoicing at thy fall] over thee: for upon whom hath not thy wickedness passed continually [for who has not suffered at your hands?]?

Habakkuk

Introduction

The ancient Chaldean's lived at Babylon and although the Babylonian Empire was named after the capital city of Babylon, the actual people who built that empire were the Chaldean's.

The Chaldean's were a very talented and artistic people associated with the Assyrians; so artistic that Babylon was the wonder of the ancient world. Remember Nebuchadnezzar of Daniel and the Hanging Gardens of Babylon which he built.

The Chaldean's were also known for being highly superstitious and heavily into all manner of magic, enchantments and general witchcraft's, including the casting of horoscopes and foretelling through various omens and methods; in short they understood dark sentences and all manner of methods of contacting demons and spiritualism.

Babylon [Chaldea] was the head of the great image of Daniel 2, and the entire image represented the successive peoples who would take over that same system until it is destroyed by Christ at his coming.

When each nation took over the empire, they replaced the people and rulers with a different race of people while each new race continued to keep the same Babylonian Empire system with its church / state system.

The Babylonian system is that of a state religion in league with the political system. This system continued through Media-Persia, Greece and the Holy Roman Empire, right down to our days when the very same system will soon be revived.

There is coming a revival of this church/state Babylonian style system in Europe, which will feature a political leader endorsed by a religious leader the Roman Pontiff.

The ancient Chaldean's were so famous for their enchantments and spiritualism [Satanism and demonic associations]; that long after the actual people migrated out of that region and into Italy, any wizard or enchanter in the successive empires was still called a "Chaldean"

We are now at the latter days when the feet of Babylon, which is also a last revival of the Holy Roman Empire; will rise up in a final revival with ten nations represented by the ten toes of the Daniel 2 statue.

We must remember that Assyria [Germany, Austria, Hungary] constitutes three of the ten nations and that this is the reviving of the Holy Roman Empire of church/state ruler ship started by the Chaldean's so very long ago in Babylon.

Regardless of the actual political leader of the now rising New Federal Europe, Germany and Austria- Hungary will have a decisive leadership role, but the system will be the Chaldean Babylonian system [see Daniel 2] to its core.

Habakkuk was inspired to prophecy about the Chaldean's in the end times. In this prophecy of the Chaldean's, the Chaldean's as the HEAD [through Nebuchadnezzar, Dan 2] of the Babylonian system, are portrayed as the entire beast system of Babylon the Great, the latter day and final Holy Roman Empire revival.

Habakkuk is a prophecy of the fall of Jerusalem and Judah to Nebuchadnezzar and ancient Babylon. The prophecy is dual also referring to the correction of physical and spiritual Judah and Jerusalem in our time.

Habakkuk 1

Habakkuk began by lamenting over the lack of godly zeal, justice and righteousness among God's people.

Habakkuk 1:1 The burden which Habakkuk the prophet did see. **1:2** O LORD, how long shall I cry, and thou wilt not hear! even cry out unto thee of violence, and thou wilt not save!

1:3 Why dost thou shew me iniquity, and cause me to behold grievance? for spoiling and violence are before me: and there are that raise up strife and contention. **1:4** Therefore the law is slacked, and judgment doth never go forth: for the wicked doth compass about the righteous; therefore wrong judgment proceedeth.

Habakkuk mourns the disregarding of God's Word, laws and commandments and all the wickedness in physical Israel of those days and in duality by today's physical and spiritual Judah/Israel. That would include our latter day nations and today's spiritually Called Out of God who commit the same sins, for God is not a respecter of persons.

God then responds that he will raise up the Chaldean's [Babylon at that time, and a type of the final Holy Roman Empire in our day] to correct the people.

1:5 Behold ye among the heathen, and regard, and wonder marvelously: for I will work a work in your days which ye will not believe, though it be told you.

1:6 For, lo, I raise up the Chaldeans, that bitter and hasty nation [called so by Habakkuk for Nebuchadnezzar's (bitter to the Jews) destruction of Jerusalem], which shall march through the breadth of the land, to possess the dwellingplaces that are not their's

In that time Nebuchadnezzar built up a tremendous empire and corrected Judah.

1:7 They are terrible and dreadful: their judgment and their dignity shall proceed of themselves.

This is referring to the Chaldean's as a type of the ten nations of the soon coming Holy Roman Empire [HRE] revival, the Chaldean's being the HEAD of the whole Daniel 2 system.

In Revelation the whole system is called Babylon the Great.

The following description of ancient military power is an allegory of the military power that the New Europe will have; when ten nations give their military and security apparatus over to a single ruler and he gains control of the massive quantities of military hardware being stored by others in Europe.

1:8 Their horses [read, armies of the New Europe] also are swifter than the leopards, and are more fierce than the evening wolves: and their horsemen shall spread themselves, and their horsemen shall come from far; they shall fly as the eagle that hasteth to eat.

1:9 They shall come all for violence: their faces shall sup up as the east wind, and they shall gather the captivity [The New Europe of Babylon the Great will defeat Israel/Judah in the end time, just like Nebuchadnezzar defeated Judah in the past and will gather their wealth to itself as one heaps up the sand.] as the sand.

1:10 And they shall scoff at the kings, and the princes [They shall scorn the power of those they attack.]. shall be a scorn unto them: they shall deride every strong hold [They shall hold in derision the strength of those they attack.]; for they shall heap dust [They shall bring the strong holds to destruction and take them, because God is against us to correct us for all our wickedness.], and take it.

All this will come upon physical and spiritual Judah/Israel because of our idolatries and sins; but then by his victories Nebuchadnezzar and the now rising Babylon the Great will become filled with pride in themselves and their miracle working religious leader [who they follow as an ultimate moral authority, a god].

1:11 Then shall his mind change, and he shall pass over, and offend [the Eternal], imputing this his power unto his god [instead of extolling the Eternal who had given him his victories].

The political leader of the New HRE will think that their victories were by their own wisdom and by their own might; thus offending the Eternal who sent them to correct his people Judah/Israel.

The Might and Holiness of God:

1:12 Art thou not from everlasting, O LORD my God, mine Holy One? we shall not die. O LORD, thou hast ordained them for judgment; and, O mighty God, thou hast established them for correction.

1:13 Thou art of purer eyes than to behold evil, and canst not look on iniquity: wherefore lookest thou upon them that deal treacherously, and holdest thy tongue when the wicked devoureth the man that is more righteous than he? **1:14** And makest men as the fishes of the sea, as the creeping things, that have no ruler over them?

1:15 They take up all of them with the angle, they catch them in their net, and gather them in their drag: therefore they rejoice and are glad.

1:16 Therefore they sacrifice unto their net, and burn incense unto their drag; because by them their portion is fat, and their meat plenteous. **1:17** Shall they therefore empty their net, and not spare continually to slay the nations?

Habakkuk 2

Habakkuk 2:1 I will stand upon my watch, and set me upon the tower, and will watch to see what he will say unto me, and what I shall answer when I am reproved.

Habakkuk speaks of the pride and sins of the Chaldean's and God gives him a vision about their latter end. This is about more than the ancient Chaldean's for God is not a respecter of persons and all who commit the same sins will also be corrected; just like the coming New Europe will correct physical and spiritual Judah/Israel and will then be corrected itself.

God plainly tells Habakkuk that this is a prophecy for the latter days, our time today.

2:2 And the LORD answered me, and said, Write the vision, and make it plain upon tables, that he may run that readeth it. **2:3** For the vision is yet for an appointed time, but at the end it shall speak, and not lie: though it tarry, wait for it; because it will surely come, it will not tarry [Once the appointed time arrives the vision will not be delayed any longer] .

This vision is for the "appointed time" at the end of this age:

> **Daniel 8:19** And he said, Behold, I will make thee know what shall be in the last end of the indignation: for at the time appointed the end shall be.

The end times of the tribulation and second coming of Christ have been appointed since the beginning. These things will surely happen at their appointed times, regardless of whether we are ready or not. Indeed they will happen when most of the brethren are NOT ready; and just like Christ caught the Mosaic Pharisees by surprise at his first coming, he will catch most people by surprise in our day for they will not heed the warnings.

The wicked are full of pride in their own ways, but the just shall live by faith and the works of faith, living by EVERY WORD of God.

Habakkuk 2:4 Behold, his soul which is lifted up is not upright in him: but the just shall live by his faith.

The proud and conceited live in sin for they trust in their own ways; but the righteous person shall live by every Word of God (Mat 4:4).

2:5 Yea also, because he transgresseth by wine [he is intoxicated with pride], he is a proud man, neither keepeth at home, who enlargeth his desire as [he is as greedy as death which devours all physical things] hell, and is as death, and cannot be satisfied, but gathereth unto him all nations, and heapeth unto him all people:

The New Europe burdens itself with subjugating the nations, but in the end his yoke will be broken.

2:6 Shall not all these take up a parable against him, and a taunting proverb against him, and say, Woe to him that increaseth that which is not his! how long? and to him that ladeth himself with thick clay!

2:7 Shall they not rise up suddenly that shall bite thee, and awake that shall vex thee, and thou shalt be for booties unto them?

2:8 Because thou hast spoiled many nations, all the remnant of the people shall spoil thee; because of men's blood [great bloodshed], and for the violence of the land, of the city, and of all that dwell therein.

God is not a respecter of persons and the warnings are for us as well as for Babylon [the New Europe].

We should take heed and quickly repent lest we share their fate. Woe to those who proudly seek to exalt themselves.

2:9 Woe to him that coveteth an evil covetousness to his house, that he may set his nest on high, that he may be delivered from the power of evil! **2:10** Thou hast consulted shame to thy house by cutting off many people, and hast sinned against thy soul.

Today in the Spiritual Ekklesia many covet to exalt themselves over others.

2:11 For the stone shall cry out of the wall, and the beam out of the timber shall answer it. **2:12** Woe to him that buildeth a town with blood [bloodshed], and stablisheth a city by iniquity! **2:13** Behold, is it not of the LORD of hosts that the people shall labour in the very fire, and the people shall weary themselves for very vanity?

Those who seek to exalt themselves will be abased (Mat 234:12), and the glory of the Eternal will be exalted above all men and gods.

2:14 For the earth shall be filled with the knowledge of the glory of the LORD, as the waters cover the sea.

Woe unto those who build a corporate church by oppressing people and demanding to be idolized above the Word of God.:You know who these folks are. Woe to those who make people drunk with pride so that they may lead them into sin and steal their crowns.

2:15 Woe unto him that giveth his neighbour drink, that puttest thy bottle to him, and makest him drunken also, that thou mayest look on their nakedness!

Woe unto those who make others drunk with pride, leading them into sin so that their garments of righteousness might be stripped away.

2:16 Thou art filled with shame for glory: drink thou also, and let thy foreskin be uncovered [The foreskin is a symbolic veil representing the sin that separates us from any sensitivity to the Word of God, which is why circumcision is a symbol of repentance and conversion.]: the cup of the LORD's right hand [the wrath of God] shall be turned unto thee, and shameful spewing shall be on thy glory.

> **Deuteronomy 10:16** Circumcise therefore the foreskin of your heart, and be no more stiffnecked.

On the spiritual plane this is talking about today's Spiritual Ekklesia intoxicating the people with false doctrine, false teachings, pride and false traditions, as well as personal and organizational idolatry; just as the final false prophet will do, using miracles to deceive and exalt himself and his associates.

Today's Spiritual Ekklesia has done this very same thing by rejecting entire sections of scripture so that they may cling to their own false traditions and lead the brethren into the idolatry of exalting men and organizations above the Word of God.

Habakkuk 2:17 For the violence of Lebanon shall cover thee, and the spoil of beasts, which made them afraid, because of men's blood [shed by the wicked], and for the violence of the land, of the city, and of all that dwell therein.

Just like the ancients had images and many still do today, we also have idols of men and the false traditions of men.

2:18 What profiteth the graven image that the maker thereof hath graven it; the molten image, and a teacher of lies, that the maker of his work trusteth therein, to make dumb idols? **2:19** Woe unto him that saith to the wood, Awake; to the dumb stone, Arise, it shall teach! Behold, it is laid over with gold and silver, and there is no breath at all in the midst of it.

The idolater and his idolatries shall not come to a good end; the end of the idolater is destruction. Therefore let us turn to live by every Word of God.

The LORD dwells in the Temple of those who live by EVERY WORD of God. The LORD does not dwell in those who follow idols of men and false teachings.

2:20 But the LORD is in his holy temple: let all the earth keep silence [do not dispute with God] before him.

Habakkuk 3

A psalm about the greatness of God

Habakkuk 3:1 A prayer of Habakkuk the prophet upon Shigionoth [rambling song] .

3:2 O LORD, I have heard thy speech, and was afraid: O LORD, revive thy work [of making a holy people] in the midst of the years, in the midst of the years make known; in wrath remember mercy.

3:3 God came from Teman, and the Holy One from mount Paran. Selah. His glory covered the heavens, and the earth was full of his praise. **3:4** And his brightness was as the light; he had horns [power, authority] coming out of his hand: and there [in his hands] was the hiding of his power.

3:5 Before him went [divine correction] the pestilence, and burning coals went forth at his feet. **3:6** He stood, and measured the earth: he beheld, and drove asunder the nations; and the everlasting mountains were scattered, the perpetual hills did bow: his ways are everlasting.

3:7 I saw the tents of Cushan in affliction: and the curtains of the land of Midian did tremble.

3:8 Was the LORD displeased against the rivers? was thine anger against the rivers [figurative of the waters of Babylon]? was thy wrath against the sea [against the wicked peoples], that thou didst ride upon thine horses and thy chariots of salvation?

3:9 Thy bow was made quite naked, according to the oaths of the tribes, even thy word. Selah. Thou didst cleave the earth with rivers.

3:10 The mountains [nations] saw thee, and they trembled: the overflowing of the water passed by: the deep uttered his voice, and lifted up his hands on high. **3:11** The sun and moon stood still in their habitation: at the light of thine arrows they went, and at the shining of thy glittering spear.

When Christ comes he will destroy the wicked

3:12 Thou didst march through the land in indignation, thou didst thresh the heathen in anger.

Messiah the Anointed One, was wounded to save the repentant, and he will destroy the idolatrous foundations of the unrepentant wicked.

3:13 Thou wentest forth for the salvation of thy people, even for salvation with thine anointed; thou woundedst the head out of the house of the wicked, by discovering the foundation unto the neck. Selah.

3:14 Thou didst strike through with his staves the head of his villages: they came out as a whirlwind to scatter me: their rejoicing was as to devour the poor secretly. **3:15** Thou didst walk through the sea [many people] with thine horses, through the heap of great waters [many peoples].

3:16 When I heard, my belly trembled; my lips quivered at the voice: rottenness entered into my bones, and I trembled in myself, that I might rest in the day of trouble: when he cometh up unto the people, he will invade them with his troops [Christ will come with his armies of holy angels and resurrected chosen].

3:17 Although the fig tree shall not blossom, neither shall fruit be in the vines; the labour of the olive shall fail, and the fields shall yield no meat; the flock shall be cut off from the fold, and there shall be no herd in the stalls: **3:18** Yet **I will rejoice in the LORD, I will joy in the God of my salvation.**

In all forms of prosperity and adversity I will cleave to my God.

3:19 The LORD God is my strength, and he will make my feet [to leap like the deer for joy at his salvation] like hinds' feet, and he will make me to walk upon mine high places [Messiah will lift up and deliver all his sincerely repentant from all their sorrows.]. To the chief singer on my stringed instruments.

Zephaniah

Zephaniah

Zephaniah is about God's judgment on the wickedness of Jerusalem which as the capital would include all of physical and spiritual Israel and their leaders.

Zephaniah is also about God's judgment on the coming New Europe of Babylon and all the world's wicked; followed by the conversion of all nations and a Song of Joy for the goodness of the Eternal.

Remember that God is no respecter of persons and we must all take any scriptural correction with serious personal self-examination to see if we fit the description. All scripture is written for US.

> **2 Timothy 3:16** All scripture is given by inspiration of God, and is profitable for doctrine, for reproof, for correction, for instruction in righteousness: **3:17** That the man of God may be perfect, thoroughly furnished unto all good works.

> **1 Corinthians 10:11** Now all these things happened unto them for examples: and they are written for our admonition, upon whom the ends of the world are come. **10:12** Wherefore let him that thinketh he standeth take heed lest he fall.

Zephaniah 1:1 The word of the LORD which came unto Zephaniah the son of Cushi, the son of Gedaliah, the son of Amariah, the son of Hizkiah, in the days of Josiah the son of Amon, king of Judah.

God utters his judgments against Judah and the nations of Israel and all of the wicked, for our many idolatries of men and false traditions and the overspreading of our many sins.

1:2 I will utterly consume all things from off the land, saith the LORD. **1:3** I will consume man and beast; I will consume the fowls of the heaven, and the fishes of the sea, and the stumbling blocks [idolizing the men who lead the people astray] with the wicked: and I will cut off man from off the land, saith the LORD.

1:4 I will also stretch out mine hand upon Judah, and upon all the inhabitants of Jerusalem; and I will cut off the remnant of Baal [destroy all idols including every false tradition of men] from this place, and the name of the Chemarims [false teachers and idol worshipers] with the [wicked priests and elders who follow idols of men and not God] priests;

Those that have divided affections calling themselves godly and boasting that they are God's people as they follow idols of men and false traditions; and all those who do not live by EVERY WORD of God will be powerfully afflicted.

1:5 And them that worship the host of heaven upon the housetops; and them that worship and that swear by the LORD, and that swear by Malcham;

1:6 And them that are turned back [away] from the LORD; and those that have not sought the LORD, nor enquired for him.

Moloch (Molech, Milcom, Malcham) the name of the national god of the Ammonites; The same idol was called Chemosh among the Moabites.

In context this is a general reference to all idol worship. Remember that worship is obedience and not some form of lip-service. If we pollute the Sabbath because some man says that it is OK, then we are obeying man rather than God; and that is idolatry!

The stern correction will begin at Jerusalem. This happened anciently and today's Spiritual Ekklesia is the spiritual equivalent of the temple at Jerusalem, being the temple of God's Spirit with the Shekinah dwelling in them. God's correction will come upon those faithless followers of men calling themselves God's church as well as on the nations.

Shekinah, Shekinah, Shechinah, Shekina, Shechina, or Schechinah, (Hebrew: שכינה) is the English spelling of a grammatically feminine Hebrew word that means "the dwelling or settling," and is used to denote the dwelling or settling of the divine presence of God, especially in the temple in Jerusalem.

This is God's Holy Spirit which rained down as fire upon Solomon's temple and has now officially moved to dwell in men.

> **2 Chronicles 7:1** Now when Solomon had made an end of praying, the fire came down from heaven, and consumed the burnt offering and the sacrifices; and the glory of the Lord filled the house. **7:2** And the priests could not enter into the house of the Lord, because the glory of the Lord had filled the Lord's house.
>
> **7:3** And when all the children of Israel saw how the fire came down, and the glory of the Lord upon the house, they bowed themselves with their faces to the ground upon the pavement, and worshipped, and praised the Lord, saying, For he is good; for his mercy endureth for ever.
>
> **Acts 2:1** And when the day of Pentecost was fully come, they were all with one accord in one place. **2:2** And suddenly there came a sound from heaven as of a rushing mighty wind, and it filled all the house where they were sitting.
>
> **2:3** And there appeared unto them cloven tongues like as of fire, and it sat upon each of them. **2:4** And they were all filled with the Holy Ghost, and began to speak with other tongues, as the Spirit gave them utterance.

After the coming correction begins on Jerusalem and the apostate Laodicean brethren of today, it will continue to spread until all wicked persons are corrected and the great battle of the Lord comes at Jerusalem.

Zephaniah uses the term "Day of the Lord" to refer to the entire last 42 months as a lead up to the actual coming of Christ with his saints; beginning the correction on Jerusalem and Judea and spreading to the Spiritual Ekklesia and all the nations of Israel.

The wicked who argue to justify their own evil ways today, shall have their mouths stopped and will be made silent before the correction of the Eternal, unable to justify themselves before the furious correction of God.

Zephaniah 1:7 Hold thy peace at the presence of the Lord GOD: for the day of the LORD is at hand: for the LORD hath prepared a sacrifice, he hath bid his guests.

1:8 And it shall come to pass in the day of the LORD's sacrifice, that I will punish the princes, and the king's children, and all such as are clothed with strange [symbolically clothed with sin and not the garments of righteousness] apparel. **1:9** In the same day also will I punish all those that leap on the thresholds [that break into or rob houses], which fill their masters' houses with violence and deceit.

1:10 And it shall come to pass in that day, saith the LORD, that there shall be the noise of a cry from the fish gate, and an howling from the second, and a great crashing from the hills.

1:11 Howl, ye inhabitants of Maktesh [the Negev], for all the merchant people are cut down; all they that bear silver are cut off.

1:12 And it shall come to pass at that time, that I will search Jerusalem with candles [God will search to find the wicked, like searching the darkness with bright lights], and punish the men that are settled on their lees [well established people who are at ease and will feel secure when the coming peace deal is ratified]: that say in their heart [which have the attitude that], The LORD will not do good, neither will he do evil [God does not see us, he is far off].

1:13 Therefore their goods shall become a booty [for their enemies], and their houses a desolation: they shall also build houses, but not inhabit them [their houses and goods will be given to others]; and they shall plant vineyards, but not drink the wine thereof.

1:14 The great day of the LORD is near, it is near, and hasteth greatly, even the voice of the day of the LORD: the mighty man shall cry there bitterly.

The great tribulation of our correction is at hand to be followed by the final great day of the Lord's coming.

1:15 That day is a day of wrath, a day of trouble and distress, a day of wasteness and desolation, a day of darkness and gloominess, a day of clouds and thick darkness, **1:16** A day of the trumpet and alarm against the fenced cities, and against the high towers.

1:17 And I will bring distress upon men, that they shall walk like blind men, because they have sinned against the LORD: and their blood shall be poured out as dust, and their flesh as the dung.

1:18 Neither their silver nor their gold shall be able to deliver them in the day of the LORD's wrath; but the whole land shall be devoured by the fire of his jealousy: for he shall make even a speedy riddance of all them that dwell in the land.

Zephaniah 2

The nations are called to sincere repentance

Zephaniah 2:1 Gather yourselves together, yea, gather together, O nation not desired; **2:2** Before the decree bring forth, before the day pass as the chaff, before the fierce anger of the LORD come upon you, before the day of the LORD's anger come upon you.

Before all these things the warning will go out to the meek, humble and faithful who zealously live by EVERY WORD of God. That warning is going out via this work now!

2:3 Seek ye the LORD, all ye meek of the earth, which have wrought his judgment; seek righteousness, seek meekness [turn to God in humble wholehearted zeal]: it may be ye shall be hid [in God's prepared refuge] in the day of the LORD's anger.

After Israel is corrected, Gaza will be corrected beginning late in the third year or during the first half of the fourth year.

2:4 For **Gaza shall be forsaken, and Ashkelon a desolation: they shall drive out Ashdod at the noon day, and Ekron shall be rooted up.**

Gaza

The correction of Gaza because they will join in the Psalm 83 confederation to afflict Judah.

2:5 Woe unto the inhabitants of the sea coast, the nation of the Cherethites [the Philistines of Gaza]! the word of the LORD is against you; O Canaan, the land of the Philistines, I will even destroy thee, that there shall be no inhabitant.

2:6 And the sea coast shall be dwellings and cottages for shepherds, and folds for flocks. **2:7** And the coast **shall be for the remnant** [proving this is about the latter days] **of the house of Judah**; they shall feed thereupon: in the houses of Ashkelon shall they lie down in the evening [the millennial kingdom at the end of the age of man]: for the LORD their God shall visit them, and turn away their captivity.

Jordan

The final judgment on Jordan because they also join the Psalm 83 confederation and attack Judah to enrich themselves and take land to enlarge their borders.

2:8 I have heard the reproach of **Moab**, and the revilings of the children of **Ammon**, whereby they have **reproached my people** [attacking Judah during the tribulation], **and magnified themselves against their border.**

2:9 Therefore as I live, saith the LORD of hosts, the God of Israel, Surely **Moab shall be as Sodom, and the children of Ammon as Gomorrah**, even the breeding of nettles, and saltpits, and a perpetual desolation: [showing that this prophecy is about the end of the tribulation and the beginning of the millennium] the **residue of my people** shall spoil them, and **the remnant of my people** shall possess them.

2:10 This shall they have for their pride, because they have reproached and magnified themselves against [against Judah and also for trying to destroy the zealous of spiritual Israel who are seeking refuge there Revelation 12] the people of the LORD of hosts.

2:11 The LORD will be terrible unto them: for he will famish [destroy all false gods and idols of men] all the gods of the earth; and [all] men shall [be brought to repentance to live by every Word of God the Eternal] worship him [the Eternal], every one from his place, even all the isles of the heathen.

All the nations will be corrected as well as Israel/Judah, Gaza and Jordan

The New Europe will take over Egypt and the Libyans and Ethiopians will serve the ten nation revival of the church state Holy Roman Empire, Babylonian system of Daniel 2.

2:12 Ye Ethiopians also, ye shall be slain by my sword.

The end of ancient Nineveh and Assyria as a fore-type of the fall of today's Germanic dominated now rising New Federal Europe.

2:13 And he will stretch out his hand against the north [the Assyrians who dwell north of Palestine], and destroy Assyria [Germany, Austria, Hungary and the rising New Europe]; and will make Nineveh [Assyria, the Germanic peoples] a desolation, and dry like a wilderness.

2:14 And flocks shall lie down in the midst of her, all the beasts of the nations: both the cormorant and the bittern shall lodge in the upper lintels of it; their voice shall sing in the windows; desolation shall be in the thresholds; for he shall uncover the cedar work.

2:15 This is the rejoicing city that dwelt carelessly [secure and without fear], that said in her heart, I am, and there is none beside me: how is she become a desolation, a place for beasts to lie down in! every one that passeth by her shall hiss, and wag his hand.

Revelation 18 explains the wrath of God towards the now rising ten nation revival of the Holy Roman Empire, Babylonian church/state system.

Zephaniah 3

Woe to all those who are full of the filthiness of rebellion against living by every Word of God, exalting wickedness above the goodness of God

Zephaniah 3:1 Woe to her that is filthy and polluted, to the oppressing city!

Nineveh as the capital and head of Assyria is a type of the whole nation of Assyria, and this prophecy is dual also applying to a second fulfillment in this latter day.

3:2 She obeyed not the voice [of God]; she received not [will not accept] correction; she trusted not in the LORD; she drew not near to her God.

3:3 Her princes within her are roaring lions; her judges are evening wolves [devouring wolves]; they gnaw not the bones till the morrow.

3:4 Her prophets are light [shallow] and treacherous persons: her priests have polluted the sanctuary, they have done violence to the law.

Making God's Word of no effect by their false traditions just as today's called out Ekklesia do, paying lip-service to God and then deciding for themselves what is right and wrong.

The Eternal is Justice and his Law is Just and Good.

3:5 The just LORD is in the midst thereof; he will not do iniquity: every morning doth he bring his judgment to light, he faileth not; but the unjust knoweth no shame.

The Eternal punishes the wicked in the hope that they will forsake their wickedness and turn to live by his righteous Word.

3:6 I have cut off [corrected] the nations: their towers are desolate; I made their streets waste, that none passeth by: their cities are destroyed, so that there is no man, that there is none inhabitant.

God is not a respecter of persons and he will correct every sinner and idolater who is not zealous to live by every Word of God, which brings life eternal. God corrects us out of his awesome love for us; afflicting our flesh to save our spirit and to turn us to righteousness, and to stop the sin which is corrupting and killing us

3:7 I said, Surely thou wilt fear me, thou wilt receive instruction; so their dwelling should not be cut off, howsoever I punished them: but they rose early, and corrupted all their doings.

3:8 Therefore wait ye upon me [ye faithful], saith the LORD, until the day that I rise up to the prey: for my determination is to gather the nations, that I may assemble the kingdoms [at Jerusalem], to pour upon them mine indignation, even all my fierce anger: for all the earth shall be devoured with the fire of my jealousy.

The espoused Husband of the "Called out Elect," is a jealous Husband who will not tolerate our adulteries with strange gods.

3:9 For then will I turn to the people a pure language, that they may all call upon the name of the LORD, to serve him with one consent.

A new universal language free from the names of idols and the deceitfulness of men will be given to all men. This is much more than some automatic change of speech patterns to one universal language.

This is accomplished by converting and placing God's Spirit in all flesh, so that all people will know and live by every Word of God. So that all people will fully internalize the mind of God and be filled with the righteousness of God. Then they will be able to discern between godliness and evil; thereby casting out all deceitfulness, false teachings and idolatry!

The tongue speaks out of the abundance of the heart: to purify the tongue, one must first purify the heart, the mind, the spirit!

When Messiah the Christ comes, the dispersed of Israel will be gathered from all the places where they have been scattered.

3:10 From beyond the rivers of Ethiopia my suppliants [the sincerely repentant], even the daughter [latter day descendants] of my dispersed, shall bring mine offering.

God will destroy the proud and those who follow idols of men to rebel against HIM; exalting their own words in haughty pride above the Word of God. In that day the people will learn that being God's people means living by every Word of God, and that God will correct those that he loves to save them from eternal death.

3:11 In that day shalt thou not be ashamed for all thy [wicked] doings, wherein thou hast transgressed against me: for then I will take away out of the midst of thee them that rejoice in thy pride, and thou shalt no more be haughty because of my holy mountain.

3:12 I will also leave in the midst of thee an afflicted and poor people, and they shall trust in the name of the LORD.

After this final correction, physical and spiritual Israel will sincerely repent and they will be forgiven and delivered and will go forward to sin no more.

3:13 The remnant of Israel shall not do iniquity, nor speak lies; neither shall a deceitful tongue be found in their mouth: for they shall feed [on every Word of God] and lie down [rest in peace], and none shall make them afraid.

The Deliverance of Jerusalem

The term daughter refers to the latter day descendants of, and in this case refers to the latter day repentant who are delivered by the Eternal. In truth all the sincerely repentant from all nations will be grafted into a kind of spiritual Israel of the New Covenant and all nations will rejoice at the salvation of the LORD!

3:14 Sing, O daughter of Zion; shout, O Israel; be glad and rejoice with all the heart, O daughter of Jerusalem.

3:15 The LORD hath taken away thy judgments [erasing the indictments against Jerusalem because the inhabitants will sincerely repent], he hath cast out thine enemy [delivering Jerusalem and making it the City of God, God's capital city over all the earth]: the king of Israel, even the LORD, is in the midst of thee: thou shalt not see evil any more.

The latter day Jerusalem will be fully wholeheartedly committed to live by every Word of God and will become the City of God, they will never again .

3:16 In that day it shall be said to Jerusalem, Fear thou not: and to Zion, Let not thine hands be slack [to work and build godliness in all the earth] .

3:17 The LORD thy God in the midst of thee is mighty; he will save, he will rejoice over thee with joy; he will rest in his love, he will joy over thee with singing.

3:18 I will gather them that are sorrowful for the solemn assembly, who are of thee, to whom the reproach of it was a burden.

God will gather those who sorrow in sincere repentance and bring them to Jerusalem to worship before God and keep God's Festivals at the Ezekiel Temple.

When Israel repents and turns to follow the Eternal with a whole heart; they will become the example for all nations that God has always intended!

The called out of today's Spiritual Ekklesia who sincerely repent and turn to live by every Word of God and turn to follow the Eternal in wholehearted zeal; will be changed to spirit and raised to eternal life and they will become teachers and examples of godliness for all peoples, as God has intended from the beginning!

3:19 Behold, at that time I will undo all that afflict thee: and I will save her that halteth, and gather her that was driven out; and I will get them praise and fame in every land where they have been put to shame.

3:20 At that time will I bring you again, even in the time that I gather you: for I will make you a name and a praise among all people of the earth, when I turn back your captivity before your eyes, saith the LORD.

Haggai

Introduction

The book of Haggai is addressed directly to Zerubbabel the governor of Judea and to Joshua the high priest to encourage them to resume building the temple after the work had stopped due to local resistance. Haggai being God's messenger to the governor and the high priest regarding the building of the temple.

This book is dual being a message to the builders of the temple at that time and a message to the end time builders of the spiritual temple of the Called Out as the dwelling place of God through the Holy Spirit, who are preparing the bride of Christ for the resurrection to spirit to become fully UNITED with God the Father and Jesus Christ at the marriage of the Lamb.

The prophecy was written during the restoration period when repentant people were returning from captivity to build the temple of God, as a shadow of the events concerning building and preparing the spiritual temple of the people of God; leading up to and including the coming of Christ to build the physical Ezekiel Temple.

The prophecy rebukes and admonishes the people for neglecting their duty to be building the temple and is also an instruction for us today.

Haggai called on the people to sincerely repent and to fulfill their duty which was to build the physical temple; similarly today's Spiritual Ekklesia is being called to sincerely repent and build ourselves into a spiritual temple through internalizing and living by every Word of God!

The book of Haggai is a picture of today's Spiritual Ekklesia, who are fixated on themselves and doing what they think is right instead of building ourselves up into a pure spiritual temple of the whole Word of God, in which God can dwell through his Spirit.

The serious issues of marrying the unconverted which in the spiritual sense means mixing true religion with the false traditions of men and Sabbath breaking, dealt with in the book of Haggai, are highly relevant for today's Spiritual Ekklesia which is full of these same sins.

Haggai, Ezra and Nehemiah cover a period of the building of the physical temple, the city and the restoration of true religion; and are prophetic of the need to build, cleanse and purify ourselves, to become a part of the true Ekklesia; the true spiritual temple of God

These books are vital instructions for us today and we should be about the vitally important business of preparing to become a part of the collective bride of Christ, and preparing for the soon coming Kingdom of God. Today's Spiritual Ekklesia needs to clean up our act and to make ourselves spiritually ONE in full UNITY with our LORD!

When an elder says that these books are only a history of a revival for that time, and rejects the corrections in them; he simply does NOT know what he is talking about.

The very same kind of revival is desperately needed for us today in our time!

ALL scriptures is written for us and for our instruction.

2 Timothy 3:16 All scripture is given by inspiration of God, and is profitable for doctrine, for reproof, for correction, for instruction in righteousness: **3:17** That the man of God may be perfect, thoroughly furnished unto all good works.

Brethren, if we do not bow to the reproofs of Holy Scripture we are NOT God's servants; and we will not have a part in the spiritual bride and spiritual temple of God through his Spirit.

If we do not restore true religion in ourselves and our assemblies today; how can we expect to be in the resurrection to spirit and have a part in restoring true religion to all Israel [and all humanity], and help to bring a vast expansion and conversion of first fruits throughout the millennium, completing the seventh day of the first fruits harvest?

Zerubbabel is identified as the governor, while Joshua is identified as the High Priest. When he comes, Jesus Christ will be both King of kings [governor] and High Priest, therefore these two offices will be united in one office and these two persons are BOTH types of the coming Christ.

Haggai 1

After Daniel was delivered from the lions den, Darius made this decree.

Daniel 6:25 Then king Darius wrote unto all people, nations, and languages, that dwell in all the earth; Peace be multiplied unto you.

6:26 I make a decree, That in every dominion of my kingdom men tremble and fear before the God of Daniel: for he is the living God, and stedfast for ever, and his kingdom that which shall not be destroyed, and his dominion shall be even unto the end.

6:27 He delivereth and rescueth, and he worketh signs and wonders in heaven and in earth, who hath delivered Daniel from the power of the lions.

Then in the second year of Darius about 520 B.C. Haggai encouraged the people to resume building the temple. At that time a letter was sent to Darius and upon finding the original edict of Cyrus he was quick to order the building of the temple to resume, without doubt having been influenced by the deliverance of Daniel.

Haggai 1:1 In the **second year of Darius the king, in the sixth month, in the first day of the month,** came the word of the LORD by Haggai the prophet unto **Zerubbabel the son of Shealtiel, governor of Judah,** and to **Joshua the son of Josedech, the high priest,** saying,

The Being who later gave up his Godhood to become flesh as Jesus Christ inspired Haggai to rebuke the people for caring about their own selves and not for building the temple according to the decree of Cyrus.

This rebuke is entirely appropriate for today's brethren!

Today, physical and spiritual Israel are both full of their own ways and they have left off and neglected any zeal to build themselves into a spiritual House of God through a zeal to internalize and live by every Word of God.

1:2 Thus speaketh the LORD of hosts, saying, **This people say**, The time is not come, the time that the LORD's house should be built.

Today the called out are intent on things like income and numbers and have forgotten the priority to which they were called; which is to build themselves into a spiritual temple, a fit dwelling place for the Holy Spirit of God; by zealously internalizing the whole Word of God through living by EVERY WORD of God.

Today we are content to sit back and follow idols of men, exalting them above the Word of God. That is what the Sabbath and Calendar issues are about; will we obey God; or will we obey idols of men exalting their ways above the Word of God.

1:3 Then came the word of the LORD by Haggai the prophet, saying,

Spiritually, is it right to be overly concerned about building our corporations and gaining numbers of attendees to bring wealth? Or should we be building ourselves spiritually and accruing spiritual wealth through a passionate zeal to live by every Word of God?

> **Matthew 6:19** Lay not up for yourselves treasures upon earth, where moth and rust doth corrupt, and where thieves break through and steal: **6:20** But lay up for yourselves treasures in heaven, where neither moth nor rust doth corrupt, and where thieves do not break through nor steal: **6:21** For where your treasure is, there will your heart be also.

Haggai 1:4 Is it time for you, O ye, to dwell in your cieled houses, and this house lie waste? **1:5** Now therefore thus saith the LORD of hosts; Consider your ways.

Jesus Christ asks us if it is time for us to build corporate entities, auditoriums and physical structures for ourselves?

Is it time for God's people to seek to collectively amass physical wealth and not to be about the business of building our spiritual house for God's Spirit; through heartfelt repentance and zeal for God's Word, including a zeal for rooting out false traditions and a zeal to embrace the purity of the true teachings of God's Word and to keep his Holy Sabbath unpolluted?

Today large sums are spent in attracting listeners in the hope of gaining numbers and contributions, and yet there is only a very tiny result. Why? Because we are NOT pleasing God! We are NOT right with God! We reject truth to cleave to false teachings and idols of men!

1:6 Ye have sown much, and bring in little; ye eat [Today we internalize only a tiny bit of spiritual milk and we are not filled with the MEAT of true sound doctrine.], but ye have not enough; ye drink, [We barely taste the Living Waters of the Word of God and we are NOT filled with the Waters of Salvation, which is living by every Word of God.] but ye are not filled with drink; ye clothe you, [We think ourselves to be dressed in the garments of righteousness and we do not see that we are spiritually naked and not clothed with righteousness(Rev 3:16)] but there is none warm; and he that earneth wages earneth wages to put it into a bag with holes.

All of our physical efforts to build up physical church entities will ultimately come to nothing because we are NOT zealous to live by every Word of God. We are distracted from the spiritual by the physical, compromising with the spiritual in the hope of physical gain.

God commands up to consider that our schisms and endless problems have come upon us because we have been about our own ways and we have not exalted the whole Word of God in order to build up our personal and collective spiritual temple of the Holy Spirit!

1:7 Thus saith the LORD of hosts; Consider your ways.

God commanded the people at that time to build his physical temple and Jesus Christ is instructing today's Spiritual Ekklesia to build themselves up into a spiritual temple today, as a fit clean place for the Spirit of God to dwell in.

> **Ephesians 2:20** And are built upon the foundation of the apostles and prophets, Jesus Christ himself being the chief corner stone;

What does this mean? Does it mean that we are to build our spiritual house on the teachings of any person who comes along claiming to be an apostle or prophet? NO! It means that we are to build our spiritual house on every Word of God as written by the ancient prophets and apostles as inspired by Jesus Christ the Lamb of God!

Any person who comes along claiming to be a prophet or apostle is to be tested and proved (Mat 7, Deu 13,18) and if he departs from any part of the Word of God and teaches people to follow his own teachings or if he claims to have the authority to decide what the brethren are to believe or do: Then he is a FALSE PROPHET, a FALSE APOSTLE and a LIAR!

If a corporate church board or leader says concerning spiritual matters "Do this because we have decided." They are not people of God; because God would never permit anyone to act contrary to his Word!

> **2:21** In whom all the building fitly framed together groweth unto an holy temple in the Lord: **2:22** In whom ye also are builded together for an habitation of God through the Spirit.

Haggai 1:8 Go up to the mountain, and bring wood, and build the house; and I will take pleasure in it, and I will be glorified, saith the LORD.

Why is today's Spiritual Ekklesia so divided? Why has our outreach for declaring the Word of the LORD been reduced into a pathetic business model approach? Why does our LORD despise our efforts?

Because we have departed from our zeal to learn, to keep and to teach; the truth, the whole Word of God!

Brethren, building the physical temple in that day was an allegory that we should be zealous about building God's spiritual temple today!

1:9 Ye looked for much, and, lo it came to little; and when ye brought it home, I did blow [If our focus is not on living by every Words of God our physical wealth will ultimately be blown away like a wind scatters the dust.] upon it. [This was true for them physically in that day and it is true for us spiritually in our day.] Why? saith the LORD of hosts. Because of mine house that is waste, and ye run every man unto his own house.

1:10 Therefore the heaven over you is stayed from dew, and the earth is stayed from her fruit.

Let us turn to Almighty God and reject the anti-biblical traditions that have enslaved us! Let us work to establish a proper relationship with our espoused Husband and God the Father.

Let every person individually and collectively BUILD our spiritual character house, which should be the Temple of the Living God!

1 Corinthians 3:16 Know ye not that ye are the temple of God, and that the Spirit of God dwelleth in you? **3:17** If any man defile the temple of God, him shall God destroy; for the temple of God is holy, which temple ye are.

Just as God brought a drought on returned Judah for neglecting to build his physical House; he has brought a spiritual drought and famine of the truth upon those who neglect his Word and his spiritual Temple today.

Haggai 1:11 And I called for a drought upon the land, and upon the mountains, and upon the corn, and upon the new wine, and upon the oil, and upon that which the ground bringeth forth, and upon men, and upon cattle, and upon all the labour of the hands.

Then the high priest and the governor obeyed the Word of God and called the people to sincerely repent and build the Temple of God.

1:12 Then Zerubbabel [the governor] the son of Shealtiel, and **Joshua** the son of Josedech, **the high priest, with all the remnant of the people, obeyed the voice of the LORD their God, and the words of Haggai the prophet, as the LORD their God had sent him, and the people did fear** [sincerely repent] **before the LORD.**

1:13 Then spake Haggai the LORD's messenger in the LORD's message unto the people, saying, I am with [God is with the sincerely repentant who keep God's commandments and do his will, to live by every Word of God.] you, saith the LORD.

Remember this is all about building the temple, it is NOT about Daniel's 70th Week prophecy about building the city and its walls.

Zerubbabel builds the temple

1:14 And the LORD stirred up the spirit of Zerubbabel the son of Shealtiel, governor of Judah, and the spirit of Joshua the son of Josedech, the high priest, and the spirit of all the remnant of the people; and they came and did work in the house of the LORD of hosts, their God,

Let us also sincerely repent and turn to zealously build up ourselves into a spiritual temple, free from all uncleanness and sin; as a fit dwelling place for the King of the entire universe; and a fitting LIGHT of godly example, for the whole world to see!

1:15 In the four and twentieth day of the sixth month, in the second year of Darius the king.

Haggai 2

Haggai 2:1 In the seventh month, in the one and twentieth day of the month, [the seventh and last day of the Feast of Tabernacles] came the word of the LORD by the prophet Haggai, saying,

The building of this physical temple in Jerusalem was an allegory of the spiritual temple that we are to build out of ourselves as a habitation for God through his Spirit.

2:2 Speak now to **Zerubbabel the son of Shealtiel, governor** of Judah, and to **Joshua the son of Josedech, the high priest, and to the residue of the people**, saying,

God encouraged the people who had seen the temple of Solomon and were discouraged by this new effort.

Brethren, I know that we may get discouraged when we see the state of the present day Spiritual Ekklesia. It is truly pathetic in terms of being a fit dwelling place for God and his Spirit, but the Master Builder is at work: He is going to get the job done by humbling God's people and bringing them to sincere repentance and a passionate zeal to live by EVERY WORD of God, which is what the correction of the great tribulation will accomplish.

Right now we are being allowed to make our mistakes, so that when reality hits us hard we will see how wrong our own ways and thoughts are and we will wake up and turn to the Eternal.

2:3 Who is left among you that saw this house in her first glory? and how do ye see it now? is it not in your eyes in comparison of it as nothing?

Then Christ encouraged them, and he encourages us today to: BE STRONG in the work before us!

Just as they were encouraged and made strong to build the physical temple; let us be encouraged and made strong through our Mighty God, for the building of the spiritual temple of the Eternal in the called out brethren!

Brethren, we are engaged in a mighty work to purify, cleanse, build and make ready the spiritual temple of God, the bride; to cleanse the bride and purify her, making the collective bride ready to become of ONE spirit in full UNITY with our espoused Husband on our Wedding Day!

2:4 Yet now be strong, O Zerubbabel, saith the LORD; and be strong, O Joshua, son of Josedech, the high priest [Both of these men were types of Jesus Christ the High Priest and King of the called out,]**; and be strong, all ye people of the land, saith the LORD, and work: for I am with you, saith the LORD of hosts:**

Being called out of physical Egypt was a type of God calling out a spiritual people from the spiritual Egypt of bondage to Satan and sin.

2:5 According to the word that I covenanted with you when ye came out of [spiritual] Egypt, so my spirit remaineth among you: fear ye not.

The prophet foretells that in the last days the nations would be shaken and a glorious new Temple will be built. This is a reference to the coming of Christ who will build the glorious Ezekiel Temple in Jerusalem.

2:6 For thus saith the LORD of hosts; Yet once, it is a little while [in future from that time]**, and I will shake the heavens, and the earth, and the sea, and the dry land; 2:7 And I will shake all nations, and the desire of all nations shall come** [All nations shall sincerely repent and their desire will be to accept the salvation of Jesus Christ and to go forward to live by every Word of God.]**: and I will fill this house** [God will fill the resurrected chosen and the Ezekiel Temple with his glory through the presence of his Holy Spirit.] **with glory, saith the LORD of hosts. 2:8 The silver is mine, and the gold is mine, saith the LORD of hosts.**

In this latter day, the spiritual temple of God, the bride: will be completed and perfected. Collectively the faithful overcomers shall be made a glorious and perfect spiritual bride, filled in full measure with the Holy Spirit as a fit spiritual temple for God to dwell in, and to be resurrected and given eternal life

2:9 The glory of this latter [The latter day Spiritual Temple of the bride, and the physical Ezekiel Temple as well.] house shall be greater than of the former [greater and more beautiful than Solomon's Temple!], saith the LORD of hosts: and in this place will I give peace, saith the LORD of hosts.

We Must Put Out ALL Sin!

Now a lesson is given to be faithful to God and his Word to dedicate ourselves to our Father's business. To be faithful we must clean up our act and start keeping the Sabbath holy! We must discard the false traditions that we rely on and we must exalt God's Word ABOVE the traditions and idols of men! We must stop idolizing our leaders and organizations and blindly obeying men instead of obeying God, when such men differ from the Word of God!

> **1 Corinthians 5:6** Your glorying is not good. Know ye not that a little leaven leaveneth the whole lump **5:7** Purge out therefore the old leaven, that ye may be a new lump, as ye are unleavened. For even Christ our passover is sacrificed for us:

Haggai 2:10 In the four and twentieth day of the ninth month, in **the second year of Darius,** came the word of the LORD by Haggai the prophet, saying,

2:11 Thus saith the LORD of hosts; **Ask now the priests concerning the law, saying,**

2:12 If one bear holy flesh in the skirt of his garment, and with his skirt do touch bread, or pottage, or wine, or oil, or any meat, shall it be holy? And the priests answered and said, No.

2:13 Then said Haggai, If one that is unclean by a dead body touch any of these, shall it be unclean? And the priests answered and said, It shall be unclean.

Even a little sin makes the whole person spiritually unclean. We must root out all sin and separate out error from truth, as soon as it is discovered.

Those who do not keep all of God's commandments and live by EVERY WORD of God; are unclean to God and they will be rejected by Jesus Christ.

It is no different in today's called out Ekklesia (Rev 3:16), because the church of God groups have made themselves unclean by mixing the spiritually unclean false teachings and false traditions of our idols of men with the pure truth of the whole Word of God! The unclean makes the clean unclean also! Even a little leaven of sin, leavens the whole person or organization!

2:14 Then answered Haggai, and said, So is this people, and so is this nation [polluted and unclean] before me, saith the LORD; and so is every work of their hands; and that which they offer there is unclean.

The whole constellation of today's Spiritual Ekklesia and professing Christianity is unclean and polluted and disgusting to Jesus Christ; if we will not live by EVERY WORD of God!

Therefore we are being cast out of his mouth, vomited out of the body of Christ into severe correction. We are full of pride and spiritually blind, unable to see ourselves as God sees us. Our Sabbaths and Feasts are disgusting to God the Father and Jesus Christ, because they are our own days kept our own way, and not kept according to the Word of God!

Consider the sincere repentance of the people at that time and how when the people began to build the Temple of God [especially spiritually, by keeping every Word of God with zeal]; God respected their repentance and cared for them.

Jesus Christ has smote today's brethren only a little, and we will not turn to him to cleanse themselves of our idolatry and sins; therefore Jesus Christ is going to eject us into the correction of the furnace of affliction so that the spirit may be saved by the affliction of the flesh.

2:15 And now, I pray you, consider from this day and upward, from before a stone was laid upon a stone in the temple of the LORD:

Let spiritual Israel consider, that for all our efforts we have become weaker and more divided. Why? Because we reject truth and any zeal for godliness in order to follow our own ways, and we will not exalt the Eternal God to live by his every Word!

2:16 Since those days were, when one came to an heap of twenty measures [of grain], there were but ten: when one came to the pressfat for to draw out fifty vessels out of the press, there were but twenty.

2:17 I smote you with blasting and with mildew and with hail in all the labours of your hands; yet ye turned not to me, saith the LORD.

Physical blessings were promised for obedience to the physical Mosaic Covenant; and spiritual blessings are promised for obedience to the spiritual New Covenant, including the blessing of being changed to spirit and receiving the gift of eternal life.

We have the promise of Jesus Christ that from the day that we begin to cleanse ourselves from our idolatry of men and false traditions and set ourselves to learn and keep and to teach the whole Word of God; God will bless us with an increase in spiritual knowledge and understanding that will prepare us for an eternal office of responsibility in God's eternal Kingdom.

2:18 Consider now from this day and upward, from the four and twentieth day of the ninth month, even from the day that the foundation of the LORD's temple was laid, consider it.

2:19 Is the seed yet in the barn? yea, as yet the vine, and the fig tree, and the pomegranate, and the olive tree, hath not brought forth: **from this day will I bless you**.

If the brethren of today's spiritual Ekklesia will turn away from their idolatry to reject all error and to embrace the truth and to live by every Word of God, to be zealous for godliness [God is truth, and God's Spirit is truth] God will bless us with spiritual blessings and a good reward for all eternity.

Zerubbabel was a type of Jesus Christ who will rule all nations at his coming; the former Zerubbabel himself will be resurrected and changed to spirit and he will have a part in the Kingdom of God.

2:20 And again the word of the LORD came unto Haggai in the four and twentieth day of the month, saying,

2:21 Speak to Zerubbabel, governor of Judah, saying, **I will shake the heavens and the earth;**

2:22 And I will overthrow the throne of kingdoms, and I will destroy the strength of the kingdoms of the heathen; and I will overthrow the

chariots [vehicles], and those that ride in them; and the horses and their riders shall come down, every one by the sword of his brother.

The physical temple builder Zerubbabel, was chosen as a type of Jesus Christ, the Master Temple Builder; who is even now working to perfect his bride who is the Father's spiritual temple!

2:23 In that day, saith the LORD of hosts, will I take thee, O Zerubbabel, my servant, the son of Shealtiel, saith the LORD, and will make thee as a signet [a sign or allegorical type]: for I have chosen thee [Zerubbabel was chosen to be a sign, and type of Jesus Christ], saith the LORD of hosts.

Zechariah

Zechariah 1

The first four chapters of Zechariah are encouragement to Joshua and Zerubbabel to rebuild the temple and look forward to the restoration of true religion and a united Israel, and the building of Jerusalem and the Ezekiel Temple by Jesus Christ in our day.

Zerubbabel and Joshua were allegorical types of Jesus Christ the resurrected Master Builder who is building a Spiritual Temple today, and will soon come to build the Ezekiel Temple in Jerusalem.

God told the people through Zechariah that he was sore displeased with the sins [Sabbath breaking and idolatry] of their fathers; just as Jesus Christ is sore displeased with our sins [Sabbath breaking and idolatry] today.

Zechariah 1:1 In the eighth month, in **the second year of Darius** (521 B.C.), came the word of the LORD unto Zechariah, the son of Berechiah, the son of Iddo the prophet, saying,

1:2 The LORD hath been sore displeased with your fathers.

A Call to Repentance for them; AND for us today!

1:3 Therefore say thou unto them, Thus saith the LORD of hosts; Turn ye unto me, saith the LORD of hosts, and I will turn unto you, saith the LORD of hosts.

Let us not be as the ancients with their idolatry and Sabbath / High Day polluting. Let us STOP cooking, working and buying food and drink or anything else on God's Sabbath and High Days; and let us observe them on the days that God has commanded, in the way that God has commanded.

Let us STOP idolizing men above the Word and commandments of Almighty God.

1:4 Be ye not as your fathers, unto whom the former prophets have cried, saying, Thus saith the LORD of hosts; **Turn ye now from your evil ways, and from your evil doings**: but they did not hear, nor hearken unto me, saith the LORD.

1:5 Your fathers, where are they? and the prophets, do they live for ever?

1:6 But my words and my statutes, which I commanded my servants the prophets, did they not take hold of your fathers? and they returned and said, Like as the LORD of hosts thought to do unto us, according to our ways, and according to our doings, so hath he dealt with us.

The Horses and the Angel of the Lord

1:7 Upon the four and twentieth day of the eleventh month, which is the month Sebat, in the second year of Darius, came the word of the LORD unto Zechariah, the son of Berechiah, the son of Iddo the prophet, saying,

1:8 I saw by night, and behold **a man riding upon a red horse**, and he stood among the myrtle trees that were in the bottom [at the bottom of the valley where the water flows]; and behind him were there [an unspecified number of] **red horses, speckled, and white**.

1:9 Then said I, O my lord, what are these? And the angel that talked with me said unto me, I will shew thee what these be.

The Explanation

1:10 And the man that stood among the myrtle trees answered and said, These are they [they are God's angelic observers] whom the LORD hath sent to walk to and fro through the earth.

1:11 And they answered the angel of the LORD that stood among the myrtle trees, and said, We [he and the horses which are angelic spirits] have walked to and fro through the earth, and, behold, all the earth sitteth still, and is at rest.

The man is an angel in charge and the horses are his angelic watchers. The specific time period is the second year of Darius 1 king of the Medes; and all the earth was at peace at that time, but the temple and the city Jerusalem were not being built.

The angel asked when the Jews would be restored.

A prophecy was given to Daniel in the first year of Darius (522 B.C.) of a coming decree to build the city and God confirmed the prophecy through Zechariah in the second year of Darius 450 B.C. that in future the city itself would be built as he had promised Daniel (Dan 9); encouraging the people in the task of building the temple and restoring true religion.

Timeline

The Building of the Temple

- The people went up to Jerusalem with Zerubbabel to build the temple according to the decree of Cyrus in 536 B.C.
- Cyrus appointed Sheshbazzar the Persian name for Zerubbabel, governor of the Jews in Jerusalem and Judea, Ezra 5:16.
- Zerubbabel and Joshua went with the people out of Babylon to Jerusalem under the governor and they build the Altar in time to sacrifice during the Feasts of the seventh month.
- Construction of the temple building began in the second year, Ezra 3.
- Little progress was made due to the opposition of the local people and construction was halted due to complaints from the local people [which came during a period of uprisings in the empire] by Artaxerxes [Darius] in 522 B.C., Ezra 5.
- Then Haggai and Zechariah began to prophesy and encourage the people and they wrote to Darius explaining that Cyrus had ordered the construction of the temple (520 B.C.)
- Darius then ordered the construction to resume in 520 B.C. and the temple was completed in 516 B.C., Ezra 6.

The Building of the City

- Artaxerxes Longimanus put away queen Vashti in his second year (461 B.C.) for her example of rebellion and disobedience.

- He became the husband of Esther in his third year (c 460 B.C.)
- In his seventh year (457 B.C.) king Artaxerxes [Ahasuerus Longimanus, disposed to hold the Jews in favor due to the influence of queen Esther and Mordachi] sent Ezra to rebuild the city Jerusalem.
- Ezra found that many Jews in Jerusalem had apostatized and therefore he concentrated on restoring true religion as a first priority before building the city walls.
- The Palestinians and other peoples greatly resisted and delayed the construction of the city walls.
- In the twelfth year (452 B.C.) of Ahaseurus the Jews were saved from Haman who was incensed by the favours granted to the Jews and conspired to destroy them.
- In 444 B.C. Artaxerxes Longimanus' 20th year of reign; Nehemiah was sent to aid Ezra in establishing true religion and to help in the rebuilding of the city Jerusalem.
- The city was completed in 408 B.C.

It was during the 49 year period from 457 B.C. when the original decree was given to build the city, that the city was built under extremely trying circumstances, being completed as the angel had foretold to Daniel in 49 years in 408 B.C. After which another 62 weeks (434 years) would pass before the revealing of the Jesus Christ when his ministry began at the age of 30 in autumn 27 A.D.

Brethren, our LORD is coming and we must rise up and be about the task of preparing the bride and making ourselves ready. We must be about the task of building ourselves into a fitting, holy, pure, spiritual temple for the habitation of God, and cleansing and purifying ourselves from all uncleanness and every defect, to become a fitting bride for our exalted LORD!

Today it is almost midnight and the cry is going out: "Behold the bridegroom cometh: Let us make ready!"

Zechariah 1:12 Then the angel of the LORD answered and said, O LORD of hosts, how long wilt thou not have mercy on Jerusalem and on the cities of Judah, against which thou hast had indignation these threescore and ten years? 1:13 And the LORD answered the angel that talked with me with good words and comfortable words.

1:14 So the angel that communed with me said unto me, Cry thou, saying, Thus saith the LORD of hosts; I am jealous for Jerusalem and for Zion with a great jealousy. **1:15** And I am very sore displeased with the heathen that are at ease: for I was but a little displeased, and they helped forward the affliction.

The correction of Judah was an example of the correction of the tribulation coming on physical AND spiritual Judah and Israel again in this latter day; and today just like in that time, the nations who will correct us will be overzealous in their correction and God will be sore displeased with them.

First restore the temple [analogous to restoring true religion and building the spiritual temple] and then build the city!

1:16 Therefore thus saith the LORD; I am returned to Jerusalem with mercies: my house shall be built in it, saith the LORD of hosts, and a line shall be stretched forth upon Jerusalem.

This is a dual prophecy for that time and also for our time.

1:17 Cry yet, saying, Thus saith the LORD of hosts; My cities through prosperity shall yet be spread abroad; and the LORD shall yet comfort Zion, and shall yet choose Jerusalem.

A prophecy of the latter day

1:18 Then lifted I up mine eyes, and saw, and behold four horns.

These four horns are not specifically identified, except that they are the Gentile nations which destroyed Israel, Judah and Jerusalem in those days, and by duality they represent destroyers in our days.

1:19 And I said unto the angel that talked with me, What be these? And he answered me, **These are the horns which have scattered Judah, Israel, and Jerusalem.**

1:20 And the LORD shewed me four carpenters;

After The Four Horns [Destroying Powers] corrected Judah; Four Carpenters [builders] would be Sent to Build the Temple, city and the nation.

These four carpenters [unidentified builders possibly Joshua, Zerubbabel, Ezra and Nehemiah] were to rebuild that which was destroyed and this was an allegory that the temple and city and nation will be built again in the latter days after the tribulation, by Jesus Christ who will deliver the captives of Israel, build the Ezekiel Temple, fully restore true religion and build Jerusalem.

As the temple, city and land were rebuilt the first time in those days; they shall be rebuilt in the fullness of beauty after the coming of Jesus Christ with his saints!

1:21 Then said I, What come these to do? And he spake, saying, These are the horns [powers] which have scattered Judah, so that no man did lift up his head: but these [carpenters, builders] are come to fray them, **to cast out the horns of the Gentiles**, which lifted up their horn over the land of Judah to scatter it.

The future millennial Israel and Judah will also be gathered back and Jerusalem rebuilt, this time by Messiah; and will prosper for they shall sincerely repent during great tribulation and God will being ALL Israel into a New Covenant with him (Jer 31:31); after which all mankind will be grafted into New Covenant Spiritual Israel (Jer 31, Joel 2:28)

Zechariah 2

Zechariah 2:1 I lifted up mine eyes again, and looked, and behold a man with a measuring line in his hand. **2:2** Then said I, Whither goest thou? And he said unto me, To measure Jerusalem, to see what is the breadth thereof, and what is the length thereof.

2:3 And, behold, the angel that talked with me went forth, and another angel went out to meet him,

This is a prophecy of the millennial Jerusalem when Messiah the Christ dwells in the city

2:4 And said unto him, Run, speak to this young man, saying, Jerusalem shall be inhabited as towns without walls for the multitude of men and cattle therein: **2:5** For **I, saith the LORD, will be unto her a wall of fire round about, and will be the glory in the midst of her.**

A prophecy of our time about Judah and Israel returning to Palestine after the coming of Messiah.

2:6 Ho, ho, come forth, and flee from the land of the north, saith the LORD: for I have spread you abroad as the four winds of the heaven, saith the LORD. **2:7** Deliver thyself, O Zion, that dwellest with the daughter [latter day descendants of] of Babylon.

Messiah is sent to deliver first spiritual and then physical Israel/Judah, which are the apple of God's eye.

2:8 For thus saith the LORD of hosts; **After the glory** [Israel the beloved of God; BOTH spiritual and physical] **hath he sent me unto the nations which spoiled you: for he that toucheth you toucheth the apple of his eye.**

Messiah the Christ will reverse things and the conquerors and masters will be made the servants of his people.

2:9 For, behold, I will shake mine hand upon them, and they shall be a spoil to their servants: and ye shall know that the LORD of hosts hath sent me.

2:10 Sing and rejoice, O daughter [the latter day descendants of BOTH physical AND spiritual Israel] of Zion: for, lo, I [Messiah] come, and I will dwell in the midst of thee, saith the LORD.

We know this is a prophecy about the Latter Days, because of the phrase "daughter of" and also by the statement below, that the surviving nations will be gathered to God as well as Israel; and that Messiah will come to deliver his people.

2:11 And many nations shall be joined to the LORD in that day, and shall be my people: and I [Messiah the Christ] **will dwell in the midst of thee, and thou shalt know that the LORD of hosts hath sent me** [Zechariah] **unto thee.**

2:12 And the LORD shall inherit Judah his portion in the holy land, and shall choose Jerusalem again.

Then the mouths of the naysayers and wicked will be stopped at the presence of the Eternal; when he stands up to deliver his people!

2:13 Be silent, O all flesh, before the LORD: for he is raised up out of his holy habitation.

Zechariah 3

The physical high priest Joshua was a type of the spiritual High Priest Jesus Christ who delivers all sincerely repentant sinners by applying his atoning sacrifice; cleansing them from all sincerely repented sin .

ALL converted people MUST live by every Word of God with true diligent zealous enthusiasm just like Jesus Christ did and does!

Salvation from eternal death is entirely conditional on true sincere repentance and on carefully following the example of Jesus Christ to live by every Word of God!

> **Zechariah 3:7** Thus saith the LORD of hosts; **If thou wilt** walk in my ways, and **if thou wilt** keep my charge, then thou shalt also judge my house, and shalt also keep my courts, and I will give thee places to walk among these that stand by.

Zechariah 3:1 And he shewed me **Joshua the high priest** standing before the angel of the LORD, and Satan standing at his right hand to resist him.

Speaking of the physical Joshua; YHVH said to Satan that the physical Joshua is a brand plucked out of the fire; that is, he was full of sin and ready to be cast into the fire, but was saved by sincere repentance and the sacrificial atonement of the Lamb of God, bearing his sins.

Jesus Christ was also covered by the sins of humanity at his death bearing the sins of the whole world; and Jesus was also saved from destruction by his perfect life, and resurrected to eternal life by God the Father.

Whenever the word "Lord" is in all capitols as "LORD," it means YHVH which can refer to either the Father or to the Being who became flesh as Jesus Christ.

3:2 And the LORD [YHVH] said unto Satan, The LORD rebuke thee, O Satan; even the LORD that hath chosen Jerusalem rebuke thee: is not this a brand plucked out of the fire?

The physical high priest Joshua then had his filthy garments [as a type of the filth of sin] removed, and he was cleansed and clothed with the garments of righteousness.

This was an allegory that Jesus Christ had the sins of the world placed on himself but was raised up from the dead because of his own perfect life and made the spirit High Priest of God the Father forever.

3:3 Now Joshua was clothed with filthy garments, and stood before the angel. **3:4** And he answered and spake unto those that stood before him, saying, Take away the filthy garments from him. And unto him he said, Behold, I have caused thine iniquity to pass from thee, and I will clothe thee with change of raiment.

The high priest's mitre or crown represents the high priest as the true ruler of Israel, a type of the eternal High Priest [Melchizedek], Messiah the Christ who is the true ruler of spiritual Israel.

3:5 And I said, Let them set a fair mitre [the headdress of a high priest] upon his head. So they set a fair mitre upon his head, and clothed him with garments. And the angel of the LORD stood by.

Then the angel of God warned the physical high priest Joshua that faithful passionate obedience to the whole Word of God was required in order to be counted among the elect!

3:6 And the angel of the LORD protested unto Joshua, saying, **3:7** Thus saith the LORD of hosts; **If thou wilt walk in my ways, and if thou wilt keep my charge**, then thou shalt also judge my house, and shalt also keep my courts, and I will give thee places to walk among these that stand by.

Jesus Christ was and is eternally faithful to live by EVERY WORD of God the Father; and we must do likewise!

If we repent and diligently walk in the ways of Christ and live by every Word of God; we shall be in the resurrection to spirit and will rule as kings and priests under the King of kings and eternal High Priest Jesus Christ.

Yes even the repentant Laodiceans!

Those who may despise correction today will lose their high reward but they may still repent in the tribulation and will then be accepted by God our Father in a diminished role as a part of the bride for his Son.

If we find ourselves being corrected in tribulation; there is still hope! God is correcting us in HOPE that we will sincerely repent; his correction has the object of bringing us to sincere repentance and so saving us!

The Branch will soon arrive to collect his bride! Let us repent and remove the blemishes of our sins so that we may be found a suitable, pure and perfect bride for our Lord.

Joshua and those with him who were zealously faithful to the whole Word of God, they and their example shall be wondered at by others, and they shall be raised up at the coming of Christ to gather his saints.

The physical Joshua is now told [as a prophecy and promise to us] of the coming of Christ the BRANCH!

3:8 Hear now, O Joshua the high priest, thou, and thy fellows [The world will be astounded when Christ comes and resurrects the faithful who sincerely repent of sin and live by every Word of God.] that sit before thee: **for they are men wondered at: for, behold, I will bring forth my servant the BRANCH** [The true vine, Jesus Christ (John 15).].

3:9 For behold the stone [the foundation stone, the chief of the corner] that I have laid before Joshua; upon one stone shall be seven eyes [the seven spirits of God, helping Christ (Rev 1:4)] behold, I will engrave the graving [the new name of Jesus Christ (Rev 3:12)] thereof, saith the LORD of hosts, and I will remove the iniquity of that land in one day.

When Christ returns WITH his saints, he will destroy the filthiness of sin and pour out his Spirit on all flesh (Joel 2:28), so that even the wild beasts will be peaceable (Is 11:5 and Is 65:25).

3:10 In that day, saith the LORD of hosts, shall ye call every man his neighbour under the vine and under the fig tree.

Zechariah 4

The Two Witnesses of God

Zechariah 4:1 And the angel that talked with me came again, and waked me, as a man that is wakened out of his sleep.

4:2 And said unto me, What seest thou? And I said, I have looked, and behold a candlestick all of gold, with a bowl upon the top of it, and his seven lamps thereon, and seven pipes to the seven lamps, which are upon the top thereof:

4:3 And two olive trees by it, one upon the right side of the bowl, and the other upon the left side thereof.

This is the lamp stand often called the Menorah. This lamp stand of seven branches, pictures the seven churches (Rev 2-3) all producing light by the oil of God's Spirit and all connected to the same foundation.

It was intended that each church would be filled with the oil of the Holy Spirit and through faithful obedience to the whole Word of God, would be a Shining Light and example for the whole world. (Mat 5, Mark 4 and Luk 11).

Right now the light of all seven churches of Revelation 2 and 3 are flickering and dying out. Yes, all seven existed together in the first century and all seven will exist together at the coming of Christ!

They all existed together in the first century and there is nothing about any mail route in Scripture, which idea is human reasoning wrongly added to scripture. They all exist together today because each one is warned to be vigilant lest Christ comes and catches them by surprise!

Today all seven attitudes exist throughout the assemblies of the Spiritual Ekklesia and their light of godliness is flickering out as they idolize the false teachings and traditions of men and live by their own ways.

The purpose of this work is to wake people up and excite a zeal for God and his Word in order to revive today's assemblies which are very near spiritual death.

The final two prophets will do the very same job at much increased power, and they will succeed in pouring the oil of God's Spirit out of themselves into the seven churches like two fruitful olive trees; turning today's Spiritual Ekklesia away from our false traditions, idolizing of men and sin; and turning us back to their LORD so that a bright shining light of godly example will be restored and that which was dying is revived.

In short, God is sending his two servants to save the seven churches before they run out of the oil of the Holy Spirit and self-destruct.

4:4 So I answered and spake to the angel that talked with me, saying, What are these, my lord?

4:5 Then the angel that talked with me answered and said unto me, Knowest thou not what these be? And I said, No, my lord.

Zechariah asked what these two olive trees who empty the golden oil [Holy Spirit] out of themselves into the seven branches of the lamp stand are; but the angel, before answering, goes into some related information.

4:6 Then he answered and spake unto me, saying, This is the word of the LORD unto Zerubbabel, saying, Not by might, nor by power, but by my spirit, saith the LORD of hosts.

Speaking to the governor of the Jews Zerubbabel, the angel informs him that the temple is being built by the power of God and not by his own strength. This is a lesson for us and for God's two servants that we are only tools in God's most capable hands.

4:7 Who art thou, O great mountain [the end time New Europe revival of Babylon the Great]? before Zerubbabel [Jesus Christ] thou shalt become a plain: and he shall bring forth the headstone thereof [properly the chief Cornerstone will be exalted and come and destroy the mountain of Babylon, flattening it. See Daniel 2.] with shoutings, crying, Grace, grace unto it.

The great mountain is the government of the Babylonian system of the New Europe, and Jesus Christ will crash the mountain of the government of Babylon the great, down to the level ground and destroy it, the cornerstone of Jesus Christ will do this with the rejoicings and shouting's of the repentant people.

Daniel 2:37 Thou, O king, art a king of kings: for the God of heaven hath given thee a kingdom, power, and strength, and glory. **2:38** And wheresoever the children of men dwell, the beasts of the field and the fowls of the heaven hath he given into thine hand, and hath made thee ruler over them all. Thou art this head of gold.

2:39 And after thee shall arise another kingdom inferior to thee, and another third kingdom of brass, which shall bear rule over all the earth. **2:40** And the fourth kingdom shall be strong as iron: forasmuch as iron breaketh in pieces and subdueth all things: and as iron that breaketh all these, shall it break in pieces and bruise.

2:41 And whereas thou sawest the feet and toes, part of potters' clay, and part of iron, the kingdom shall be divided; but there shall be in it of the strength of the iron, forasmuch as thou sawest the iron mixed with miry clay. **2:42** And as the toes of the feet were part of iron, and part of clay, so the kingdom shall be partly strong, and partly broken. **2:43** And whereas thou sawest iron mixed with miry clay, they shall mingle themselves with the seed of men: but they shall not cleave one to another, even as iron is not mixed with clay.

2:44 And in the days of these kings shall the God of heaven set up a kingdom, which shall never be destroyed: and the kingdom shall not be left to other people, but it shall break in pieces and consume all these kingdoms, and it shall stand for ever.

2:45 Forasmuch as thou sawest that the stone [the Messiah, Jesus (Yeshua) the Christ] was cut out of the mountain without hands, and that it brake in pieces the iron, the brass, the clay, the silver, and the gold; the great God hath made known to the king what shall come to pass hereafter: and the dream is certain, and the interpretation thereof sure.

The mountain [government and religious system] of Babylon will be utterly destroyed!

> **Jeremiah 51:25** Behold, I am against thee, O destroying mountain [government of Babylon, the New Europe], saith the LORD, which destroyest [Babylon the destroyer, will be destroyed] all the earth: and I will stretch out mine hand upon thee, and roll thee down from the rocks, and will make thee a burnt mountain. **51:26** And **they shall not take of thee a stone for a corner, nor a stone for foundations; but thou shalt be desolate for ever**, saith the LORD.

Jesus Christ is the foundation stone of salvation, the chief cornerstone of godliness! Jesus Christ is building his Father's Spiritual Temple and Christ is the cornerstone of that Spiritual Temple!

> **Ephesians 2:20** And are built upon the foundation of the apostles and prophets, Jesus Christ himself being the chief corner stone;

Zechariah 4:8 Moreover the word of the LORD came unto me, saying,

4:9 The hands of Zerubbabel [The building of the physical temple succeeded, as a type of Jesus Christ building and completing the faithful into a fit dwelling place for God through the Holy Spirit!] have laid the foundation of this house; his hands shall also finish it; and thou shalt know that the LORD of hosts hath sent me unto you.

What is the foundation of the Spiritual Temple of God? The foundation of the Spiritual Temple of God the Father is: The Whole Word of God, as inspired by Jesus Christ!

> **Ephesians 2:19** Now therefore ye are no more strangers and foreigners, but fellowcitizens with the saints, and of the household of God; **2:20** And **are built upon the foundation of the apostles and prophets** [those who wrote the scriptures], **Jesus Christ himself being the chief corner stone**; **2:21** In whom all the building fitly framed together groweth unto an holy temple in the Lord: **2:22** In whom ye also are builded together for an habitation of God through the Spirit.

Zechariah 4:10 For who hath despised the day of small things? for they shall rejoice, and shall see the plummet in the hand of Zerubbabel [a type of Christ the Master Builder] with those seven; they are the eyes [The seven spirits (servants and helpers) of YHVH, Jesus Christ (Rev 3:1, 5:6).] of the LORD, which run to and fro through the whole earth.

Zerubbabel was a type of Jesus Christ, he began to build and completed building a physical temple; and Jesus Christ laid the foundations of the Spiritual Temple, which consists of those who internalize and live by every Word of God: Jesus Christ: WILL COMPLETE THE JOB!

Jesus Christ is God the Father's Master Builder and he will complete what he began six thousand years ago!

The last days WILL begin on God's schedule, whether we are ready or not; the resurrection will take place on God's schedule whether are ready or not, and there shall by much weeping and gnashing of teeth by those who have not made themselves ready.

The Kingdom WILL COME, on God's schedule, regardless of whether we think we are ready, or whether we think we have finished our work or not!

This plan is on God's schedule and NOT our schedule! And the Master Builder will finish the Father's Spiritual Temple ON TIME!

NO! Zerubbabel is not a type of some mere mortal man with a swelled head! He was a type of the true Cornerstone who laid the foundation of the Kingdom of God forever! and which will destroy Babylon the Great of Daniel 2!

We are to STAND ON that FOUNDATION and not on the shifting sands of organizational traditions and the teachings of men contrary to scripture!

4:11 Then answered I, and said unto him, What are these two olive trees upon the right side of the candlestick [lampstand, menorah] and upon the left side thereof?

And Zechariah asked a third time.

4:12 And I answered again, and said unto him, What be these **two olive branches** which through the two golden pipes **empty the golden oil out of themselves**? **4:13** And he answered me and said, Knowest thou not what these be? And I said, No, my lord.

Zechariah asked a total of three times: What are these two olive trees?

4:14 Then said he, **These are the two anointed ones, that stand by the LORD of the whole earth.**

The two olive trees are the two anointed ones who stand by Jesus Christ whatever the cost, whatever anyone else says; and they do whatever God tells them to do!

They are two prophets who will come in the spirit of Moses and Elijah in their dedication and zeal for the Eternal and every Word of God. Read Matthew 17 where God shows us who stands beside our Lord in a vision.

There are yet coming two prophets to complete the preaching of the gospel by men and they will also pour the oil of God's Spirit out of themselves and into the seven churches which are all about to die; so as to revive them and fill them with the oil of God's Spirit! (Rev 11). See also Revelation 11.

Zechariah 5

A series of visions about Babylon the Great and the latter days

Zechariah 5:1 Then I turned, and lifted up mine eyes, and looked, and behold a flying roll [scroll]. **5:2** And he said unto me, What seest thou? And I answered, I see a flying roll; the length thereof is twenty cubits [30 feet], and the breadth thereof ten cubits [15 feet].

This is the curse for breaking the Word of God, that will fall on the wicked over all the earth.

5:3 Then said he unto me, **This is the curse that goeth forth over the face of the whole earth: for every one that stealeth shall be cut off as on this side according to it; and every one that sweareth shall be cut off as on that side according to it.**

5:4 I will bring it forth, saith the LORD of hosts, and **it shall enter into the house of the thief, and into the house of him that sweareth falsely by my name:** and it shall remain in the midst of his house, and shall consume it with the timber thereof and the stones thereof.

Zechariah is told that the woman [the Babylonian Mysteries] of wickedness will be set up in Shinar [Babylon] and will be established there. This woman is the Babylonian Empire church state system represented by the statue of Daniel 2.

The modern Babylonian religion today has moved and is based in Rome as the iron of the Daniel two stature and will soon bring a new revival of the Holy Roman Empire system of Babylon the Great.

This is a very real political religious system and in the spiritual sense it is representative of anyone who rebels against God and decides right and wrong for themselves instead of doing as God has commanded, exalting the words of men above the Word of God. That would include those adopting her hierarchical Nicolaitane "Primacy of Peter" governance system of Babylon the Great, including anyone and everyone who follows idols of men instead of living by every Word of God.

5:5 Then the angel that talked with me went forth, and said unto me, Lift up now thine eyes, and see what is this that goeth forth.

5:6 And I said, What is it? And he said, This is an ephah [a container of about a bushel] that goeth forth. He said moreover, This is their resemblance through all the earth.

5:7 And, behold, there was lifted up a talent of lead: and this is a woman [the mystery religion of Babylon] that sitteth in the midst of the ephah.

Wickedness is cast into the jar and sealed inside with lead. This means that the woman [the false religion of the Babylonian Mysteries] was founded in Babylon.

5:8 And he said, **This is wickedness. And he cast it into the midst of the ephah; and he cast the weight of lead upon the mouth thereof.**

The only place in the Bible that angels appear as women.

5:9 Then lifted I up mine eyes, and looked, and, behold, there came out two women, and the wind was in their wings; for they had wings like the wings of a stork: and they lifted up the ephah between the earth and the heaven.

This wickedness depicted as a woman is the Babylon the Great church state religious system of Daniel 2; with its final fulfillment in our time by the final revival of the Holy Roman Empire [regardless of the name it calls itself].

5:10 Then said I to the angel that talked with me, Whither do these bear the ephah?

5:11 And he said unto me, **To build it an house in the land of Shinar** [The Babylonian system was set up and established beginning with

Nebuchadnezzar in Babylon]: **and it shall be established, and set there upon her own base.**

Babylon was in Shinar, and the woman of wickedness is the Babylonian Mysteries church state system of the statue of Daniel 2. Its final manifestation is described as the Holy Roman Empire system in Revelation 17, the Babylonian Mystery Religion which had its beginnings in Babylon.

Zechariah 6

The vision of the four chariots; chariots being war machines.

Zechariah 6:1 And I turned, and lifted up mine eyes, and looked, and, behold, there came **four chariots** out from between two mountains; and the mountains were mountains of brass.

6:2 In the **first chariot were red horses**; and in the **second chariot black horses**;

6:3 And in the **third chariot white horses**; and in the **fourth chariot grisled and bay horses.**

6:4 Then I answered and said unto the angel that talked with me, What are these, my lord?

6:5 And the angel answered and said unto me, **These are the four spirits of the heavens, which go forth from standing before the LORD [YHVH] of all the earth.**

The Father is Lord of all; therefore the term LORD of the earth refers to Jesus Christ who will rule over all the earth as King of kings. These four spirits are sent out on the earth to enforce the curse and quiet the anger of the Eternal.

6:6 The **black horses** which are therein go forth into **the north country**; and **the white go forth after them**; and the **grisled go forth toward the south country** [the King of the South,. Egypt and Israel].

6:7 And the bay went forth, and sought to go that they might walk to and fro through the earth: and he [YHVH] said, Get you hence, walk to and fro through the earth [find out what is happening on the earth]. So they walked to and fro through the earth.

In this latter day, the Babylonian Mysteries has been moved to Rome and the New Europe is also the latter day seat of the king of the NORTH, the now rising Babylonian the Great empire system which will occupy Judea and Egypt.

Then after 42 months God will deliver his people from Babylon.

6:8 Then cried he upon me, and spake unto me, saying, **Behold, these that go toward the north country have quieted my spirit** in the north country.

The Godly Chosen

6:9 And the word of the LORD came unto me, saying, **6:10** Take of them of the captivity, even of Heldai, of Tobijah, and of Jedaiah, which **are come from Babylon,** and come thou the same day, and go into the house of Josiah the son of Zephaniah;

Those who came out of Babylon in those days made crowns for Joshua the high priest who was a type of the spirit High Priest, Jesus Christ. The men who had come out of Babylon and returned to Jerusalem are an allegory of those who come out of spiritual Babylon and its idolatry of men; to love and zealously keep the whole Word of God and will be among the chosen to be resurrected and to rule with Christ.

Today's Spiritual Ekklesia is very much a part of Babylon the Great belief system, holding to the very same abominable practice of exalting men and the word and traditions of men, above the Word of God as their ultimate moral authority! This is why Christ admonishes us to:

> **Revelation 18:4** And I heard another voice from heaven, saying, Come out of her [We MUST sincerely repent of following her false doctrine of placing men between the brethren and God and teaching the brethren to follow idols of men above any zeal to live by every Word of God.], my people, that ye be not partakers of her sins, and that ye receive not of her plagues.

At the coming of Christ, the crowns of the earth will pass to HIM; and he shall be crowned King of kings and LORD of lords!

In those ancient days, the several crowns were placed on the head of Joshua the high priest; prophetically indicating that the High Priesthood and the King-ship will be united and conferred on Messiah the Christ at his now soon coming.

There is no doubt that Joshua [the name meaning Salvation, the very same name as the Messiah Yeshua] was a type of Jesus [Hebrew: Yeshua] the Messiah, the Christ!

Zechariah 6:11 Then take silver and gold, and **make crowns, and set them upon the head of Joshua the son of Josedech, the high priest;**

This pictures Jesus Christ being crowned King of kings! Then Joshua as a type of Jesus [Hebrew: Yeshua] is declared to be the Branch as a type of that ultimate True Vine, Yeshua [Christ] Messiah! John 15.

> **Isaiah 11:1** And there shall come forth a rod out of the stem of Jesse, and **a Branch shall grow out of his roots:**
>
> **11:2** And the spirit of the LORD shall rest upon him, the spirit of wisdom and understanding, the spirit of counsel and might, the spirit of knowledge and of the fear of the LORD;
>
> **11:3** And shall make him of quick understanding in the fear of the LORD: and he shall not judge after the sight of his eyes, neither reprove after the hearing of his ears:
>
> **11:4** But with righteousness shall he judge the poor, and reprove with equity for the meek of the earth: and he shall smite the earth: with the rod of his mouth, and with the breath of his lips shall he slay the wicked.

Zechariah 6:12 And speak unto him [speak to Joshua], saying, Thus speaketh the LORD of hosts, saying,

The Branch [Jesus Christ] is to build God's Spiritual Temple the Spiritual Ekklesia, and will also build the Ezekiel Temple at Jerusalem!

Behold the man whose name is The BRANCH; and he shall grow up out of his place [he shall be exalted], and he shall build the temple of the LORD:

This presentation of Joshua as not only high priest but also king; is an instructional type, an allegorical picture, of Jesus Christ; who will build the Spiritual Temple and will come to sit upon his throne in Jerusalem as

King of kings and also as the High Priest and the ONLY Mediator between God the Father and humanity.

6:13 Even he [Messiah the Christ] **shall build the temple of the LORD; and he shall bear the glory** [for building the Spiritual Ekklesia into a Spiritual Temple and delivering them into eternal life], and shall sit and rule upon his throne; and he shall be a priest upon his throne: and the counsel of peace shall be between them both.

Brethren, the Babylonian Mysteries church state system which follows idols of men, is a counterfeit of God's church state system; where all people follow, obey and live by every Word of God!

Zerubbabel the governor was a type of Christ in his role as governor and ruler and Joshua the high priest was a type of Jesus Christ as our High Priest.

The High Priest, Jesus Christ, will merge the office of King of kings with his office of High Priest and there shall be no more contention between kings and priests.

The crowns given to Joshua by those who came out of Babylon represent their acceptance of Joshua's authority, as a type of the acceptance of the authority of Messiah the Christ by those who come out of spiritual Babylon and given themselves in full submission to the Eternal. They will be given crowns under the King of kings, to rule the nations.

6:14 And the **crowns shall be to Helem, and to Tobijah, and to Jedaiah, and to Hen** the son of Zephaniah, for a memorial in the temple of the LORD.

The four men who came out of Babylon are singled out for their zeal for God, as a type of those who have a zeal for the whole Word of God and have come out of spiritual Babylon.

6:15 And they that are far off shall come and build in the [the second temple in that day, and today the Ezekiel Temple] temple of the LORD, and ye shall know that the LORD of hosts hath sent me unto you. And this shall come to pass, **if ye will diligently obey the voice of the LORD your God**

Brethren, many have turned away from their zeal for God and joined the Babylonian Mystery Religion by accepting the foundational false doctrine of the Primacy of Peter; which is a hierarchical governance system that places men between God and the brethren; making idols out of men and their teachings and false traditions: and so falling into the pit of wickedness and destruction.

We must come out of that system of idolatry and sincerely wholeheartedly REPENT of exalting men above the Word of God!

Do not misunderstand, I am not against organization or ministry; all godly authority is from God! Therefore when men go contrary to the Word of God; they are in rebellion against the authority of God, and they lose their ministerial authority.

Almighty God comes first and we are to follow men, ONLY as they follow God!

When they exalt the word and traditions of men above the Word of God, today's Spiritual Ekklesia is, spiritually speaking just another part of the Babylonian Mysteries,

> **Revelation 18:4** And I heard another voice from heaven, saying, **Come out of her, my people, that ye be not partakers of her sins** [stop accepting her idolatry by allowing anyone or anything to come between us and the Word of God], **and that ye receive not of her plagues.**

Zechariah 7

God reveals the way to the Mosaic Covenant promise of physical prosperity; a type of spiritual prosperity for those Called Out to the spiritual New Covenant: Keep the commandments and be zealous to build the house [especially the Spiritual Temple] of God and to live by every Word of God!

Zechariah 7:1 And it came to pass in **the fourth year of king Darius**, that the word of the LORD came unto Zechariah in the fourth day of the ninth month, even in Chisleu;

7:2 When they had sent unto the house of God Sherezer and Regemmelech, and their men, to pray before the LORD, **7:3** And to speak unto the priests which were in the house of the LORD of hosts, and to the prophets, saying, Should I weep in the fifth month, separating myself, as I have done these so many years?

Then Messiah the Christ told the people that their fasting was in vain because they did not rise up to: go and sin no more.

How like the vain fasting of today's brethren who fast for what they want and then rise up to call God's Sabbath holy while proceeding to pollute God's Sabbath and High Days, and returning to idolize men and many other sins!

7:4 Then came the word of the LORD of hosts unto me, saying,

7:5 Speak unto all the people of the land, and to the priests, saying, When ye fasted and mourned in the fifth and seventh month, even those seventy years, did ye at all fast [in sincere repentance to God] unto me, even to me?

7:6 And when ye did eat, and when ye did drink [at the Festivals], did not ye eat for yourselves, and drink for yourselves?

Today we use God's Festivals to satisfy personal pleasures instead of being zealous to consume (internalize) sound doctrine and to learn of God. Even the sermons are all about us and how great we are and how great a reward we will have.

7:7 Should ye not hear the words which the LORD hath cried by the former prophets [Should we not teach the sound doctrines of the whole Word of God, to sincerely repent and follow the Eternal to keep and live by his every Word?]**, when Jerusalem was inhabited and in prosperity, and the cities thereof round about her, when men inhabited the south and the plain?

Sincere repentance from all sin and living by every Word of God is the way to prosperity, peace and eternal life!

7:8 And the word of the LORD came unto Zechariah, saying, **7:9** Thus speaketh the LORD of hosts, saying, **Execute true judgment, and shew mercy and compassions every man to his brother: 7:10 And oppress not the widow, nor the fatherless, the stranger, nor the poor; and let none of you imagine evil against his brother in your heart.**

Our unrepentant sins will bring strong correction from Jesus Christ upon us

Brethren, the wrath of Christ came down upon them in times past for their sins against the Word of God; and the New Covenant Ekklesia are supposed to have the Spirit of God and are supposed to know better!

How much greater will his wrath be upon us for committing the very same sins?

7:11 But they refused to hearken, and pulled away the shoulder, and stopped their ears, that they should not hear.

7:12 Yea, they made their hearts as an adamant stone, lest they should hear the law, and the words which the LORD of hosts hath sent in his spirit by the former prophets: therefore came a great wrath from the LORD of hosts.

The soon coming tribulation is the climax of God's correction upon his wayward people: BOTH physical AND spiritual Israel/Judah and after them, all the nations.

Physical Israel was and will again be corrected and we of today's Spiritual Ekklesia who are not zealous to learn, to keep and to teach the whole Word of God, will also be corrected and our organizational idols will be destroyed.

7:13 Therefore it is come to pass, that as he cried, **and they would not hear** [the Word of God to learn, keep and teach it]; so they cried, and I would not hear, saith the LORD of hosts:

7:14 But I scattered them with a whirlwind among all the nations whom they knew not. Thus the land was desolate after them, that no man passed through nor returned: for they laid the pleasant land desolate.

God is not a respecter of persons, and today he will treat those lukewarm and lax for his Word just as he did in the days of old: With a great correction!

Yet, he is a merciful God who deeply loves his people, and he will quickly forgive us when we have sincerely repented and learned the lessons that God wants to teach us by afflicting us.

Our espoused Husband is jealous because of all our adulteries with our idols of men and false traditions; and he will correct his wayward people. Yet when they sincerely repent and turn to him; he will come to gather up his bride tenderly into his arms and taking her to the Wedding Feast in heaven (Rev 15, Rev 7:9 and Rev 19), and will then return with them to bring peace to the whole earth.

Zechariah 8

The coming of Christ, and the millennial Kingdom

Zion and Jerusalem are a type of the spiritual bride, being often unfaithful; but in the end becoming as full of godliness as the sea is full of water.

> **Revelation 21:2** And I John saw the holy city, new Jerusalem, coming down from God out of heaven, prepared as a bride adorned for her husband.
>
> **21:3** And I heard a great voice out of heaven saying, Behold, the tabernacle of God is with men, and he will dwell with them, and they shall be his people, and God himself shall be with them, and be their God.
>
> **21:4** And God shall wipe away all tears from their eyes; and there shall be no more death, neither sorrow, nor crying, neither shall there be any more pain: for the former things are passed away.

Zechariah 8:1 Again the word of the LORD of hosts came to me, saying,

When our affliction has resulted in our sincere repentance, then the Eternal will rise up to deliver us.

8:2 Thus saith the LORD of hosts; **I was jealous for Zion with great jealousy, and I was jealous for her with great fury.**

Jesus [Hebrew: Yeshua] will come to rule the earth.

8:3 Thus saith the LORD; **I am returned unto Zion, and will dwell in the midst of Jerusalem: and Jerusalem shall be called a city of truth; and the** [Temple Mount; and the government of God] **mountain of the LORD of hosts the holy mountain.**

During the tribulation we may despair but we can trust in the promise of God. Jerusalem [representing both physical and spiritual Israel] will yet be delivered and built up in godliness!

8:4 Thus saith the LORD of hosts; **There shall yet old men and old women dwell in the streets of Jerusalem, and every man with his staff in his hand for very age. 8:5 And the streets of the city shall be full of boys and girls playing in the streets thereof.**

There is nothing too hard for our Master to accomplish! What is amazing and unbelievable to man is obvious and true to Almighty God! He will accomplish his purpose!

8:6 Thus saith the LORD of hosts; If it be marvellous in the eyes of the remnant of this people in these days, should it also be marvellous in mine eyes? saith the LORD of hosts.

When we are in correction and we repent and lament for our sins our deliverance might seem far off and impossible to us; yet there is nothing too hard for God the Father and Jesus Christ our Lord Husband, to accomplish!

When Christ comes Judah and Israel will return to their land, which is a type of Spiritual Israel returning to their God and entering the Promised Land of eternal life!

8:7 Thus saith the LORD of hosts; Behold, I will save my people from the east country, and from the west country; **8:8** And **I will bring them, and they shall dwell in the midst of Jerusalem: and they shall be my people, and I will be their God, in truth and in righteousness.**

The people who returned from ancient Babylon were encouraged to build the physical temple; and this was only a type of the building of the Ezekiel Temple; and both are a type of the building of a Spiritual Temple of godliness in humanity!

When Christ comes the nations will seek out the Eternal and will contribute to building the Ezekiel Temple. These physical temples are types of the collective bride, the Spiritual Temple in whom the Spirit of God dwells!

Today, the brethren MUST be about the business of building our personal dwelling place for God's Spirit; building ourselves into a Temple of the Spirit of the Living Eternal God!

We MUST sincerely repent and turn to our espoused Husband, Jesus Christ, in enthusiastic zeal for him and to live by every Word of God!

We MUST love God the Father and the Son Jesus Christ like No Other; loving them enough to obey them and to do everything we can to please them!

And if we love the Son we will love the Father also.

Let us therefore Be Strong to turn to our Mighty Deliverer to Learn, to Keep, to Teach and to live by every Word of God! Let us be STRONG in the Eternal to purge out all leaven of sin and to internalize the whole Word of God, to build up ourselves with God's power, into a fitting dwelling place for the Holy Spirit of our Mighty God!

8:9 Thus saith the LORD of hosts; **Let your hands be strong, ye that hear in these days these words by the mouth of the prophets**, which were in the day that the foundation of the house of the LORD of hosts was laid, that the temple might be built.

Today we have departed from the Word of God, therefore there has been NO spiritual growth these many years. God will now correct us in the furnace of affliction if we do not quickly repent.

These ancients were impoverished physically because they neglected the building of God's physical temple. Today we are spiritually impoverished because we neglect building the Spiritual Temple of the Holy Spirit, rejecting truth to cleave to our false traditions of men.

8:10 For before these days there was no hire [money for wages] for man, nor any hire for beast; neither was there any peace to him that went out or came in because of the affliction: for I set all men every one against his neighbour.

Our Lord will bless us if we turn to him, and if we dedicate ourselves to live by every Word of God we shall truly become his Spiritual Temple, God dwelling in us; but if we do not destroy all sin from ourselves, God will surely correct us.

1 Corinthians 3:17 If any man defile the temple of God, him shall God destroy; for the temple of God is holy, which temple ye are.

In that day when Christ returns with his resurrected chosen, he will bring a blessing for ll those who sincerely repent on the earth (Joel 2:28-29).

Zechariah 8:11 But now I will not be unto the residue of this people as in the former days, saith the LORD of hosts. **8:12** For the seed shall be prosperous; the vine shall give her fruit, and the ground shall give her increase, and the heavens shall give their dew; and I will cause the remnant of this people to possess all these things.

The seed is a type of the Word of God which will be prosperous and bring much fruit. The true vine, Jesus Christ, will have many branches bringing forth much fruit (John 15). The dew of heaven is a type of the pouring out of the Holy Spirit of God upon the sincerely repentant.

8:13 And it shall come to pass, that as **ye were a curse among the heathen, O house of Judah, and house of Israel; so will I save you, and ye shall be a blessing**: fear not, but let your hands be strong.

Just as physical and spiritual Israel were a curse upon the earth when they lived contrary to the Word of God; when they turn to God in sincere repentance they shall become a real blessing on the earth.

When they become zealous to Learn, to Keep and to Teach the whole Word of God; they shall become a true Shining Light of example to the earth!

8:14 For thus saith the LORD of hosts; As I thought to punish you, when your fathers provoked me to wrath, saith the LORD of hosts, and I repented not: **8:15** So again have I thought in these days to do well unto Jerusalem and to the house of Judah: fear ye not.

After our correction and sincere repentance, Jesus Christ will come to his people with a blessing! This is speaking of spiritual Israel/Judah as well as the physical nations.

8:16 These are the things that ye shall do; Speak ye every man the truth to his neighbour; execute the judgment of truth and peace in your gates: 8:17 And let none of you imagine evil in your hearts against his neighbour; and love no false oath: for all these are things that I hate, saith the LORD.

Let spiritual and physical Israel/Judah turn away from the false traditions and errors of the past and embrace and live by every Word of God!

8:18 And the word of the LORD of hosts came unto me, saying, **8:19** Thus saith the LORD of hosts; The fast of the fourth month, and the fast of the fifth, and the fast of the seventh, and the fast of the tenth, shall be to the house of Judah joy and gladness, and cheerful feasts; therefore love the truth and peace.

Yeshua Messiah [Jesus Christ] promises to turn our mourning into rejoicing!

The ancient fasts of the captivities and the destruction of the physical temples and our fasts of sincere repentance will be turned into joy when Almighty God has delivered us.

Then all the earth will seek the Eternal with a whole heart!

8:20 Thus saith the LORD of hosts; It shall yet come to pass, that there shall come people, and the inhabitants of many cities: **8:21** And the inhabitants of one city shall go to another, saying, **Let us go speedily to pray before the LORD, and to seek the LORD of hosts: I will go also. 8:22** Yea, **many people and strong nations shall come to seek the LORD of hosts in Jerusalem, and to pray before the LORD.** [YHVH]

All nations and all languages shall turn to the Eternal in wholehearted sincerity! Oh, what a glorious time!

8:23 Thus saith the LORD of hosts; **In those days it shall come to pass, that ten men shall take hold out of all languages of the nations,** even shall take hold of the skirt of him that is a Jew [spiritually faithful to God], saying, **We will go with you: for we have heard that God is with you.**

God's Spirit will be poured out on all flesh (Joel 2:28)

Zechariah 9

That day will surely come when Christ will come WITH the resurrected godly faithful and Israel/Judah will repent and wholeheartedly turn to God; then the knowledge of God will fill Jerusalem and spread out from there to fill the whole earth!

Then Damascus will have peace and shall be subject to God.

Zechariah 9:1 The burden of the word of the LORD in the land of Hadrach, [Syria] and Damascus [In the millennium Damascus and Syria will turn to God and will be at peace with Israel.] shall be the rest [peace] thereof: **when the eyes of man [ALL humanity], as of all the tribes of Israel, shall be toward the LORD**.

In the millennium the northern border of Israel will be at Homs on the Euphrates, and will extend from the Euphrates to Lebanon. United Israel under the resurrected king David will dominate Tyre and Lebanon as well as Syria.

9:2 And Hamath also shall border thereby; Tyrus, and Zidon, though it be very wise.

Lebanon in spite of their political wisdom will be within the borders of Israel along with Damascus and Hamath [modern Homs].

9:3 And Tyrus did build herself a strong hold, and heaped up silver as the dust, and fine gold as the mire of the streets. **9:4** Behold, the LORD will cast her out, and he will smite her power in the sea; and she shall be devoured with fire.

During the tribulation Tyre will become very rich through trade with Babylon [Europe] and shipping commerce. The wealth of Tyre will be destroyed and the city burned with fire in the last year by the invading armies of Asia. Those who remain will be deported to India (Joel 3:8).

The people of Gaza are the descendants of the Philistines and are not Arabs or Palestinians. Today the one million true Gazans have been joined by about 800,000 Palestinian refugees from the Jewish State.

Gaza, which will join the Psalm 83 confederation against Judah when the Extremist Settler Movement overthrows the coming peace deal; will be defeated and occupied by the coming Asian armies and the pride of the Philistines will be crushed. Then the people of Gaza will turn to accept the Messiah at his coming and will become a peaceful tributary of Israel.

9:5 Ashkelon shall see it, and fear; Gaza also shall see it, and be very sorrowful, and Ekron; for her expectation shall be ashamed; and the king shall perish from Gaza, and Ashkelon shall not be inhabited. **9:6** And a bastard shall dwell in Ashdod, and I will cut off the pride of the Philistines.

The words of blood [words of HATE] shall perish and the remnant of the Philistines will turn to the Eternal in sincerity of heart when Christ comes.

9:7 And I will take away his blood [violent words] out of his mouth, and his abominations from between his teeth: but **he that remaineth, even he, shall be for our God,** and **he shall be as a governor in Judah** [Gaza shall be a province of Judah with its own local governor], and Ekron as a Jebusite [The Jebusites of Jerusalem who anciently became subject to Judah].

Christ will dwell at Jerusalem the city of the Ezekiel Temple, and all Israel will be protected by Messiah the King!

9:8 And I will encamp about mine house because of the army, because of him that passeth by, and because of him that returneth: and **no oppressor shall pass through them any more:** for now have I seen with mine eyes.

The Coming of the King of kings

A prophecy of Christ entering Jerusalem on the foal of a donkey

9:9 Rejoice greatly, O daughter of Zion; shout, O daughter of Jerusalem: behold, thy King cometh unto thee: he is just, and having salvation; lowly, and riding upon an ass, and upon a colt the foal of an ass.

The armies of the enemies of Ephraim [representing all Israel] and Jerusalem, will be dismantled by Christ; and Messiah will bring a millennial Sabbath of peace to all Israel and to the whole earth.

9:10 And I will cut off the chariot [war machine] from Ephraim, and the horse [war horse, military vehicles] from Jerusalem, and the battle bow [military weaponry] shall be cut off: and **he shall speak peace unto the heathen** [all the nations]: **and his** [Christ's] **dominion shall be from sea even to sea, and from the river even to the ends of the earth.**

War will be banished and the dominion of Messiah will extend over all the earth; then through the blood of the New Covenant sacrifice of Jesus Christ, and all peoples who sincerely repent will be delivered.

9:11 As for thee [the dead will come forth from the graves] also, by the blood of thy covenant I have sent forth thy prisoners [the Chosen Elect will be delivered from the shackles of death] out of the pit [the grave] wherein is no water.

Those who have been faithful and have overcome and died in hope [FAITH]; will receive a good reward and eternal life.

9:12 Turn you to the strong hold, ye prisoners of hope [the saints who lived and died in hope will be delivered the prison of the grave]: even to day do I declare that I will render double [the godly faithful will have a double reward] unto thee;

Greece is to be punished for their complicity and alliance with the New Europe against Judah; and the captives being held by Greece will be delivered.

9:13 When I have bent Judah for me, filled the bow with Ephraim, and **raised up thy sons, O Zion, against thy sons, O Greece,** and made thee as the sword of a mighty man.

9:14 And the LORD shall be seen over them, and his arrow shall go forth as the lightning: and the LORD God shall blow the trumpet, and shall go with whirlwinds of the south.

9:15 The LORD of hosts shall defend them [Messiah the Christ will rise up to deliver his people]; and they shall devour, and subdue with sling stones; and they shall drink, and make a noise as through wine; and they shall be filled like bowls, and as the corners of the altar.

The Day of Deliverance

9:16 And the LORD their God shall save them in that day as the flock of his people: for they shall be as the stones [precious to God like jewels] of a crown, lifted up as an ensign upon his land. **9:17** For how great is his goodness, and how great is his beauty!

Then the famine of the land and of the Word of God will be lifted, and the people will eat and drink in plenty. This is analogous to the famine of the Word of God being lifted and all the people eating and drinking very deeply of the whole Word of God.

. . . corn [grain, food] shall make the young men cheerful, and new wine the maids.

Zechariah 10

Let us all pray for the rain of God's Spirit to be poured out on all the earth (Joel 2:28).

Zechariah 10:1 Ask ye of the LORD rain in the time of the latter rain; so the LORD shall make bright clouds, and give them showers of rain, to every one grass in the field.

God's anger against the shepherds, the leaders and elders of today's Spiritual Ekklesia (Ezekiel 34).

There is in particular a great anger against those who are supposed to know better and are supposed to: Cry Aloud and show the people their sins in this latter day (Isaiah 58:1)!

God's anger is waxed very hot against today's Spiritual Ekklesia and their business model outreach, because they refuse to present the true Gospel of warning, sincere repentance, and the Gospel of salvation through living as Jesus Christ lived; BY every Word of God the Father (Mat 4:4)]; which is the ONLY way into the Kingdom of God.

Speaking of today's church of God elders and leaders which have made idols out of themselves:

10:2 For the idols [many church leaders and elders] have spoken vanity, and the diviners [self-proclaimed apostles and prophets] have seen a lie, and have told false dreams; they comfort in vain: therefore they went their way as a flock, they [the flock] were troubled, because there was no [godly] shepherd.

The national and church of God leaders and elders are like goats, each one going his own way and not living by every Word of God, while the godly faithful follow God the Father and Jesus Christ!

10:3 Mine anger was kindled against the shepherds, and I punished the goats: for the LORD of hosts hath visited his flock the house [BOTH physical and spiritual] of Judah, and hath made them as his goodly horse in the battle.

Messiah the Christ will rebuke today's evil shepherds and deliver the people from them.

The True Good Shepherd

The true good shepherd, Jesus Christ, will destroy every oppressor in the tribulation, including the present church of God leaders and elders, if they refuse to repent. When Messiah comes he will raise up the faithful of spiritual Judah and Israel under His Banner and destroy every oppressor in the earth.

10:4 Out of him [Judah] came forth the corner [Stone], out of him the nail, out of him the battle bow, out of him [he shall destroy] every oppressor together.

When Christ comes with his resurrected chosen, physical Judah and Israel will not only be repentant and accept Christ to live by every Word of God, they will rise up and join Christ to fight with him against the oppressors as a part of the army of the Lord.

10:5 And they shall be as mighty men, which tread down their enemies in the mire of the streets in the battle: and they shall fight, because the LORD is with them, and the riders on horses [soldiers with their war machines] shall be confounded [defeated, overcome].

When Christ comes all Israel will sincerely repent and the remnant of Israel shall be saved.

10:6 And I will strengthen the house of Judah, and I will save the house of Joseph, and I will bring them again to place them [in their land]; for I have mercy upon them: and they shall be as though I had not cast them off: for I am the LORD their God, and will hear [their cries of repentance and calls for deliverance] them.

In the time of Christ's coming all Israel will turn to accept and rejoice at the coming of Messiah the Christ, the KING of kings and teh High Priest of our Salvation!

10:7 And they of Ephraim [the Anglo Saxon people] shall be like a mighty man, and their heart shall rejoice [at their deliverance] as through wine: yea, their children shall see it, and be glad; **their heart shall rejoice in the LORD**.

10:8 I will hiss [against the enemies] for them, and gather them; for I have redeemed them: and they shall increase as they have increased.

The people of Israel/Judah will remember the Eternal in their captivity, and they will turn to him in mass repentance when Messiah comes.

10:9 And I will sow them among the people: and they shall remember me in far countries; and they shall live with their children, and turn again [to sincerely repent and turn to a zeal for God to live by God's Word].

10:10 I will bring them again also out of the land of Egypt, and gather them out of Assyria; and **I will bring them into the land of Gilead and Lebanon**; and place shall not be found for them [there will be no space for their great numbers].

Ephraim and Israel will be given the land of the ten tribes and Lebanon/Syria, and there will still not be enough land for these repentant survivors.

10:11 And he shall pass through the sea with affliction, and shall smite the waves in the sea, and all the deeps of the river [the Euphrates where ancient Assyria was located Rev 16:12] shall dry up: and the pride of Assyria shall be brought down, and the sceptre of Egypt shall depart away.

10:12 And I will strengthen them in the LORD; and they shall walk up and down in his name, saith the LORD.

Zechariah 11

When Christ comes a united Israel under the resurrected king David will rule over Gaza, Lebanon, Syria, Jordan and Turkey as tributary states.

The trees falling are emblematic of the nations falling. Lebanon, Syria, Jordan, Gaza and Bashan [Golan] will fall first to the Asian armies, and then after Christ comes with the resurrected godly the remnant of those nations will be subject to the resurrected king David and a reunited Israel/Judah will dominate the entire Middle East.

Zechariah 11:1 Open thy doors, **O Lebanon,** that the fire may devour thy cedars [the strength of Lebanon as symbolized by the cedars] .

11:2 Howl, fir tree; for the cedar is fallen; because the mighty are spoiled: howl, O ye oaks of Bashan [Golan Plateau]; for the forest of the vintage [the mighty men and strength of these nations will be brought down by the armies of Asia] is come down.

This speaks of the shepherds [leaders] of the modern nation of Jordan.

11:3 There is a voice of the howling of the shepherds; for their glory is spoiled: a voice of the roaring of young lions; for **the pride of Jordan is spoiled**.

Messiah will deliver the flock of Israel who are captive and he will give them the wealth of their oppressors.

The oppressor's will be turned against one another and Israel will be delivered.

11:4 Thus saith the LORD my God; Feed the flock of the slaughter [the nations of Israel]; **11:5** Whose possessors slay them, and hold themselves not guilty: and they that sell them say, Blessed be the LORD; for I am rich: and their own shepherds pity them not.

11:6 For I will no more pity the inhabitants of the land, saith the LORD: but, lo, I will deliver the men every one into his neighbour's hand, and into the hand of his king: and they shall smite the land, and out of their hand I will not deliver them.

Beauty

The Mosaic Marriage Covenant between Israel and Messiah the Christ is here called Beauty; the death of the Husband of Israel broke the Mosaic Marriage Covenant [Beauty] between him and Israel/Judah.

Zechariah 11:7 And I will feed the flock of slaughter, even you, O poor of the flock. And I took unto me two staves; the one I called Beauty, and the other I called Bands; and I fed the flock.

11:8 Three shepherds also I cut off [from their authority over Israel/Judah] in one month [the first month]; and **my soul lothed them, and their soul also abhorred me.**

The Mosaic Covenant ended with the death of the Husband of Israel and Moses Seat was transferred to "That Prophet" Jesus Christ, at his resurrection! Three shepherds were cut off at the time that the Mosaic Marriage Covenant ended with the death of Israel's Husband.

This prophecy was fulfilled in the first century, with the cutting off of the Mosaic Covenant shepherds of Israel/Judah: who were **the Levitical Priesthood, the Scribes** [who became the modern Karaites] **and the Pharisees** [which developed into today's Rabbins]. These leaders in the first century rejected Messiah and God the Father for their own traditions, and were therefore rejected by God.

The Mosaic Covenant being ended by the murder of the Husband, the resurrected Yeshua [Jesus] was freed from the physical Mosaic Marriage Covenant to physical Israel/Judah, and formally espoused himself in a New Covenant (Jer 31, Ezek 36:26) to a spiritual people of a spiritual Israel who were zealous to keep the whole Word of God.

11:9 Then said I [to the widowed Mosaic Israel/Judah], I will not feed you [support you as your husband any longer]: that that dieth, let it die; and that that is to be cut off, let it be cut off [God's Mosaic Covenant ended with the cutting off of the husband Yeshua [Jesus] Christ]; and let the rest eat every one the flesh of another [depend on themselves].

The Mosaic Marriage Covenant between physical Israel/Judah and Yahweh which was made at Sinai, was BROKEN by the death of the Husband of Israel, Yahweh; the Being who gave up his Godhood to be made flesh as Jesus Christ.

11:10 And I took my staff, even Beauty [the Beautiful Mosaic Covenant that the people would not keep], and cut it asunder, **that I might break my covenant** [the Mosaic Marriage Covenant] **which I had made with all the people.**

When Christ was crucified those poor in spirit, humble, [as opposed to the proud and self-centered] and submissive to the whole Word of God which God the Father called to himself through Christ, entered into a spiritual espousal to full unity with Messiah on a spiritual level in a New Marriage Covenant promised in Jeremiah 31:31 and:

> **Ezekiel 36:24** For I will take you from among the heathen, and gather you out of all countries, and will bring you into your own land.
>
> **36:25** Then will I sprinkle clean water [the Water of the Word and Spirit of God Ephesians 5:26] upon you, and ye shall be clean: from all your filthiness, and from all your idols, will I cleanse you.
>
> **36:26** A new heart also will I give you, and a new spirit will I put within you: and I will take away the stony heart out of your flesh, and I will give you an heart of flesh.
>
> **36:27** And **I will put my spirit within you**, and cause you to walk in my statutes, and ye shall keep my judgments, and do them. **36:28** And ye shall dwell in the land that I gave to your fathers; and ye shall be my people, and I will be your God.

This is also a prophecy of spiritual Israel, that the proud and self-centered in the Spiritual Ekklesia will not enter into the marriage of the Lamb at the resurrection.

Only those spiritually humble enough to exalt the whole Word of God, and to follow the Lamb whithersoever he goeth (Rev 14:4); will be in the resurrection to spirit and receive eternal life as a part of the collective bride of the New Marriage Covenant!

Zechariah 11:11 And it was broken in that day [The Mosaic Marriage Covenant "Beauty" was ended on the day of the death of the Husband of Israel]: and so the poor of the flock [the poor in spirit (humble before God)] that waited upon me knew that it was the word of the LORD.

The following verse clinches this prophecy of "Beauty" being about the Mosaic Marriage Covenant with Christ.

11:12 And I said unto them, If ye think good, give me my price; and if not, forbear. **So they weighed for my price thirty pieces of silver. 11:13** And the LORD said unto me, Cast it unto the potter: a goodly price that I was prised at of them. And I took the thirty pieces of silver, and cast them to the potter in the house of the LORD.

Brethren, the three shepherds that were cut off in the first month at Passover were **the Levitical Priesthood, the Scribes** [who became the modern Karaites] **and the Pharisees** [which developed into today's Rabbins]: And no, NONE of these three shepherds sit in Moses seat today.

It is the resurrected Jesus Christ who now sits in Moses seat and who has replaced the priesthood of Aaron with the High Priesthood of Melchizedek!

BANDS; the brotherhood of Israel and Judah

11:14 Then I cut asunder mine other staff, even Bands, that **I might break the brotherhood between Judah and Israel.**

The brotherhood between Israel and Judah was broken immediately after the death of Solomon (1 Kings 11:11)].

The foolish shepherds are described; which exactly describes the leaders and elders [shepherds] of today's Spiritual Ekklesia.

11:15 And the LORD said unto me, Take unto thee yet the instruments of a foolish shepherd.

Rehoboam as an example of bad spiritual shepherds

11:16 For, lo, I will raise up a shepherd [Rehoboam of Judah 1 Kings 12] in the land, which shall not visit those that be cut off, neither shall seek the young one, nor heal that that is broken, nor feed that that standeth still: but he shall eat the flesh of the fat, and tear their claws in pieces. [rend the sheep in pieces for personal advantage]

Spiritually the shepherd who does not faithfully give the flock the solid meat of sound doctrine and diligent instructions to zealously and without compromise live by every Word of God: Is a FOOLISH shepherd and will be destroyed by the Eternal.

11:17 Woe to the idol shepherd that leaveth the flock! [To seek his own advantage, and does not teach a passionate zeal for the whole word of God.] the sword shall be upon his arm [against him], and upon his right eye: his arm shall be clean dried up, and his right eye shall be utterly darkened [blind].

The next three chapters are about the last days and the coming of Christ.

The Pharisees [Rabbins] do NOT sit in Moses Seat today! Today the resurrected Jesus Christ sits in the seat of authority over the New Covenant people! The seat of spiritual authority has been restored to the original Melchizedek and now belongs to "That Prophet" Jesus Christ and the Word of God!

There are many who claim that the modern Pharisees or Rabbins have authority over the Calendar and perhaps other issues; then they deny the Rabbins in dating the Passover and Pentecost, and refuse to follow the Rabbins in much else!

Which is it gentlemen? Do we bow to the falsely supposed and nonexistent authority of those who reject our LORD; or do we accept the authority of the Word of God and Jesus Christ; the true spiritual High Priest of the New Covenant!

The choice is before you brethren: Will you follow idols of men, or will you follow the Lamb [the Word] of God?

Zechariah 12

The Day of The Lord can be the time when Babylon [the new Europe] and the nations of the East are gathered at Jerusalem, at the coming of Jesus Christ.

A prophecy of Jerusalem at the coming of Messiah the Christ: The prophecy begins by exalting the Eternal and then quickly turns to Jerusalem

Zechariah 12:1 The burden of the word of the LORD **for Israel,** saith the LORD, which stretcheth forth the heavens, and layeth the foundation of the earth, and formeth the spirit of man within him.

The prophet says that many people will be gathered against Jerusalem at the day of the Lord and they will all be destroyed when Christ comes to Jerusalem to save Jerusalem and Judah.

12:2 Behold, I will make Jerusalem a cup of trembling unto all the people round about, **when they shall be in the siege both against Judah and against Jerusalem. 12:3** And **in that day** will I make Jerusalem a burdensome stone for all people: all that burden themselves with it shall be cut in pieces, though all the people of the earth be gathered together against it.

In the day of Messiah the King of kings, he will smite all nations who are gathered against Jerusalem to battle.

12:4 In that day, saith the LORD, I will smite every [war] horse with astonishment, and his rider with madness: and I will open mine eyes upon the house of Judah, and will smite every [warrior and war machine] horse of the people with blindness.

There will yet be Jews remaining in Jerusalem who will turn to him and rejoice in him: Rising up to turn on their oppressors with the help of the Deliverer, Messiah the King!

When Christ comes and stands on the Mount of Olives in that day, the leaders of Judah and Jerusalem will rejoice at their deliverance and they shall rise up to fight in the city and across Judea; as the Eternal destroys the armies fighting against Jerusalem.

12:5 And the governors of Judah shall say in their heart, The inhabitants of Jerusalem shall **be my strength in the LORD of hosts their God**.

Christ will destroy the massed armies and Judah shall sincerely repent and turn to embrace the one that they had pierced, and Judah will fight in that day against the wicked occupiers of Jerusalem and Judea and their attackers.

12:6 In that day will **I make the governors of Judah like an hearth of fire among the wood, and like a torch of fire in a sheaf; and they shall devour all the people round about, on the right hand and on the left: and Jerusalem shall be inhabited again in her own place, even in Jerusalem.**

The people of Judah will be saved first and they shall rise up to rejoice in him and they will fight their oppressors by the power of their God; they will be reunited with the ten tribes and the broken Bands between Judah and Israel will be healed.

12:7 The LORD also shall save the tents of Judah first, that the glory of the house of David and the glory of the inhabitants of Jerusalem do not magnify themselves against Judah.

When Messiah the Christ comes and Judah repents and turns to him; Jesus Christ will destroy the armies gathered to fight at Jerusalem and he will then empower the people of Judah to rise up in the strength of Almighty God to mop up and drive the nations out of the land.

12:8 In that day shall the LORD defend the inhabitants of Jerusalem; and he that is feeble among them at that day shall be as David; and the house of David shall be as God, as the angel of the LORD before them.

Messiah will raise up Judah to defeat all the nations that have tormented Judah.

12:9 And it shall come to pass in that day, that **I will seek to destroy all the nations that come against Jerusalem.**

The Repentance of Judah/Israel and the great mourning over their sin!

A great repentance will come; and Judah and all Israel will accept the Messiah the Christ and be brought into the spiritual New Covenant of Jeremiah 31 and Ezekiel 36:26. Then both Judah and Israel will be united with God and being of like mind they will be united with each other again. Repenting before God and being reconciled to God will heal the broken Bands between Judah and Israel.

Brethren this is the only way that the broken bands between the assemblies of today's Spiritual Ekklesia can and will be healed!

Every person needs to sincerely repent of idolizing the false traditions of men and turn to live by every Word of God; then every person will be reconciled to God, which is the ONLY foundation for true godly unity with one another!

12:10 And **I will pour upon the house of David, and upon the inhabitants of Jerusalem, the spirit** [the Holy Spirit, Joel 2:28] **of grace and of supplications: and they shall look upon me whom they have pierced, and they shall mourn for him, as one mourneth for his only son, and shall be in bitterness for him, as one that is in bitterness for his firstborn.**

12:11 In that day shall there be a great mourning in Jerusalem, as the mourning of Hadadrimmon in the valley of Megiddon.

12:12 And the land shall mourn [repent], **every family apart**; the family of the house of David apart, and their wives apart; the family of the house of Nathan apart, and their wives apart;

12:13 The family of the house of Levi apart, and their wives apart; the family of Shimei apart, and their wives apart; **12:14** All the families that remain, every family apart, and their wives apart.

After Judah and Israel repent; all humanity will also repent and turn to live by every Word of God. Then justice and peace shall cover the earth!

> **Habakkuk 2:14** For the earth shall be filled with the knowledge of the glory of the Lord, as the waters cover the sea.

Zechariah 13

A fountain of pure water will spring forth from the Temple Mount, which is representative of the water of life, the Holy Spirit being given freely to the people in the New Covenant of Jeremiah 31:31, Ezekiel 36:26-28 and Joel 2:28!

Zechariah 13:1 In that day there shall be a fountain opened to the house of David and to the inhabitants of Jerusalem for [to cleanse from sincerely repented sin and bring holiness] sin and for uncleanness.

Satan and all evil spirits will be removed and restrained! No more will men deceive people away from God to follow idols of men!

13:2 And it shall come to pass in that day, saith the LORD of hosts, that I will cut off the names of the idols out of the land, and they shall no more be remembered: and also I will cause the [false] prophets and the unclean spirit to pass out of the land.

No deceitful teaching contrary to the Word of God [as is done even in the Ekklesia today], will be permitted. Even those closest to them will reject them! Today the assemblies are FULL of false prophets and false teachers, teaching their own ways contrary to the Word of God; while falsely claiming to represent God as they lead people away from any zeal for God to follow idols of men.

13:3 And it shall come to pass, that when any shall yet prophesy [falsely and teach false doctrine], then his father and his mother that begat him shall say unto him, Thou shalt not live; for thou speakest lies in the name of the LORD: and his father and his mother that begat him shall thrust him through when he prophesieth.

The false religious leaders and deceitful elders in today's Spiritual Ekklesia, as well as all other false teachers will be ashamed of their false teachings

13:4 And it shall come to pass in that day, that the [false] prophets shall be ashamed every one of his [false] vision, when he hath prophesied [and his prophecies have failed]; neither shall they wear a rough garment [pretend to be humble or godly] to deceive:

13:5 But [today's false prophets will repent and deny their previous claims of greatness] he shall say, I am no prophet, I am an husbandman; for man taught me to keep cattle from my youth.

Jesus Christ will forgive his sincerely repentant people and those who hated him and have sincerely repented will become his friends.

13:6 And one shall say unto him, What are these wounds in thine hands? Then he shall answer, **Those with which I was wounded in the house of my friends.**

An inset prophecy of Jesus Christ who was smitten, and God's flock scattered. Yet he is risen and will save God's faithful little ones.

13:7 Awake, O sword, against my shepherd, and against the man that is my fellow, saith the LORD of hosts: smite the shepherd, and the sheep shall be scattered: and I will turn mine hand upon the little ones.

This correction and humbling will begin with the great tribulation from which only a third of Israel/Judah will be delivered alive.

13:8 And it shall come to pass, that in all the land, saith the LORD, two parts therein shall be cut off and die; but **the third shall be left therein**.

That third will suffer terribly and they will be corrected and molded and humbled and brought to a sincere wholehearted repentance. This speaks of physical Israel, AND today's Spiritual Ekklesia.

13:9 And **I will bring the third part through the fire, and will refine them as silver is refined, and will try them as gold is tried: [then] they shall call on my name, and I will hear them: I will say, It is my people: and they shall say, The LORD is my God.**

Zechariah 14

The Day of the Lord's coming

The armies of Europe and her allies of Psalm 83 will take Jerusalem at the start of the tribulation and hold it for 42 months.

Zechariah 14:1 Behold, the day of the Lord cometh, and thy spoil shall be divided in the midst of thee.

14:2 For I will gather all nations against Jerusalem to battle; and the city [the whole city of Jerusalem will be trodden down of the Gentiles [the New Federal Europe and the nations of Psalm 83] for 42 months Rev. 11:2] shall be taken, and the houses rifled, and the women ravished; and **half of the city** [half of the Jewish population will be removed from Jerusalem] **shall go forth into captivity, and the residue of the people shall not be cut off from the city**.

Then the armies of Asia will gather outside the city and at the end of 42 months Christ will come with his resurrected chosen and deliver Jerusalem and Judah first!

14:3 Then shall the Lord go forth, and fight against those nations, as when he fought in the day of battle.

Christ will come WITH his resurrected chosen (Jude 1:14) and 144,000 of them will stand on the Mount of Olives. Then a great earthquake will split the Mount and the people, the women and children, will flee the battle. See an explanation of the 144,000.

14:4 And **his feet shall stand in that day upon the mount of Olives,** which is before Jerusalem on the east, and the mount of Olives shall cleave in the midst thereof toward the east and toward the west, and there shall be a very great valley; and half of the mountain shall remove toward the north, and half of it toward the south.

14:5 And ye shall flee to the valley of the mountains; for the valley of the mountains shall reach unto Azal [the king's (Uzziah's) garden at the base of the southernmost point of the Mount of Olives *Nahal Atzal* (נחל אצל)]: yea, ye shall flee, like as ye fled from before the earthquake in the days of Uzziah king of Judah: and the LORD my God shall come, and all the saints with thee.

This day will be one of dark cloud and the gloominess of battle, and the light of the Eternal shall illuminate the night and the day.

14:6 And it shall come to pass in that day, that the light shall not be clear, nor dark: **14:7** But it shall be one day which shall be known to the LORD, not day, nor night: but it shall come to pass, **that at evening time it shall be light.**

When Christ comes there will be a great earthquake and a spring of water will rise up out of the Temple Mount; then our LORD will build the Ezekiel Temple and the Altar will be built over the spring of water. This will indicate that the application of the sacrifice of Christ will bring the Living Waters of the Holy Spirit from God.

14:8 And it shall be in that day, that **living waters shall go out from** [the third Temple] **Jerusalem**; half of them toward the former sea, and half of them toward the hinder sea: in summer and in winter shall it be.

These physical waters are a picture of the flowing of the Living Waters of the Holy Spirit from the Altar of God in the heavenly Temple down upon all flesh (Joel 2:28).

> **Ezekiel 47** Afterward he brought me again unto the door of the house [the Ezekiel Temple]; and, behold, waters issued out from under the threshold of the house eastward: for the forefront of the house stood toward the east, and the waters came down from under

from the right side of the house, at the south side of the altar. **Read the whole chapter.**

Zechariah 14:9 And **the LORD shall be king over all the earth**: in that day shall there be one LORD [all humanity will worship YHVH (God the Father and the Son) and there will be no other God worshiped by man in all the earth], and his name one.

14:10 All the land shall be turned as a plain from Geba to Rimmon south of Jerusalem: and it shall be lifted up [Jerusalem will be lifted up as a high plateau, so that Jerusalem will be exalted above the surrounding land], and inhabited in her place, from Benjamin's gate unto the place of the first gate, unto the corner gate, and from the tower of Hananeel unto the king's winepresses.

14:11 And **men shall dwell in it, and there shall be no more utter destruction; but Jerusalem shall be safely inhabited.**

The armies of Asia which come up against the army of the New Federal Europe based at Jerusalem will be consumed by Christ at his coming.

> **Revelation 14:19** And the angel thrust in his sickle into the earth, and gathered the vine of the earth, and cast it into the great winepress of the wrath of God. **14:20** And the winepress was trodden without [the Asian army will be destroyed outside the city] the city, and blood came out of the winepress, even unto the horse bridles [in pools 3 to 4 feet deep], by the space of a thousand and six hundred furlongs [200 miles].

Zechariah 14:12 And this shall be the plague wherewith the LORD will smite all the people that have fought against Jerusalem; **Their flesh shall consume away while they stand upon their feet, and their eyes shall consume away in their holes, and their tongue shall consume away in their mouth.**

14:13 And it shall come to pass in that day, that a great tumult [overwhelming panic and terror] from the LORD shall be among them; and **they shall lay hold every one on the hand of his neighbour, and his hand shall rise up against the hand of his neighbour**.

When God has destroyed the armies of the wicked outside the city, the men of Judah will rise up against the army of the New Federal Europe and the nations of Psalm 83 that occupy the city.

14:14 And **Judah also shall fight at Jerusalem;** and the wealth of all the heathen round about shall be gathered together, gold, and silver, and apparel, in great abundance.

Even the animals of the invaders will be destroyed.

14:15 And so shall be the plague of the horse, of the mule, of the camel, and of the ass, and of all the beasts that shall be in these tents, as this plague.

Then ALL nations will repent and they will know the Eternal (Joel 2:28).

14:16 And it shall come to pass, that **every one that is left of all the nations which came against Jerusalem shall even go up from year to year to worship the King, the LORD of hosts,** and to keep the feast of tabernacles.

All flesh shall observe God's seventh day [Friday sunset to Saturday sunset] Sabbaths and the New Moons.

> **Isaiah 66:23** And it shall come to pass, that **from one new moon to another, and from one sabbath to another, shall all flesh come to worship before me, saith the Lord.**

Zechariah 14:17 And it shall be, that whoso will not come up of all the families of the earth unto Jerusalem to worship the King, the LORD of hosts, even upon them shall be no rain.

14:18 And if the family of Egypt go not up, and come not, that have no rain; there shall be the plague, wherewith the LORD will smite the heathen that come not up to keep the feast of tabernacles.

Keeping the Sabbath and the New Moons is reckoned with keeping the Feast of Tabernacles! Jesus Christ the King of kings will require these three things and to live by every Word of God, after he comes!

Why do supposedly converted leaders and brethren reject the sanctity of the Sabbath and High Days buying in restaurants and otherwise polluting God's Holy Sabbath and High Days, and reject the new moons today? Why do they condemn those who are zealous in these things which God obviously wants us to do? Because they are NOT godly men! They make the Word of God of no effect by the false traditions of men!

14:19 This shall be the punishment of Egypt, and the punishment of all nations that come not up to keep the feast of tabernacles.

14:20 In that day shall there be upon the bells of the horses, HOLINESS UNTO THE LORD; and the pots in the LORD's house shall be like the bowls before the altar.

The pots shall be holy so that the sacrifice of the peace offerings may be cooked in them, and there shall be peace between mankind and the Eternal God!

14:21 Yea, every pot in Jerusalem and in Judah shall be holiness unto the LORD of hosts: and all they **that sacrifice shall come and take of them, and seethe therein**: and in that day there shall be no more the Canaanite [The Canaanite was a allegorical type of sin, therefor spiritually this means that no more sin will be tolerated!] in the house of the LORD of hosts.

Malachi

Introduction

The Book of Malachi is the last Book of the Mosaic Scriptures, and the last Book of the Prophets called during the Mosaic Covenant. Malachi was sent to prophesy about the times just before the first coming of Christ; and much in this is an applicable lesson about the situation just before Christ's second coming.

Jude is the New Testament companion book to Malachi, explaining the meaning of Malachi for the New Covenant.

The situation and the problems before both the first and second comings of Christ are very much alike. Both comings were [or are] preceded by a leaning to the traditions and reasoning's of men, with a laxity of zeal for God's Word when it interfered with the traditions of the groups.

Both had leaders who say "sin is the transgression of the law" while exalting their own false traditions above the Word of God.

For many leaders then and today, the main concern is to occupy the chief place among the people while neglecting the weightier matters of the law.

Matthew 23:23 Woe unto you, scribes and Pharisees, hypocrites! **for ye pay tithe of mint and anise and cummin, and have omitted the**

weightier matters of the law, judgment, mercy, and faith: these ought ye to have done, and not to leave the other undone.

1 Timothy 3:16 All scripture is given by inspiration of God, and is profitable for doctrine, for reproof, for correction, for instruction in righteousness: 3:17 That the man of God may be perfect, thoroughly furnished unto all good works.

We are commanded to be [or become] perfect before God; and both Malachi and Jude reveal very much about what needs to be worked on in this latter day.

Matthew 5:48 Be ye therefore perfect, even as your Father which is in heaven is perfect.

Malachi wrote mainly about the conditions before the first coming and Jude wrote the last Book before the final Revelation of Jesus Christ; the last Book before the second coming.

Malachi reveals certain physical problems and sins; and Jude reveals the conditions just prior to the final hour of trial and the second coming of Christ.

Malachi and Jude are very much complimentary books, both writing of conditions before the coming of Christ.

For Malachi, I will be using and English translation of the **Masoretic** text.

In the Masoretic text, Malachi is divided into three chapters only, although it contains the same full four chapters of scripture that is contained in the KJV.

Malachi 1

Malachi 1:1 The burden of the word of the LORD to Israel by Malachi.

A prophecy against Esau [modern Turkey]. God is against Esau because he despised his birthright selling it for a bowl of stew, just as so very many today despise the birthright of their calling trading it for the pleasures of worldliness.

1;2 I have loved you, saith the LORD. Yet ye say: 'Wherein hast Thou loved us?' Was not Esau Jacob's brother? saith the LORD; yet I loved Jacob;

1:3 But Esau I hated, and made his mountains a desolation, and gave his heritage to the jackals of the wilderness.

1:4 Whereas Edom saith: 'We are beaten down, but we will return and build the waste places'; thus saith the LORD of hosts: They shall build, but I will throw down; and they shall be called the border of wickedness, and the people whom the LORD execrateth for ever.

1:5 And your eyes shall see, and ye shall say: 'The LORD is great beyond the border of Israel.'

Esau sold his birthright for a bowl of food. He did not value what he had. Even so the saint that thinks little of his birthright through the Father's calling and compromises fearing what men may do; will be despised like Esau. As Esau despised his birthright, God despised his attitude.

If we will not zealously treasure our birthright as that Pearl of Great Price, giving everything for it; God will also despise us.

We have been called to a birthright of eternal life as the children of the Most High God; it is our birthright to be spiritually united with the Son of God for all eternity. God the Father in his mercy has given us the right to call him "Father" to be totally at one with him and his son and to inherit ALL things!

Will we despise that birthright as Esau despised his?

What we have been called to is worth all the suffering and persecution that this world and its god has to offer. It is WORTH fighting for; WORTH suffering for; WORTH enduring for! It is the pearl of Great Value which is worth everything in this world put together.

Why would anyone throw it away to go back into the Egypt of bondage to the sin which we were delivered out of?

We call God our Father and yet we have no respect or fear of him, that we should live by His Word.

1:6 A son honoureth his father, and a servant his master; if then I be a father, where is My honour? and if I be a master, where is My fear? saith the LORD of hosts unto you, O priests, that despise My name. And ye say: 'Wherein have we despised Thy name?'

Today's leaders and elders are just like these priests.

They offered polluted bread; the unleavened bread of the offerings being representative of the Unleavened Bread of Life the Word of God; and today's leaders and elders offer polluted spiritual bread by mixing God's Word with their own false traditions.

They hold the truth of God in contempt, even willing to exalt themselves above God by claiming that they have the right to bind and loose God's Word as they see fit; deciding right and wrong for themselves like Eve and Adam.

Today the assemblies often observe Passover on the wrong day by the wrong method and we use polluted bread which is white flour instead of whole grain, made without salt or the oil of the Holy Spirit; and we dare to think that God accepts us! These physical things are indicative of our attitude towards spiritual things!

1:7 Ye offer polluted bread upon Mine altar. And ye say: 'Wherein have we polluted thee?' In that ye say: 'The table of the LORD is contemptible.

Today's leaders and elders offer false teachings and demand to be idolized above God's Word by the brethren, and then imagine that God will accept this great evil. and bless them.

1:8 And when ye offer the blind for sacrifice, is it no evil! And when ye offer the lame and sick, is it no evil! Present it now unto thy governor; will he be pleased with thee? or will he accept thy person? saith the LORD of hosts.

Our correction will come upon us because of our own wickedness; therefore quickly and sincerely repent and turn to love the Eternal and live by his Word. Exalt the Eternal God above our own imaginations and idols of men, reject error and embrace truth and justice.

1:9 And now, I pray you, entreat the favour of God that He may be gracious unto us!–this hath been of your doing.–will He accept any of your persons? saith the LORD of hosts.

The altar is the table of the Lord upon which the sacrifice is laid. Each type of sacrifice is a type of an aspect of the work and sacrifice of Jesus Christ. When we say that we cannot overcome sin and then continue in sin, believing that we as sinners will be accounted righteous; we make a mockery of the sacrifice of Christ.

When we are full of the spots and blemishes of sin and still insist that God sees us as pure; we delude ourselves. Like Esau we do not value our calling because we are simply not willing to make the effort to overcome.

1:10 Oh that there were even one among you that would shut the doors [so that we would stop traveling, buying, working or paying others to work on the Sabbath], that ye might not kindle fire on Mine altar in vain! I have no pleasure in you, saith the LORD of hosts, neither will I accept an offering at your hand.

We seek the application of the sacrifice of Christ in vain by continuing in our sins.

1:11 For from the rising of the sun even unto the going down of the same My name is great among the nations; and in every place offerings are presented unto My name, even pure oblations; for My name is great among the nations, saith the LORD of hosts.

Jesus Christ loved his wife Israel with a deep and abiding love.

Though she played the whore by going after other gods many times and left him many times, he forgave and forgave them each time they returned to him. In spite of her unfaithfulness he was NEVER unfaithful to her and remained faithful right up until that marriage was dissolved by his very literal death.

Even so he loves those now called by God the Father to be espoused to him. Yet he does not want to go through that kind of marriage ever again. He is testing us and judging us as to whether he really wants us as a part of his bride.

No person who is lax for sin which really means lax in obedience to him, will qualify to have a part in his bride. No, he has had one bad marriage and he does not want another.

He wants as his dream bride someone to love and cherish and delight in; who will love and cherish and delight in him. He wants a bride who will value what he values, love what he loves; and always and forever cooperate and work together with him. He wants a bride that will be a true and real help to him and not a burden of sorrows.

He does not want a bride who does not acknowledge his Love and Authority; who does what she wants instead of what he commands. Those, who will justify sin [disobedience] now cannot be trusted to be obedient and zealously faithful in the future.

1:12 But ye profane it, in that ye say: 'The table of the LORD is polluted, and the fruit thereof, even the food [the Word of God] thereof, is contemptible.'

We prefer the words of our idols of men to the truth, twisting the Word of God to try and justify remaining in or tolerating willful sin.

1:13 Ye say also: 'Behold, what a weariness is it!' and ye have snuffed [we turn up our noses at the truth of God to exalt the words of our idols of men above the Word of God] at it, saith the LORD of hosts; and ye have brought that which was taken by violence, and the lame, and the sick; thus ye bring the offering; should I accept this of your hand? saith the LORD.

The altar is the table of the Lord upon which the sacrifice is laid. Each type of sacrifice is a type of an aspect of the work and sacrifice of Christ.

Rejecting the "Table of the LORD" is a reference to rejecting Jesus Christ as our authority in order to follow our own vain imaginations, like rejecting the scriptures concerning the Sabbath and calendar to do as WE decide.

The sacrificial animals are types of Christ, it is not fit that his perfection be represented by the sick, blind and lame.

For them to offer the sick, blind and lame as representations of Christ shows contempt for the Lamb of God! Today we show our contempt for Jesus Christ and God the Father by exalting the words of idols of men above the Word of God.

Today it is WE who are spiritually sick, blind and lame and we know it not (Rev 3).

Today the sacrifice of Christ is presented to God the Father on behalf of the sincerely repentant, yet we must also bring a sacrifice! We must sacrifice ourselves and our sinful nature; denying ourselves and taking up our cross [burden] and living by every Word of God. We must kill the old sinful self in the water of baptism and arise a NEW being in Christ, totally dedicated to godliness, totally faithful and obedient to our Husband and his Father in heaven.

Has zealous obedient service to our espoused Husband become such a weariness to us that we lift up our noses at those who are filled with enthusiastic zeal for our God?

Why are we lax and lukewarm in living by every Word of God, considering it a burden; while we are filled with zeal for some man or institution instead of our Lord?

> **1 Corinthians 7:23 Ye are bought with a price; be not ye the servants of men.**

We are no longer our own, we have been purchased at a great price; we belong to Jesus Christ and God the Father! We have no right to do our own things our own way, we are to bring ourselves as a living sacrifice to live by every Word of God.

> **Romans 12:1** I beseech you therefore, brethren, by the mercies of God, that ye present your bodies a living sacrifice, holy, acceptable unto God [through living by every Word of God], which is your reasonable service.
>
> **12:2** And be not conformed to this world: but be ye transformed by the renewing of your mind [replacing worldliness with godliness],

that ye may prove what is that good, and acceptable, and perfect, will of God.

We are to be a living sacrifice; which refers to a life of service to Jesus Christ and God the Father.

If we present a lax and lukewarm sacrifice of obedience and service to Christ and God the Father we the same as those who offered the sick, blind and lame, the valueless sacrifice.

> When we admit that we are full of the spots and blemishes of sin and then insist that God sees us as pure; we delude ourselves. We do not value our calling, like Esau we are simply not willing to make the effort to overcome. Like the Pharisees we are presenting an unworthy sacrifice of service to our mighty God.
>
> **James 1:22 But be ye doers of the word, and not hearers only, deceiving your own selves.**
>
> **1:23** For if any be a hearer of the word, and not a doer, he is like unto a man beholding his natural face in a glass: **1:24** For he beholdeth himself, and goeth his way, and straightway forgetteth what manner of man he was.
>
> **1:25** But whoso looketh into the perfect law of liberty [which delivers us from sin, by teaching us to avoid sin], and continueth therein, he being not a forgetful hearer, but a doer of the work, this man shall be blessed in his deed.

The over-comer will receive the reward of his calling.

Almighty God places a difference between the Holy and the Profane; and NO person unclean by reason of sin may enter his kingdom. He will not overlook continuing in sin and the mocking of his sacrifice.

> **Galatians 6:7** Be not deceived; God is not mocked: for whatsoever a man soweth, that shall he also reap. [Jesus Christ will not overlook any sin, nor will he forgive sin which we fail to stop doing.]

We are to grow and overcome as we learn, but if we stop sincerely trying and just say, "I don't worry about it, Christ will forgive" we have made the sacrifice of Christ into a license to continue in sin; we have made a mockery of the sacrifice of Christ.

> **1 Corinthians 6:9** Know ye not that the unrighteous shall not inherit the kingdom of God? Be not deceived: neither fornicators, nor idolaters, nor adulterers, nor effeminate, nor abusers of themselves

with mankind, **6:10** Nor thieves, nor covetous, nor drunkards, nor revilers, nor extortioners, shall inherit the kingdom of God.

Galatians 5:19 Now the works of the flesh are manifest, which are these; Adultery, fornication, uncleanness, lasciviousness, **5:20** Idolatry, witchcraft, hatred, variance, emulations, wrath, strife, seditions, heresies, **5:21** Envyings, murders, drunkenness, revellings, and such like: of the which I tell you before, as I have also told you in time past, that they which do such things shall not inherit the kingdom of God.

No, Christ is not going to overlook these things and just pronounce "you are forgiven" without any real genuine effort to overcome on our part.

1 John 3:7 Little children, let no man deceive you: he that doeth righteousness is righteous, even as he is righteous.

3:8 He that committeth sin is of the devil; for the devil sinneth from the beginning. For this purpose the Son of God was manifested, that he might destroy the works of the devil.

3:9 Whosoever is born of God doth not commit sin; for his seed remaineth in him: and he cannot sin, because he is born of God.

Even as these people despised the sacrifice on the altar [God's table], offering the sick, blind and lame as shadows of the Lamb of God; even so those who are lax, lukewarm and soft on sin; also make a mockery of the sacrifice of Christ.

Malachi 1:14 But cursed be he that dealeth craftily, whereas he hath in his flock a male, and voweth, and sacrificeth unto the Lord a blemished thing [gives a half-hearted service]; for I am a great King, saith the LORD of hosts, and My name is feared among the nations.

The sacrifice of Christ is to be RESPECTED and exalted; we are to sorrow to the point that we loathe our sin and turn from it in absolute disgust; completely broken up in sincere repentant contrition over the evil that required the death of PERFECTION because of our wickedness.

Jesus Christ the Lamb of God gave a PERFECT sacrifice for us: we MUST provide a true LIVING SACRIFICE of service and faithful loving passionate obedience to him. We must not offer a living sacrifice of laxity, lukewarmness, complacency and carelessness.

We must not exalt others above He who purchased us and delivered us. No, we must not break God's Word because some man or organization told us to!

WE MUST study the scriptures and think on them night and day to see how we can better serve and please he who delivered us. We must be always faithful to the Mediator of our New Covenant which is our espoused Husband.

We MUST NOT replace zeal for God with zeal for a man or institutions, falsely thinking that we are pleasing God by doing so! That is like a wife giving herself to some other man, thinking that she is pleasing her husband in doing so!

Surely, this is NOT pleasing to Jesus Christ! It is IDOLATRY and it is SPIRITUAL ADULTERY! It is NOT serving Jesus Christ our espoused Husband, but serving another!

> **John 8:34** Jesus answered them, Verily, verily, I say unto you, Whosoever committeth sin is the servant of sin.

> **Romans 12:1** I beseech you therefore, brethren, by the mercies of God, that ye present your bodies a living sacrifice, holy, acceptable unto God, which is your reasonable service. **12:2** And be not conformed to this world: but be ye transformed by the renewing of your mind, that ye may prove what is that good, and acceptable, and perfect, will of God.

Almighty God is NOT soft on sin, because sin destroys that which he loves so very deeply: His people! Jesus Christ is NOT soft on sin, because sin destroys that which he loves so very deeply: His Bride!

Malachi 2

Malachi 2:1 And now, this commandment is for you, O ye priests.

This is especially for the leaders, elders and ministry of today's Spiritual Ekklesia, yet every one of us is called to train to become priests of the priesthood of Melchizedek. Therefore this message is to all of the New Covenant Called Out.

2:2 If ye will not hearken, and if ye will not lay it to heart, to give glory unto My name,

A name represents the person bearing that name and we are to exalt the Eternal in BOTH word and deed. Words and lip-service are meaningless without the deeds of total faithful obedience and zeal to live by every Word of God to back them up; for faith without works is dead (James 2).

. . . saith the LORD of hosts, then will I send the curse upon you, and I will curse your blessings; yea, I curse them [already], because ye do not lay it to heart.

Because we are zealous for our idols of men and have no zeal to live by every Word of God, today's Spiritual Ekklesia is under a curse.

> **Revelation 3:15** I know thy works, that thou art neither cold nor hot: I would thou wert cold or hot.

3:16 So then because thou art lukewarm, and neither cold nor hot, I will spue thee out of my mouth.

3:17 Because thou sayest, I am [spiritually] rich, and increased with goods [we think we know it all and will not listen to God's Word], **and have need of nothing; and knowest not that thou art** [spiritually] **wretched, and miserable, and poor, and blind** [willfully blind to truth], **and naked** [naked of godly righteousness]

3:18 I counsel thee to buy of me gold [knowledge of God] **tried in the fire** [when we are afflicted in the fire of correction], **that thou mayest be** [become spiritually rich] **rich; and white raiment, that thou mayest be clothed** [with godly righteousness], **and that the shame of thy nakedness** [sincerely repent that our sins might be covered by Christ] **do not appear; and anoint thine eyes with eyesalve** [we must open our eyes to truth and accept truth rejecting all error], **that thou mayest see** [spiritual things].

3:19 As many as I love, I rebuke and chasten: be zealous therefore, and repent.

3:20 Behold, I stand at the door, and knock: if any man hear my voice, and open the door, I will come in to him, and will sup with him, and he with me.

Malachi 2:3 Behold, I will rebuke the seed [prevent any increase] for your hurt, and will spread dung upon your faces, even the dung of your sacrifices; and ye shall be taken away unto it.

We will be rejected, cast away and spewed out for our spiritual laxity and lukewarmness (Rev 3).

What does it mean to have dung on our faces? It is worse than having someone spit in our face: it is a shame and a disgrace to us. It is the strongest possible rebuke that a person can give to another without resorting to violence. Indeed we would resist such a rebuke with violence if it came from a man. When it comes from God it is a stunning rebuke.

God Almighty regards our lax, complacent, careless service to him; desiring our own ways and following our idols of men, and exalting men and their organizations above his Word as excrement!

2:4 Know then that I have sent this commandment unto you, that My covenant might be with Levi [a covenant of a priesthood with Levi and his descendants, because he loved and respected God], saith the LORD of hosts.

2:5 My covenant was with him of life and peace, and I gave them [the covenant and commandments] to him, and of fear, and he feared [greatly respected God] Me, and was afraid [RESPECTED and OBEYED God] of My name.

2:6 The **law of truth** was in his mouth, and unrighteousness was not found in his lips; he walked with Me in peace and uprightness, and did turn many away from iniquity

Despite ONE mistake, Levi was zealous for God and God's ways; setting a godly example and teaching righteousness.

The priests are now brought into this message.

2:7 For the priest's lips should keep [teach] knowledge, and they should seek [the people should be able to seek the truth from a priest] the law at his mouth; for he is [a priest is supposed to be] the messenger of the LORD of hosts

The spiritually Called Out of the New Covenant are also commanded to teach the true knowledge of God to all people, and to teach all people to live by every Word of God (Mat 28).

2:8 But **ye are turned aside out of the way; ye have caused many to stumble** [Today many elders teach the brethren to compromise with and break God's Word.] in the law; ye have corrupted the covenant of Levi, saith the LORD of hosts.

Just like many ancient Levitical priests corrupted their covenant to be priests of God, many elders of the New Covenant of Melchisedec have corrupted their calling as well.

2:9 Therefore have I also made you contemptible and base before all the people, according as ye have not kept My ways, but have had respect of persons in the law.

Because we exalt idols of men, false traditions and organizations above the Word of God; obeying them instead of God's Word and respecting them above God and his Word; many in today's ministry have become contemptible in the eyes of God and man.

2:10 Have we not all one father [God the Father]? Hath not one God created us? Why do we deal treacherously every man against his brother, profaning the covenant of our fathers?

Why the infighting and power politics? Why the abuse of brethren? Why the splitting, division and confusion?

2:11 Judah [spiritual Judah/Israel, as well as physical Judah/Israel] hath dealt treacherously [against their Husband, the Eternal], and an abomination is committed in Israel and in Jerusalem; for Judah hath profaned the holiness of the LORD which He loveth, and hath married the daughter of a strange god.

Spiritual New Covenant Judah/Israel has left off from our love and zeal for the Husband of our baptismal commitment to follow idols of men; exalting them and their false ways above the Word of God!

Yes, we have exalted the organizations of men above God the Father and above the Son the Husband of our New Covenant of espousal to marriage.

We are no longer faithful to every Word that comes out of the mouth of the Living God, making for ourselves idols of men! We believe the LIE that following men contrary to the Word of God is following God and we fall astray. When people say "just support the church, just do what we say and you are being loyal to Christ" they lie.

Turn from this abominable LIE and repent quickly, lest a jealous God [our Mighty espoused Husband] cast us into great affliction!

This means anyone who reject Jesus Christ as the ONLY Mediator between God the Father and man and who reject his admonition to live by every Word of God!

There is NO Mediator between man and God the Father except the eternal spirit High Priest Melchizedek [Jesus Christ]! We are NEVER to make an idol out of an elder or leader to follow them contrary to the Word of God! By exalting their word above God's Word, such wicked men are exalting themselves above God himself!

NO man has the authority to sit in judgment of God's Word to decide for himself and others what to bind and loose and what is right and wrong as Eve and Adam did in the garden! Such men are son's of wickedness and damnation and all who follow them are rushing to their own destruction!

> **1 Timothy 2:5** For there is one God, and one mediator between God and men, the man Christ Jesus; **2:6** Who gave himself a ransom for all, to be testified in due time.

NO ONE can intercede for you with God the Father! NO ONE!

We are to love and live by every Word of God the Father and Jesus Christ, who is the High Priest of the New Covenant and the ONLY mediator between God the Father and man.

We are to repent of all sin, and sin is the breaking of any of part of the Word of God (1 John 3:4). Then after sincere repentance and a baptismal commitment to live by every Word of God, we may be reconciled to God the Father and approach him directly in the name of our sacrifice and High Priest; the ONLY Mediator: Jesus Christ.

For Christ himself commanded us to pray directly to God the Father in his name; we are not to pray to any so called intercessor that they may approach the Father on our behalf; we are to pray directly to the Father in the name of Jesus Christ.

> **Matthew 6:9** After this manner therefore pray ye: **Our Father which art in heaven, Hallowed be thy name**. **6:10** Thy kingdom come, Thy will be done in earth, as it is in heaven. **6:11** Give us this day our daily bread. **6:12** And forgive us our debts, as we forgive our debtors. **6:13** And lead us not into temptation, but deliver us from evil: For thine is the kingdom, and the power, and the glory, for ever. Amen.

> **John 16:23** And in that day ye shall ask me nothing. Verily, verily, I say unto you, Whatsoever **ye shall ask the Father in my name**, he will give it you.

Malachi 2:12 May the LORD cut off to the man [may God destroy (cut off) out of the assembly, every person who follows idols of men (Mal 2:11)] **that doeth this, him that calleth and him that answereth out of the tents of Jacob, and him that offereth an offering unto the LORD of hosts.**

This is a profound curse; that any person who does not repent of exalting organizations and institutions and men, and doing what mere human beings say instead of living by every Word of God will be cut off from among God's people.

Those who buy food and drink on the Holy Sabbath days of Almighty God; saying "the church permits this" are obeying idols of men and they will be cut off from God for this double sin: first of polluting the Sabbath, and second for obeying anyone other than God the Father and our espoused Husband. We are not to blindly follow any man who LIES claiming that he can bind or loose God's Word; we are to love God and live by EVERY WORD of God!

May the Eternal "CUT OFF" anyone who allows ANYTHING to come between him and the Eternal Almighty God!

2:13 And this further ye do: ye cover the altar of the LORD with tears, with weeping, and with sighing, insomuch that He regardeth not the offering any more, neither receiveth it with good will at your hand.

Those wicked elders and leaders who make themselves into idols for the brethren, filling the people with sorrows by their false teachings and leading them into all manner of sins, are anathema to God.

2:14 Yet ye say: 'Wherefore?' Because the LORD hath been witness between thee and the wife of thy youth, against whom thou hast dealt treacherously, though she is thy companion, and the wife of thy covenant.

Relationships between husbands and wives are also an allegory of our relationship with our espoused husband Jesus Christ and we are not to be disloyal to him in following idols of men.

Today many husbands have abused their wives and many wives have abused their husbands. This is about abuse and adultery, and our physical marriage covenant to love, cherish and care for one another.

It is also about our spiritual marriage covenant with Jesus Christ to love, cherish, obey and follow him wherever he goes.

One of the purposes of physical marriage is to teach us loyalty, respect and tender concern for our spouses, so that we may learn loyalty and passionate love for our spiritual Husband Jesus Christ.

The Nicolaitane bullying and dominating of people by leaders and elders, and the same kind of conduct between husbands and wives is despised and hated by Almighty God.

2:15 And not one hath done so who had exuberance of spirit!

Those that do such sins are not enthusiastic, zealous or exuberant to live by every Word of God!

He or she who is not faithful to their covenant of marriage now, would not be faithful to a spiritual Marriage Covenant with Jesus Christ for all eternity. To such people the world revolves around them. Everything is about them and about their advantage, it is pure selfishness and not about the loving and faithful service to their mate which God requires.

Those who are zealous and exuberant, loving to live by every Word of God, are loving, faithful and loyal!

> **Matthew 23:12** And whosoever shall exalt himself shall be abased; and he that shall humble himself shall be exalted.

God wants us to produce godly children, and to do that requires godly parents instructing their children in godliness; and the setting of a godly example. If the parents abuse one another and live in constant strife; how does that teach godliness to children?

Today the Ekklesia is full of abuse and the sin of divorce and remarriage; and the root of these sins is our spiritual adultery against the espoused Husband of our baptismal commitment; for if we lived a godly life in faithfully living by every Word of God we would love one another according to godly love.

Malachi 2:15. . . For what seeketh the one? a seed [children] given of God. A godly increase and blessing [of family and children]. Therefore take heed to your spirit, and let none deal treacherously against the wife of his youth.

Divorce is the hiding of a sinful unrepentant nature by one or both sides; it is hiding our violence against godly love. Divorce is an admission that we cannot live in godly love and peace; and it is the breaking of our vows made in the presence of God.

2:16 For I hate putting away, saith the LORD, the God of Israel, and him that covereth his garment with violence, saith the LORD of hosts; therefore take heed to your spirit, that ye deal not treacherously.

God hates adultery, intimidation, coercion, bullying and abuse; both between husbands and wives and between elders and brethren, and in any human relationship. Such a relationship is NOT about love and peace, but is one of violence, fear, suffering and sorrow.

Brethren; God hates divorce; and that is especially true of our separating ourselves from God by following idols of men and refusing to live by every Word of God, as we committed to do at baptism.

2:17 Ye have wearied the LORD with your words. Yet ye say: 'Wherein have we wearied Him?' In that **ye say: 'Every one that doeth evil is good in the sight of the LORD, and He delighteth in them; or where is the God of justice?'**

We have wearied the Eternal by saying that we are a righteous people when we are full of sin.

When we say that God will forgive and then we feel free to be lax and soft on sin, we make a mockery of God's Word and we waste his time with our many words of prayer. We are a weariness and a vexation of spirit to God if we say "sorry" and then continue to sin.

We pour out our words to him and then feel justified in abusing our flock, our brethren, or our wives and children.

We speak great prideful words, calling ourselves God's people while we pollute God's Sabbaths and do many other wicked deeds, and still we believe that God will accept and bless us; overlooking our blemishes of sin and the ugliness of our deeds.

Matthew 7:21 Not every one that saith unto me, Lord, Lord, shall enter into the kingdom of heaven; but he that doeth the will of my Father which is in heaven.

7:22 Many will say to me in that day, Lord, Lord, have we not prophesied in thy name? and in thy name have cast out devils? and in thy name done many wonderful works?

7:23 And then will I profess unto them, I never knew you: depart from me, ye that work iniquity.

7:24 Therefore whosoever heareth these sayings of mine, and doeth them, I will liken him unto a wise man, which built his house upon a rock:

Malachi 3

Malachi 3:1 Behold, I send My messenger [John Baptist (Elijah), and the end time Elijah], and he shall clear the way before Me; and the Lord [Messiah, the Christ], whom ye seek, will suddenly come to His temple [Christ will come unexpectedly by most, to the spiritual temple, the people in whom God's Spirit dwells], and the messenger of the covenant [Jesus Christ is the Messenger of the New Covenant], whom ye delight in, behold, he cometh, saith the LORD of hosts.

3:2 But who may abide the day of his coming? And who shall stand when he appeareth? For he is like a refiner's fire, and like fullers' soap;

3:3 And he shall sit as a refiner and purifier of silver; and he shall purify the sons of Levi [The descendants of Zadok of physical priesthood of Levi will be brought into the New Covenant and will become New Covenant priests of God of the order of Melchizedek.], and purge them as gold and silver; and there shall be they that shall offer unto the LORD offerings in righteousness.

The descendants of Zadok will enter the New Covenant and will offer sacrifices in the Ezekiel Temple (Ezekiel 40-48).

Many will be corrected, refined and purified through a trial by fire (Rev 3). Levi will also be turned back to his God, for at least 12,000 of Levi shall be Called, Sealed and made Pure before God (Rev 7:7. Rev

7:14). After this trial by fire, when the Kingdom will have come, God's Spirit will be poured out on all flesh (Joel 2:28), and a new physical temple will be built in Jerusalem (Ezek 41-42).

God's Spirit will remain in no one who sins knowingly-willfully. The wicked will be rejected from being a part of God's spiritual temple

> **1 Corinthians 3:16 Know ye not that ye are the temple of God, and that the Spirit of God dwelleth in you? 3:17 If any man defile the temple of God, *him shall God destroy*; for the temple of God is holy, which temple ye are.**

Malachi 3:4 Then [because of sincere repentance and faithful diligence to live by every Word of God] shall the offering of Judah and Jerusalem be pleasant [acceptable to] unto the LORD, as in the days of old, and as in ancient years.

Jerusalem will become the capital of the earth and Judah will be brought back to her land; and Israel shall also be brought back to her land.

The new physical Ezekiel Temple will be built and the physical sacrifices will be reinstated along with a new and full understanding of their spiritual implications. The physical priests will be filled with God's Spirit and also the whole people and they shall all know the Eternal and obey him, making him their delight.

> **Jeremiah 31:33** But this shall be the covenant that I will make with the house of Israel; After those days, saith the LORD, **I will put my law in their inward parts, and write it in their hearts; and will be their God, and they shall be my people.**
>
> **31:34** And they shall teach no more every man his neighbour, and every man his brother, saying, Know the LORD: for they shall all know me, from the least of them unto the greatest of them, saith the LORD: for I will forgive their iniquity, and I will remember their sin no more.

Malachi 3:5 And I will come near to you to judgment; and I will be a swift witness against the sorcerers, and against the adulterers [those who are unfaithful to God], and against false swearers; and against those that oppress the hireling in his wages, the widow, and the fatherless, and that turn aside the stranger from his right, and fear not Me, saith the LORD of hosts.

3:6 For I the LORD change not; and ye, O sons of Jacob, are not consumed.

The Eternal Keeps His Promises!

God will not totally destroy the people for their wickedness, but will correct them until they are turned back to him! He will swiftly judge the wicked and the oppressor!

The Head of the Spiritual Ekklesia is Jesus Christ and his head is God the Father, NO person has the right to exalt himself to judge God's Word to decide right and wrong for himself. Today's Spiritual Ekklesia has followed our own ways while claiming to be godly. We must turn to a wholehearted zeal to live by every Word of God.

3:7 From the days of your fathers ye have turned aside from Mine ordinances, and have not kept them. **Return unto Me, and I will return unto you, saith the LORD of hosts**. But ye say: 'Wherein shall we return?'

Today the robbers of God's tithes and offerings in the Ekklesia are not the brethren; they are the ministry who take God's monies and then teach against any zeal for God, rather teaching a zeal to exalt idols of men above the Word of God.

3:8 Will a man rob God? Yet ye rob Me. But ye say: 'Wherein have we robbed Thee?' In tithes and heave-offerings.

3:9 Ye are cursed with the curse, yet ye rob Me, even this whole nation.

The Pharisees demanded a complete tithing, as does today's Spiritual Ekklesia; and so they think that they are guiltless in this matter and that this rebuke only applies to others. Yet today's ministry does indeed rob God; by diverting God's funds to finance ungodly enterprises and taking wages that they have not earned. Loving their big salaries and fat expense accounts while not teaching the people to live by every Word of God with zeal; indeed condemning anyone who is zealous for God, as being "over righteous."

> **Ezekiel 34:2** [see the whole chapter, and Jeremiah 23] Son of man, prophesy against the shepherds of Israel, prophesy, and say unto them, Thus saith the Lord GOD unto the shepherds; Woe be to the shepherds of Israel that do feed themselves! should not the shepherds feed the flocks? **34:3** Ye eat the fat, and ye clothe you with the wool, ye kill them that are fed: but ye feed not the flock.

Malachi 3:10 Bring ye the whole tithe into the store-house, that there may be food [the Gospel and the Word of God may be preached] in My house [spiritual food for the people], and try Me now herewith, saith the LORD of hosts, if I will not open you the windows of heaven, and pour you out a blessing, that there shall be more than sufficiency.

Let us start rejecting error and start using God's tithe to begin to teach the truth; let us begin to live by every Word of God.

3:11 And I will rebuke the devourer for your good, and he shall not destroy the fruits of your land; neither shall your vine cast its fruit before the time in the field, saith the LORD of hosts.

3:12 And all nations shall call you happy; for ye shall be a delightsome land, saith the LORD of hosts.

We will be a delight to the Eternal IF we live by every Word of God and proclaim righteousness throughout the world as he has commanded in Matthew 28, instead of taking God's tithe while teaching our own false traditions.

3:13 Your words have been all too strong against Me, saith the LORD. Yet ye say: 'Wherein have we spoken against thee?'

Today most elders, leaders and many brethren call those who are zealous to live by every Word of God; foolish.

3:14 Ye have said: 'It is vain to serve God; and what profit is it that we have kept His charge, and that we have walked mournfully [repentantly mourning our sins] because of the LORD of hosts?

The wicked make it their delight to go out and buy food and drink, polluting God's holy Sabbath day; our chief topic of conversation on the Sabbath is NOT God and his Word.

We do not think and meditate, filling our heart and mind with God's Word night and day. Our heart is not set on our God, but on our organization, leader, elder or the social pleasures around meeting together. I am speaking now to those in this condition and not to those to whom this does not apply.

Today we look up to and envy the arrogant and proud, because they are lifted up; not realizing that God will bring them down to destruction for their great pride.

3:15 And now we call the proud happy; yea, they that work wickedness are built up; yea, they try God, and are delivered.

Yes, we exalt the men and organizations even when they abuse and dominate us by bullying and intimidation, taking and taking while telling us to compromise with God's Word by doing whatever they say, and causing many to exalt such men above God's Word in the sin of idolatry.

We exalt those who play power politics, above the faithful elders who speak the truth, for we delight in being told that we have it made if we only obey the elder. We delight in being told how good and righteous we are as we do our own thing instead of enthusiastically living by every Word of God: Thinking that somehow we can crash the Wedding Feast without a garment of righteousness.

> **Matthew 22:11** And when the king came in to see the guests, he saw there a man which had not on a wedding garment [was not clothed with godly righteousness] : **22:12** And he saith unto him, Friend, how camest thou in hither not having a wedding garment [not being clothed with godly righteousness]? And he was speechless.
>
> **22:13 Then said the king to the servants, Bind him hand and foot, and take him away, and cast him into outer darkness, there shall be weeping and gnashing of teeth.**
>
> **22:14 For many are called, but few are chosen.**

Malachi 3:16 Then they that feared the LORD spoke one with another; and the LORD hearkened, and heard, and a book of remembrance was written before Him, for them that feared the LORD, and that thought upon His name.

God IS WATCHING US! He knows what we do and what we say. He is looking for those with open eyes, who see the reality and who cry and sigh over the evils among his people: those who genuinely CARE, who truly LOVE God enough to actually DO what God has commanded.

> **Ezekiel 9:4** And the LORD said unto him, Go through the midst of the city, through the midst of Jerusalem, and set a mark upon the foreheads of the men that sigh and that cry for all the abominations that be done in the midst thereof.
>
> **9:5** And to the others he said in mine hearing, Go ye after him through the city, and smite: let not your eye spare, neither have ye pity: **9:6** Slay utterly old and young, both maids, and little children, and women: **but come not near any man upon whom is the mark;**

and begin at my sanctuary. Then they began at the ancient men which were before the house.

We have now come to a time when Almighty God is sifting out those who turn to him in zealous, passionate, enthusiastic, abundant LOVE for God and his Word; separating them out before correcting the lax, faithless and lukewarm.

We are at the time of Malachi 3:16, Ezekiel 9:4 and Revelation 11:1-2 where the Holy is being separated from the profane, so that the outer courtyard of the spiritual temple [people of God] can be given over to the Gentiles for their correction; while the inner court or Holy Place [the faithful] is preserved.

> **Revelation 11:1** And there was given me a reed like unto a rod: and the angel stood, saying, Rise, and measure the temple of God, and the altar, and them that worship therein.
>
> **11:2** But the court which is without the temple leave out, and measure it not; for it is given unto the Gentiles: and the holy city shall they tread under foot forty and two months.

Malachi 3:17 And they [those who love God enough to zealously DO what he says] shall be Mine, saith the LORD of hosts, in the day that I do make, even Mine own treasure; and I will spare them, as a man spareth his own son that serveth him.

3:18 Then shall ye again discern between the righteous and the wicked, between him that serveth God and him that serveth Him not.

It is the people who LOVE God and his Word to keep it with all their hearts (Mat 22:36-38) who are upset and sorrow over the evils. Those who repent and seek to serve Almighty God with a whole heart are the true pillars and they will be spared and delivered as a part of the Bride of the Lamb.

It is those who have learned the difference between the Holy and the Profane and have chosen to live by every Word of God who will be accounted worthy to judge the nations in God's Kingdom!

Malachi 4

Malachi 4:1 For, behold, the day cometh, it burneth as a furnace; and all the proud, and all that work wickedness, shall be stubble; and the day that cometh shall set them ablaze, saith the LORD of hosts, that it shall leave them neither root nor branch.

It is:

- Those who exalt men and institutions, obeying them above obeying God,
- Those who compromise with the holiness of God's Sabbath and Holy Days,
- Those who follow the teachings of the unconverted for their prophecy and some of their doctrine;
- Those who lack any zeal for their espoused Husband and his Father,
- Those who are not passionately burning with zeal for their Deliverer, and
- Those who cling to their false traditions and refuse to accept the increase of spiritual knowledge promised to them by the Eternal in Daniel 12;

Who will be cast in to the furnace of affliction so that they might be humbled to contrite repentance.

The wicked who follow idols of men and false traditions, having no zeal to live by every Word of God; will be tried in the fire of affliction to see if they will sincerely repent or if they must have the birthright of their calling taken away from them.

4:2 But unto you that fear [have RESPECT for God to do his will] My name shall the sun [literally "sun;" properly: A brilliant LIGHT] of righteousness arise with healing in its [his] wings; and ye shall go forth, and gambol [dance in rejoicing like a youth] as calves of the stall.

4:3 And ye shall tread down the wicked; for they shall be ashes under the soles of your feet in the day that I do make, saith the LORD of hosts.

The Eternal will deliver and exalt all those who are humble before him, who truly LOVE him and DO his will. They will be persecuted and attacked as Pharisaic and self-righteous by their brethren, NOW; but the Eternal will be our reward and the pillars will receive a double portion.

> **Isaiah 61:6** But ye shall be named the Priests of the LORD: men shall call you the Ministers of our God: ye shall eat the riches of the Gentiles, and in their glory shall ye boast yourselves.
>
> **61:7** For your shame [because the faithful have been mocked by the wicked] ye shall have double; and for confusion they shall rejoice in their portion: therefore in their land they shall possess the double: everlasting joy shall be unto them.
>
> **61:8 For I the LORD love judgment, I hate robbery for burnt offering; and I will direct their work in truth, and I will make an everlasting covenant with them.**

God hates the taking of offerings through coercion and intimidation and mental extortion. He loves righteousness and just judgment.

God will direct the feet of all those who passionately love him and live by EVERY WORD of God; and they will live in complete unity with God the Father and Jesus Christ for ALL eternity!

The righteous who live by every Word of God and zealously keep every Word of God; will inherit eternal life!

Malachi 4:4 Remember ye the law of Moses My servant, which I commanded unto him in Horeb [Sinai] for all Israel, even statutes and ordinances.

The foundation of turning parents and children to each other is for parents and children to base their lives on the same foundation, which is UNITY

WITH GOD through a passionate exuberant zeal to live by every Word of God!

4:5 Behold, I will send you Elijah the prophet before the coming of the great and terrible day of the LORD. **4:6** And he shall turn the heart of the fathers [God the Father] to the children [the people], and the heart of the children [the people] to their fathers [God the Father]; lest I come and smite the land with utter destruction.

Elijah will turn the hearts of today's Spiritual Ekklesia to God the Father, and God the Father's heart will be turned to all those who sincerely repent and turn to live by his every Word.

God's law is a law of love and through keeping it the fruits of love, true unity and peace are obtained. Elijah will turn the hearts of parents and children to each other, by turning the hearts of BOTH children and parents to the Eternal God and to passionately living by every Word of God.

> **Luke 1:17** And he shall go before him in the spirit and power of Elias, to turn the hearts of the fathers [God the Father] to the children, and [will turn the disobedient to sincere repentance] **the disobedient to the wisdom of the just; to make ready a people prepared for the Lord.**

Visit Our Website

theshininglight.info